Praise for Irving Brecher

"Reading The Wicked Wit of th[e] [...]
spending Tuesdays With [...]
Last Tape!"
　　　—Don Foster, Emmy- [...]
　　　　producer of "Two- [...]

"I love Irv. He's a live [...]
　　—Robert Wagner

"The only good thing about making the movie *At the Circus* was beginning my friendship with Irv Brecher."
　　—Groucho Marx

"If you're interested in groundbreaking television, look no further than Irv Brecher. Thank God for this book—at 94, Irv is truly the last of the Joke-hicans."
　　—Liz Tuccillo (co-author of *He's Just Not That Into You*, writer for *Sex and the City*)

"Irv of the incomparable wit!"
　　—Ben Hecht (screenwriter, *The Front Page*)

"Wit is defined as the ability to perceive and express in ingeniously humorous manner the relationship between seemingly incongruous things. My own definition is infinitely simpler.
I define wit as Irving Brecher."
　　—Larry Gelbart

Praise for Hank Rosenfeld

"Hank Rosenfeld is a smart, funny, utterly singular force of nature.
>   —Kurt Andersen (Editor of *Spy*, author of "Heyday", host NPR's Studio 360)

"This guy Hank is smart and funny"
>   —Peter Bergman, Firesign Theater

"Hank has an uncanny ability to experience all the nooks and crannies in life that the rest of us often miss. (In another life, maybe he was an English muffin. Good thing for us that in this one, he's a writer.)"
>   —Andy Cowan, Producer "Seinfeld" and "Cheers"

"Hank is a superlative storyteller."
>   —Diana Nyad (Host of Public Radio's "Savvy Traveler")

"Here's the chance to know something about the heavyweights that entertained your parents when they went to the Tivoli or the Odeon or even the Bijou: Groucho, Gleason, Tracy, Wayne, Garland.

"Please buy my son's book."
>   —Norman Rosenfeld

The Wicked Wit of the West

The last great Golden-Age screenwriter shares the hilarity and heartaches of working with Groucho, Garland, Gleason, Burns, Berle, Benny and many more

by Irving Brecher

as told to **Hank Rosenfeld**

Ben Yehuda Press

Teaneck, New Jersey

Published by Ben Yehuda Press
430 Kensington Road
Teaneck, NJ 07666

http://www.BenYehudaPress.com

Cover illustration by Drew Friedman.

Ben Yehuda Press books may be purchased for educational, business or sales promotional use. For information, please contact:
Special Markets, Ben Yehuda Press,
430 Kensington Road, Teaneck, NJ 07666.
markets@BenYehudaPress.com.

pb ISBN   1-934730-23-8
pb ISBN13 978-1-934730-23-2
Library of Congress Control Number & CIP pending

20081020
08 09 10   / 10 9 8 7 6 5 4 3 2 1

For Norma

It was a Grande Collusion.

> *– Irv*

For my parents Norman and Dulcie, who enjoy books even more than movies, and movies even more than me. (Wait. Irv, help! That didn't come out right…)

> *– Hank*

Contents

"Ladies and gentlemen...and I guess that takes in most of you."
> — Groucho Marx

An aged man is but a paltry thing
A tattered coat upon a stick, unless
Soul clap its hands and sing, and
    louder sing.
> — W.B. Yeats

Chester A. Riley: *I've been in some deep holes, but I'll never be in any deeper than I am right now!*
Digger O'Dell: *Would you care to bet? I have a job for you! Come, we'd better be shoveling off...*
> — Irving Brecher

Have you got a pencil? I left my typewriter in my other pants.
> — J. Cheever Loophole

This is either a day for writing, the early stages of a honeymoon, or fifteen grains of opium.
> — Groucho in a letter to Brecher

IRV'S OEUVRE

1914 Irving Sidney Brecher is born on January 17th in Bronx, NY

1933 begins writing at 19 for young phenom Milton Berle on stage and radio

1934-36 writes gags for Henny Youngman and other Vaudeville acts

1937 brought west by Mervyn LeRoy, writes Berle into movie *New Faces of 1937*

1938 contributes humor to Metro-Goldwyn-Mayer's *The Wizard of Oz* (uncredited)

1939 writes *The Marx Brothers At The Circus*

1940 writes *The Marx Brothers Go West*

1941 writes *Shadow of the Thin Man* starring William Powell, Myrna Loy

1942 writes *Du Barry Was a Lady* starring Red Skelton, Lucille Ball, Gene Kelley & writes a play, "Sweet Charity"

1943 writes *Best Foot Forward* starring Lucille Ball & sketches for movie *Ziegfeld Follies of 1943*

1944 writes *Meet Me in St. Louis* starring Judy Garland
creates *The Life of Riley* radio show on NBC

1945 writes *Yolanda and the Thief* starring Fred Astaire

1948 writes *Summer Holiday,* his last script at MGM

1949 writes and directs *The Life of Riley* movie at Universal Pictures, & TV version

1950 wins Emmy award ("Best Filmed Comedy") for *The Life of Riley TV* series

1952 sells *Life of Riley* TV rights to NBC

1952 writes and directs *Somebody Loves Me* at Paramount Pictures

1955 creates *Peoples Choice* for CBS starring Jackie Cooper, "Cleo" the hound

1960 writes *Cry for Happy* at Columbia Pictures with Glenn Ford, Donald O'Connor

1961 directs *Sail a Crooked Ship* at Columbia with Ernie Kovacs, Robert Wagner

1962 writes *Bye Bye Birdie* at Columbia starring Dick Van Dyke, Ann-Margret

2008 standup comic, sit-down curmudgeon (Where is everybody?)

Part I

Meet Irv the Nerve

First Words

```
Hank: Irv, you're 92 years old. Listening to you
is like hanging out with Methuselah!
Irv: Methuselah lived to be 900. But that's
because in those days there were no doctors.
```

Groucho Marx and S.J. Perelman were once asked whom they found to be fastest with the "one-line impromptu."

Perelman and Marx agreed: "George S. Kaufman, Oscar Levant and screenwriter Irving Brecher."

So who was Irving Brecher and how did he come up with all those funny things everybody else ended up saying? And why didn't anybody in the 21st century know about him? And if I were to find all this out, what could I tell you about Brecher that he couldn't tell you a hell of a lot funnier?

So, Irv is telling most of the story. He didn't want to go down the memoir-with-ghostwriter route. Irv isn't putting down that genre; some of his best friends have written some of my favorite memoirs. But when Irv Brecher sat down to write a Marx Brothers movie single-handedly, it had never previously been attempted. When Irv Brecher created the first television situation comedy, that hadn't been done previously, either.

Now, with his first book, Brecher is again creating something different. Not a memoir or biography, Irv calls it "a freak," this collaboration between a writer and a fan-turned-friend.

Our typesetter calls it nastier names and goes a little "font crazy." He uses these italics for my observations and narrations, a regular Roman face for Irv, **bold face for my side of our conversations,** and `this typewriter face for Irv's stand-up routines.`

A straight memoir would have been simpler. The way I see it, though, a little typographical turmoil is a small price to pay for the chance to meet "the wicked wit of the West," personally, as he holds court at a Hollywood roundtable.

"Get the pickled tongue on corn rye," Brecher is insisting. "I want you to be strong."

In the few months since I first met Irv, I've come to value his advice almost as much as I've admired his sharp, robustly funny attitude about life. Could pickled tongue be the secret for how octogenarians like Irv stay young? Unlikely, but I take the advice.

We're at the Friar's Club on Little Santa Monica Boulevard in Beverly Hills. It used to be one of his favorite haunts. Now it's under new management and Brecher hates it.

I'm talking to him about his maybe, possibly, writing a book. He fires off right away his idea about it:

Listen to me, kid. Steve Allen wrote eight hundred books. Sometimes he wrote a book a day. One day he took a break short enough to say to me, "Irv, why not write one?"

I told him that I was embarrassed to quote myself saying funny things. I've never been reluctant to entertain in front of people, at a lectern or wherever. I just didn't want to talk about myself in that way.

Steve Allen said, "You can find a way if you try. Say it up front, as a disclaimer."

You know, Steve may be right. So here it is. I'm saying it. I admit I am very funny. I don't like to quote myself but unfortunately everybody I know who should be quoting me is dead. Fine friends *they* turned out to be.

The Disclaimer

The Friar's Club was once the West Coast hangout for comedians. Large pictures of famous members Bob Hope and George Burns are all over the walls. But most prominent of all is Milton Berle. I ask Irv why:

Berle had a long run, in which he built up the club and attracted lots of members because he arranged and entertained periodically hilarious stags. Then he had a mild stroke. Actually just a few weeks before my 85th birthday. To my delight, he came anyway.

After his stroke? Really?

Yeah. It was a lovely gesture. I had a real fondness for Milton because in a way, he put me into show business. If it weren't for him, I might have been a dentist or an accountant or some other inflicter of pain.

Berle's written a zillion books. Where's *Irv Brecher's Hollywood*?

I've been thinking about this for a while now.

Books about Hollywood that sell are those where the author, usually an actor, screwed dozens of other actors in vivid detail. Or was a drinker, or on drugs. You need a Joan Crawford gothic horror tale of a childhood.

But I want to be honest with you—my father never molested me. My father never molested my mother. I was not locked in a closet for twelve years and fed under the door with matzos. They did not starve me. During the Depression we all starved together. My sweet father, mother, sister, brother and grandmother...

I confess—at the risk of offending the evangelicals—we never prayed together. Except for food.

Now, George Burns wrote six books. He never read them. He actually never wrote them. He had them written for him and they sold because he was George Burns, a name with a great deal of public notice and appeal. He's a very good friend of mine—even though he's not here anymore.

(Scooping more coleslaw onto his rye.)

Look kid, Lassie has a book. Rin Tin Tin has a book. The gatekeeper at MGM in 1939 wrote a thesis in which he claimed he could recognize every star without demanding their I.D. Don't hold your breath. In fact, suck on a mint, the corned beef here has a lot of garlic.

> "Life gets the last laugh."
> —Irv Brecher

Our lunch became an article in the Forward *newspaper, a story about getting to know an old man with fresh insights who doesn't act old at all, but has a comic's ability to make cantankerous tirades come across playful as hell.*

I read the story aloud over the phone.

Did you like it, Irv?

Kiddo, you're in love with me, aren't you?

Um, yes. But who *wouldn't* be? Don't you think people should have a chance to learn more about you?

Don't count on it.

Just when I thought I'd never talk him into it, Brecher calls me to come to his office—a single room he rents on the second floor of his apartment building in Westwood.

Okay. You didn't talk me into it, but my wife and daughter have been nagging me for years. They're pretty sore at me, so it would be a nice thing if one day they could say, "He made us happy, he wrote a book. Nobody bought it, but he made us happy."

Okay.

I don't know much about you, except that you're a nice Jewish boy who likes pastrami. But you know when you get to this age, very few things happen in your life that are that good. Because people are dying. People you care about. Staying alive is like trying to fight a war. You wonder: who's next? When the fucking phone rings you don't know where the hell it's coming from. The truth is, I could have ignored my daughter, much as I care about her, but it was hard to say no when my wife insisted she'd pull a Lysistrata act on me.

What do you mean?

No sex!

And not just me. With anybody!

So we gotta do the book.

Okay.

And call me Irv instead of Irving. We'll get these sessions over faster. I'll test my memory and you can write it down. But on one condition.

What's that?

If it turns out to be a book, I don't have to read it.

In the end, he's kept his word. And he's given me his words, although he's now blind from glaucoma and has to have them read back to him. But he's listening keenly as ever, making sure I stay true to the story. He's particularly attentive that my efforts to highlight his catch phrases don't turn them into cliches, thus embarrassing the master wordsmith.

At the Friar's Club with Milton Berle (*l*), who put me into show business and never had the decency to apologize.

Hello, I Must Be Going

Hank: I wanna tape you so I can be accurate.
Irv: Well, if you wanna be accurate you're going
to have a lot of trouble being a journalist.

I met Irv for the first time in a 14th floor suite at the Century Park Hotel.

As a folk journalist armed with audiotape, I try to make a buck by sticking a microphone in front of somebody's face and getting the human interest angle. One day I got a call from a friend saying that the Turner Classic Movie channel was coming to film a batch of archival interviews with Golden Age Hollywood actors, producers, stunt persons, and stylists. She added: "I know that you're in love with the Marx Brothers, so you may be interested in dropping in while they film a fella named Irving Brecher. There may be a story in it. He wrote two Marx Brothers movies."

Of course I went. I was a huge Marx Brothers fan. Their movies got me through sophomore year at Wesleyan. They showed the entire student body Marx Brothers movies and It's a Wonderful Life the week before exams so we would be able to come out of our self-obsessed shells and laugh at the world.

The first thing I see is this elderly gentlemen sitting in the hotel room. He was tall, very lean—let's say skinny—with whispy white hair. He had huge hands with long fingers, knuckles like boulders, and he had some kind of mischief in his blue eyes. I thought he was holding up pretty well under hot movie lights.

Holding up? He was holding court! He gave quite a performance, co-starring Judy Garland, L.B. Mayer, Nick and Nora, and the Marx Brothers.

"I'm afraid I'm the last living MGM writer," he was telling the interviewer. "And I hope I get through this interview..."

I was struck immediately: this fellow Brecher, he sounded exactly like Groucho Marx—that distinctively edgy launching of an expertly aimed zinger. (Groucho said he never told jokes, he just told the truth, which was funnier).

Suddenly, a beeping sound broke the scene. "Cut," said the producer.

"Unless there's a canary in here," Brecher said, "my hearing aid just died."

"How long do those batteries last?" asked the interviewer.

"About two weeks," he told her. "Longer, if you don't do any listening."

Groucho, A Dangerous Companion

Brecher reached inside his smart blue blazer for a replacement battery. While he fixed his hearing aid, the TCM crew changed film reels. When they resumed, he told them a story that he repeated to me a few weeks later. It was the one about the time he traveled down south with Groucho Marx, whom he labeled "a dangerous companion." Here is his version direct from my tape recorder.

Irv: I loved the nihilism of Groucho. Fucking with the big shots. I'm a complainer, a dissenter and a put-downer, and Groucho was my alter ego. I liked the anarchism. Groucho was also my champion. He always defended my scripts against less than talented producers.

The truth is, Groucho hated being an actor. He would refer to his mother Minnie, "pushing us into acting." He wanted to be a writer, "but she screwed me up," is what he'd say. He had no fun remembering his vaudeville days as a kid with his brother Adolph who was Harpo, Leonard who was Chico, and Herbert who was Zeppo. Groucho, who would answer to the name Julius, was basically withdrawn and serious. But he could and did explode verbally with great accuracy. He was interested in politics, by which I mean he had a contempt for most politicians. He was a Roosevelt Democrat, and outspokenly critical of the red baiting super-patriots like Senator Joe McCarthy and the House Un-American Activities Committee. A bunch of un-Americans wiping their ass with the Constitution.

But Groucho could be murder. He used to do something that I never quite understood: when we dealt with strangers, he would recklessly create danger in some weird effort to make me laugh, which I never did, because the things he said or did would scare the hell out of me. He'd destroy a situation to put me in peril! All for an audience of one. He couldn't resist. Maybe it was because I was twenty-four and he was in his forties? No, he was just a dangerous companion. A menace. His tongue was an unguided missile. Worse than in his movies.

About five weeks after completing **At The Circus**, my first Marx Brother's picture, we went to a sneak preview in Huntington Beach. That meant the studio executives, the director and stars, and even the lowly writer went in limousines to a coastal theater south of Los Angeles. Everybody else was calm; they'd all done this before. But I was practically catatonic.

It seemed to me that my whole life, my future was riding on what would happen once the movie was shown. I felt that because I was getting solo screen credit, I'd have nobody else to blame if it turned out to be a flop. Which in my state I was sure it would be.

Thank God I was wrong. The film got all the laughs we'd hoped for. The cards that the audience was given to fill out as they exited, came back mostly positive. So it was a happy trip back to Hollywood.

The next morning, I got a call from Groucho asking if I'd like to join him on a trip to Europe. "And how!" I said. "If the studio lets me take off some time. Can I take my wife along?"

Groucho said, "Obviously you're sex crazy. But okay."

After booking passage to cross the Atlantic on the SS Liberte, in the spring of 1939, Groucho, my wife Eve and I took the train to New York. We got there and checked into the Sherry-Netherlands hotel. We'd planned to spend a few days seeing some Broadway shows and friends.

A couple of days before we were to set sail, Groucho got a telegram from a friend of his in the State Department. They must have picked it up from the Hollywood Reporter or Variety that he was going (Variety always had a little box called "On The Go" where it had "Clark Gable Goes Hunting." So it must have had "Groucho Goes To Paris.") The telegram said it would be inadvisable to go to Europe at this time, under present conditions. The situation vis-à-vis Hitler was getting scary.

"It could be dangerous," Groucho said. "Hitler may have seen one of my movies."

Then he got serious. "No Paree, kid. Now what the hell will we do?"

My wife, who was born in Virginia and knew her way around the South, mentioned a famous resort in White Sulfur Springs, West Virginia, called The Greenbrier. "It's quite beautiful," she told us. "You can play golf." Groucho said yeah, he'd heard Sam Snead was the golf pro.

I said I thought I'd heard something about the hotel being restricted. They didn't like Jews. But Eve had been there and never had a problem. Of course, Groucho and I didn't look like Eve. But he wasn't concerned. He pranced happily across the room and told me in a brogue: "You worry too much, Paddy me bye. Shure and they'll be nice or they'll know the wrath of me sainted father, Bishop McMarx, begorrah!"

So I sent a telegram down to The Greenbrier asking them to reserve two rooms for the following day, signing the request "I. Brecher" rather than "Irving." I hoped this would outwit any anti-Semite reservations clerk. I got a confirmation later that day by telegram; they were looking forward to our arrival. My wife had business in New York—Eve said she'd join us in the hotel in a couple of days.

The next evening, we boarded the Chesapeake & Ohio sleeper train out of Grand Central Station. And here's where I started to worry—I've always been a fucking terrible worrier—because I'd traveled with Groucho before. When he wasn't disruptive or embarrassing, he simply complained. We'd taken the train from Los Angeles to New York and I discovered he was a world-class insomniac, always griping that he never got any sleep in the lower bunk of whatever sleeping car we were in. This particular car kept being shunted back and forth around the Grand Central train yards as if some maniac was using it as a toy. Evidently this individual coach had to be hooked onto the train heading south. And for what seemed like hours, I listened to Groucho whine pathetically. (Funny as hell of course, inventing new words of hatred for the engineer or praying that we'd be derailed.)

"This is a fucking bowling alley, Brecher! I curse the day you married that sadist wife. 'Go to Greenbrier!' she says. That shrike! Any woman who would sentence a beloved comedian, international idol, to a night like this should be flogged!"

"Okay! I'll flog her. You let me sleep!"

"You promise?"

We didn't sleep on the way down, we were laughing and complaining so much.

Finally, the train made it to West Virginia—arriving just after dawn. With Groucho bleary-eyed, I commandeered a taxi to take us to the Greenbrier Hotel. Beautiful country; there was frost on the ground. The beauty alone should have made me happy, except I had a growing apprehension that kept me from enjoying the scene. I felt I was in enemy territory with a loose cannon as my companion. Yes, a man adored by millions of moviegoers—men mostly—who saw him do and say what they didn't dare express on their jobs or in their own lives. You may think he was doing a great public service. But the man needed a keeper.

We get to the hotel and it is a stunning place with huge golf courses as far as I can see, and not a soul in sight. I decided to play it clever, cool.

"Grouch," I say. "Why don't you take care of the fare and the baggage, and I'll run ahead and check in."

"Begorrah, 'tis a foine plan, me bye!" he says in that cockamamie burr.

Now I started running up the driveway, up the long path to the huge doors of this magnificent antebellum edifice—I had a right to be worried.

I heard footsteps padding close behind me: the s.o.b. was tailing me in his Groucho crouch, as if the cameras were rolling. His crouch about to pounce, meant disaster was ahead. If I could only check us in....

I made it inside into a huge lobby and rushed to the check-in counter. Three men in black suits stood stiff as statues behind a long desk. They just stared into space. No greeting. They looked like they had just come from a lynching, and would probably enjoy a pogrom. Then they looked at this thin, pale stripling—me—followed by an even stranger, toadying creature smoking a cigar.

I held out the telegram and said: "Good morning, I have this confirmation—." But before they could take it, Groucho leaned on the counter, and in a voice that I can still remember as being very sharp, said:, "Is it true gentlemen, that you operate a chain of brothels from coast to coast?"

No laughs.

"Let me put it another way. Are you your brothel's keeper?"

Only the sound of my stomach dropping. The middle clerk smiled icily. Solemn as an oak, he spoke. "Afraid there's been some error. We have no reservation."

I waved the telegram at him. "But you sent this…"

"Sorry, there must be some mistake."

Then, pain-in-the-ass Groucho came to the rescue.

"How'd you boys like to be in the movies?" he beamed. "I've got some mighty big connections at MGM. They're looking for a trio to compete against the Three Stooges."

The cabbie had set down our two overstuffed suitcases by now, so Groucho sat down on one. "I demand a lawyer!" he shouted, echoing off every cranny in that lobby. I felt myself sweating. I noticed the elbows of the clerks' black jackets glistening. I noticed how they all had the same face with long blue noses. Groucho had made his joke, he had had his fun, but nobody laughed and we had no place to go.

Suddenly a fellow appeared, asking if there was a problem. The manager. I appealed to him.

"This man is sick," I explained, going on how "my friend was trying to be funny, you know how it is with comedians. Look at this telegram, please sir, please?"

He seemed to listen to my tears. Grimly, he nodded to the clerks, and one of them located a vacancy.

"Two-twenty-two," I heard him tell the bellhop.

My heart started beating again. It was sixteen hundred miles back to

New York. We ended up in, not really a room; it was more of a broom closet with two cots. Pipes running overhead, no windows. Sort of an air vent with a sink. American plan. The can was down the hall. Groucho flopped on a cot. I could have killed him.

"Your joke didn't quite go over," I said to him instead of killing him.

He just nodded cheerfully. "Those morning audiences were always tougher," he said, a reference to Vaudeville theater days. "But you'll see when I do it again later, it'll get a belly."

But I had some revenge. Groucho didn't get five minutes sleep that night. Neither did I; it was a miserable dump.

The next morning my wife arrived from New York. After the shock of seeing our plight, she used her feminine wiles and Southern accent on the manager of the manor, and we got two decent rooms. There was a convention of newspaper and magazine cartoonists staying at the hotel, including many famous cartoonists of the day. Most of them enjoyed meeting Groucho. One of them, Rube Goldberg, possibly the most famous, was an old friend, a man known for drawing insanely funny inventions, impossible to describe, but memorable. We had a great time with them. I remember the delightful lunch in the hotel where we had been persona non grata.

But you want ironic? The following night the hotel ran a new movie for its guests: the Marx Brothers in *At The Circus*. Evidently, they let the *movie* in the Greenbrier. They just didn't want Groucho.

Groucho is across the table and I'm next to Rube Goldberg who is pulling a new invention out of his pants at a cartoonists' luncheon in White Sulphur Springs at the Greenbrier Hotel.

Take Me to Your Reader

> Irv: When I first got out here the orange-
> blossom scent would knock you down in Pasadena.

Back at the hotel in Century City, Brecher had turned a planned half-hour interview into ninety-minutes of tales spun from some marvelous Eden he called, "Los An-geleez," reeling off other anecdotes—why Danny Thomas was the best stem-winding storyteller he ever heard; how he tricked Judy Garland into doing "Meet Me in St. Louis"; how an undertaker character he created saved his life.

When it ended, I stalked him from the fourteenth floor down through the hotel lobby and out to the door of the limousine Turner had provided. I awkwardly tried to get his attention.

Um, Mr. Brecher, I love the Marx Brothers and—
It's a free country. You're entitled to your opinion.
I freelance for the *L.A.* **Times and magazines like the** *Shambhala Sun...*
I read the *Shambhala Sun* religiously. Every time I'm in the ashram. *Relentless.*
Is there any chance I can call you for an interview and—
Sure, call. If I don't answer, I may be dead. In that event, I may not call you back. Death tends to interfere with anything else you want to do.

Pitch to the LA Times calendar section: "Irving Brecher, Hollywood wonder, alive and witting! A well-quipped octogenarian like one of those ancient Sri Lankan elephants holding all native memory between his ears, with a big bite o' Marxian mischief in his voice. And why not? He wrote two of their movies. All Hail Brecho! What can I say, he had me at 'Hello, I must be going.'"
They ran with it. I telephoned.

Mr. Brecher?
It could be.
The *Times* **editor said I could do eight hundred words on you.**
An obituary?
I laughed. That's how our friendship started: Irv made me laugh about death.

No. A feature for the entertainment section.
Well, whom am I supposed to entertain? I'd like a guest list.

After they ran it, a story recapping the dazzling routine he'd done for Turner, he answers the phone:
Who the hell is it…?
Mr. Brecher?
Probably.
Did you read the story?
Unfortunately, yes.
Uh-oh.
Yeah. I got a number of calls from people surprised that I'm not dead. One sounded chagrined. Some of them were from people who I thought were dead. Anyway, I appreciate that I didn't come off too badly. Thanks to your interview, my wife finds me more interesting now. And you were so nice to me, I'd like to reward you with a lunch. You're a light eater, I trust.

Last of the Hillcrest Roundtable

Equipped with my recorder, I arrived at Brecher's condo on Wilshire Boulevard in Westwood, a cream-colored twelve-story high-rise called "The Westholme." A Latino doorman in blue "Westholme" jacket and pants opened the glass double-door entrance and directed me to the elevators. On the tenth floor at the end of a long, wide hallway, I rang the buzzer at Apartment 1001 and was greeted warmly by Brecher's lovely wife Norma. Sunshine poured in from huge windows all around as she led me to the man, pausing to show me the views, which were stunning. I could look down and see, just a few blocks from their place, the campus of UCLA. A mile to the south, huge office buildings, hotels, and a water tower that said "Fox," signalled the little satellite of commerce called Century City. Visible to the north were the hills of Hollywood, and to the west was the Pacific Ocean, all the way to Catalina.

"On a clear day," Norma said, "you can see forever, you know..." trailing a laugh that had its own little song to it. We passed two walls lined with books from the floor to the ceiling. On red carpeting spread throughout the large living room sat a grand piano at an angle with a family photograph and flowers in a vase on top of it. Next to the flowers was a golden statuette that I took to be an Emmy award, knowing Brecher received such a winged angel in 1950 for "The Life of Riley."

In the adjoining study sat the very image of a writer-in-retirement. Brecher's perch was a high-backed red Barcelona armchair and behind him were red curtains he no doubt drew to watch movies on a large TV screen across the room, with more books behind it on white shelves six rows high. Across from the flower-print sofa where I eventually sprouted roots was a wall full of photographs of people from Brecher's life. Some I recognized: William Bendix on a parade float with a very young Brecher, maybe in his 30s; Jack Benny and Brecher dressed like Canadian Mounties; Groucho Marx around a table of men, each with a cigar; Milton Berle in later years in a loud suit, beaming at Brecher and arched slightly back holding a cigar; another shot of Groucho and a much younger Brecher holding cigars; Irv sitting looking sideways over the top of a typewriter holding a cigar; one of a young child in a snow suit in front of an old house; and one of Norma standing with another woman, both young and stunning and there was Louis Armstrong smiling between the two of them.

I had time to check all this out because upon entering his lair, Norma and I were shushed by Brecher, who waved his arm frantically to show us he was on the phone. He uttered a couple mm-hmms and then pressed the speaker-phone button.

"—Well, I'll be glad to, sir," projected a voice trying hard to sound silky smooth. "Gospel Light is a company catering to folks like yourself who enjoy those beautiful melodies..."

"Yes indeedy!" Brecher smiled wide with a strange glee I hadn't seen at his Turner performance. "I saw your offer here on my television set," he said impishly, "and knew I would just have to be able to hear some of Jesus' favorite songs."

"Then you will love the CDs," said the voice. "Just give me your name and address."

"Surely, brother," said Brecher.

"And credit card number—"

"Amen!" Brecher said, building energy. "Now I am legally blind, so I couldn't make out all that was on my TV—how much are the CDs again?"

"Only nineteen ninety-five, sir."

"Do you take VISA?"

"Yes," the voice said. "And just add four ninety-five for shipping and handling."

"What did you say, brother?" Brecher's face was shining.

"Only nineteen ninety-five, plus four ninety-five for shipping and handling."

"Oh Lord!" said Brecher. "The church only pays me twenty dollars a week for picking up beer cans in the parking lot..."

"Only nineteen ninety-five," said the voice, now put into purr mode. "Plus, as I said, the shipping and handling..."

"I'll tell you what, ," Brecher said. "Never mind the CDs. I'll just take the shipping and handling."

A pause from the peddler. And then: "You... just want to pay for shipping and handling?"

"Yes. Want my credit card? I can't read it to you. But my seeing eye dog will. Here, Jasper!"

Click!

Brecher sat upright, relaxing his role as a born-again imposter.

"That takes care of that shit," he said, the mad glint still in his eye. "You know what s-h-i-t stands for? 'Shipping and Handling in Television.'"

Was this odd performance for my personal amusement? Or was this just how one peculiar old codger amuses himself?

"People call them pranks," Brecher said as he wriggled out of his red seat and reached for a cane Norma held in front of him. "It's more than that. It's an expression of fucking quiet outrage."

Actually, I'd thought it sounded like something that Groucho would say: "Well then [cigar high, eyes rolling], just send me the shipping and handling..."
But I didn't tell Brecher that as we headed out to lunch.

Finally we're in my Toyota and Brecher directs me (Norma calls him "The Director") to Hillcrest, the legendary Jewish country club. It is a central part of his life, having been a member for more than fifty years. (Just don't call it "Hillside" around aging Angelinos—Hillside is the Jewish cemetery.)
In less than ten minutes, we pass 20th Century Fox Studios on Pico Boulevard and make a right turn into Hillcrest's hidden driveway.
Brecher notices the flag is at half-mast.
"Somebody died," he says. "I have to go see if it's me."
"Mr. Brecher, hello!" says a valet, approaching the car.
"Mr. Brecher! Hello, Mr. Brecher!" says another man who helps him out of the front seat.
The valet takes my Toyota.
We enter a magnificent brown-trimmed palace with gleaming floors and fine wooden wainscoting.
"Hello Mr. Brecher. Two in the Grill Room?"
This is Renaldo, in a blue jacket adorned with the club crest. He leads us through a vast spread of sumptuous golden carpets and tablecloths—there's Monty Hall, host of TV's Let's Make a Deal walking past the buffet!—to a table overlooking the golf course. Seated at a table for four, Brecher immediately turns into a Jewish mother. He severely recommends against the veal, even though I was only kidding about ordering it. I make a note: "senses of humor could clash."
We end up partaking of his vouched-for smorgasbord of brisket, turkey, rolls, and fish. Hillcrest's buffet is famous he says, and unreal—every plate I get comes gravy-enhanced. I'm able to finish off two bowls of gazpacho, a dish of honeydew, half a dozen cantaloupe and watermelon slices, a brownie, an ice cream sundae and two chocolate chip cookies (for later). Irv ends up picking off some of my raspberries and having a Hebrew National dog with tomato soup.

I know Brecher is a man of a million stories. Where to begin? Groucho? Television? Radio? I start by asking him when he joined Hillcrest.

1943. I was 29.

The club burned down right after that.

Really?

Yes! It was closed for a while. They started repairing it. People could play golf, they just couldn't go inside.

I understand it was the first club in L.A. to admit Jews.

You understand correctly. But it wasn't that they admitted Jews. It was that a group of German Jews, many of them immigrants, decided to build their own club because they were barred from the Los Angeles and Wilshire country clubs. So in 1920 they bought a hundred-and-fifty acres and built a clubhouse.

All Jewish members, right?

Wrong. They hated being discriminated against, so the members wanted to demonstrate they were not bigots. At the Wilshire and the L.A. clubs, bigotry was par for the course.

A fitting phrase.

Think nothing of it. *I don't.*

Did they pick this spot because 20th Century Fox was across the street?

No. Fox was there, a small place making silent movies. But they built here because the land was—you might say—dirt cheap. There was nothing else here. This was prairie! They bought it from the city. I think the real estate agent was a Navajo.

(I look across the Grill Room at one round table that looks like it could seat a dozen people, but at the moment is without a single diner.)

Is that the table?

That's it. *[He nods.]* Where some of the greatest comedians ever would eat and try to top each other.

With jokes.

Sometimes. Sometimes an experience they had playing vaudeville or Broadway, or maybe radio, TV, the movies...

How often did they meet?

What do you mean? They ate lunch here whenever they were in town! And every Sunday night, especially in the 1940s. This was sensational. Wouldn't it be nice if they were all over there now? Groucho Marx, Harpo, George Burns, Al Jolson, Jack Benny, George Jessel, Lou Holtz, Milton Berle, the three Ritz Brothers… and can you believe it? Me!

How did you break into such a hallowed assemblage?

To my everlasting pleasure, I was invited by Groucho to have lunch at the table shortly after I joined the club. Groucho and I had become very close while doing *At The Circus* and *Go West*. I really was flattered to be accepted by these giants. I was there for so long; I watched them go, one by one...

(Irv drinks his coffee. I try to pick up the mood.)

I've always loved Jack Benny...

(Putting down the coffee, he picks right up again.)

I did too. As a friend. He was really sort of naïve and gentle. A softy. I'll tell you. Surprisingly, because he was so great on radio and TV, Jack Benny never made us laugh. Regardless of his tremendous importance—anywhere he went in America, he was recognized by strangers—Jack Benny was really a very unassuming guy. Not like most comics. And this was fresh to me. A helluva lot of them do a lot to hold everyone's attention, to remind them of their importance. He was an extremely appreciative listener and a particularly good audience, especially for George Burns, his closest friend. Burns had a quirky streak and did little shtick on Jack that would send him into hilarity.

Like what?

It wouldn't be funny if I told you. But Benny would collapse laughing.

Okay. Who else sat over there?

Harry Ritz. He made us laugh. He did very funny body movements, remarkable eye-rolling and very funny ways of dealing with food. Plunging a forkful of steak in his ear. Harry liked to be on.

Who was the funniest?

I would say the funniest man at the table was George Jessel. You don't hear much about him because he never made it big in TV or the movies. He was great doing stand-up at Broadway theatres such as the Roxy or the Palace. He had a stab at movies at Fox because the studio head, Darryl Zanuck liked him. Jessel had self-destructed his career early on, around 1930 I would guess, when he starred in a smash hit on Broadway, **The Jazz Singer**. He was the toast—or matzo, maybe—of the town. And then Warner Brothers, a struggling studio in Hollywood, bought the rights to **The Jazz Singer**, figuring to make a movie that could possibly save them. Naturally, they offered Jessel the lead. Success had made him very confident, so he demanded a fee far in excess of what Warner could possibly pay. They offered him stock in the company instead. He said, "Shove it." To his dismay, Warner signed Al Jolson to play the lead. Jolson had demanded a hefty fee, but Warner successfully convinced him to take stock, instead. Jolson became a millionaire in that deal. And Jessel and Jolson were not good pals after that. I liked Jessel. He was really funny at the table, talking about troubles with women and all the human frailties that afflicted him.

I imagine club members got a kick out of being in the same room with these men.

Just the opposite. At one point, a few other patrons started a small revolution. They decided it was un-democratic for us to have a table where they were not welcome. I overheard rumors of some kind of revolt in the locker room. One of them said: "Why don't we go to the board of directors and tell them to pass a rule?" The other said: "They'd never do it. They're afraid of those big shots." The first said: "There's gotta be some way to break up that table."

"You're crazy," said the other guy. "You're gonna take an axe and chop up the table? The club will buy a new one!"

So the insurgents never got anywhere. The table is still here, and all of them are gone. In 1996, when George Burns died, that was the end of the lively Hillcrest round table of great wits. Now I'm the last man standing. Except I'm sitting.

How did the gang here compare with the group of writers you sat with at Metro-Goldwyn-Mayer?

It was totally different! Here the comedians usually talked about themselves, and they were all aging performers. At the MGM writers' table, we talked about everything, primarily: the incompetence of producers; the lack of talented directors; and anything else that was negative.

Who were the Ritz Brothers?

They started in vaudeville clubs and then made movies and had a fairly good career.

Remember any of their routines?

Sure. One of their best-known bits went: "I have a sinus problem." –You do? "Yeah, I need an agent to sign us."

Old style.

Harry Ritz was irrepressible.

What were the other Ritz Brothers like?

The other two were dolts. You want dessert?

Golf is Not a Game

After lunch, we walk through the "Men's Card Room." He promises to join the players "as soon as I get rid of this young man. He's a free-lunch journalist."

The game seems tame enough, but I know gin wasn't always a gentleman's game in Irv's circles. The Friar's Club was the scene of a scandalous episode where members were fleeced by crooked rummy players for thousands of dollars.

I imagine your card games here aren't like the ones at the Friar's.

Some members had the game rigged using marked cards to fuck their friends. Some even ended up in jail. But their cheating was good for one thing: It gave me the chance to make Jack Benny laugh.

One day I went into the steam room and Jack was in there getting boiled. He said, "Irv, you're a member of the Friar's, aren't ya?" I replied, "I'm an honorary member." And then Jack said, "Somebody told me that the Friar's were planning to move to a place where they could have their own golf course."

"It could be true," I said, "I was over there yesterday and I saw some of the gamblers marking their balls."

He fell on the floor.

Did you play a lot of golf here?

I wouldn't say *play*. I suffered through it because I enjoyed the company of Jack Benny, Harpo Marx, George Burns. But the golf is boring. Besides, it's not a game.

Not a game?

You can call it an *activity*. A time-killer, a hobby, a way to avoid your wife. But a game? That's where you have competition, where somebody's trying to beat you. Tennis, football. Even checkers is a game. There's an opponent trying to prevent you from whatever you're trying to achieve. Golf is not a game. It's something you can do all by your lonesome. Like masturbation: the player does his thing, only with two balls instead of one. He holds his club in one hand instead of two, and concentrates on achieving the desired result with as few strokes as possible. There are some differences, of course. The club is probably shorter than the ones in the golf bag. Maybe three *feet* shorter.

You've sold me, Irv. I'm gonna quit.

Oh? Golf... or what?

Funny guy.

Irv, on the answering machine: "Hank? Irv. Are
we there yet? I don't want to have to read this
fucking book post-humorously."

*On our way out of Hillcrest, a man dressed casually in a yellow cotton sweater
comes up and kisses Brecher hello.*

"Irv," he says, "I guess you saw the flag was at half-mast."

"Tell me the good news."

"Manny passed away."

"Has anyone told him?"

When the man leaves, Brecher fills me in:

Guy was ninety-nine years old. He was a pawnbroker and the cheapest
son-of-a-bitch I ever knew. Once it was my bad luck to run into him on
Hollywood Boulevard. As we were walking along, a panhandler stopped
him and said, "Please, mister. Three days I ain't ate. I'm so hungry." Manny
gave him an appetite suppressant.

Come on, you're making that up.

Put it down as creative conversation.

*From then on, I began to assume that some of what Brecher told me was his
purely off-the-cuff fictional impromptus. Other things were real, yes. Either
way, it kept me coming back for more. I looked forward to these solo flights of
putdowns, some of which I caught on my tape recorder after Brecher grudgingly
granted permission.*

You can tape me. But I reserve the right to add a laugh track.

*On our drive back to his place, we got onto politics. Calling him a liberal is
an understatement. And on the subject of George W. Bush, who had been in
office just a few months, he said:*

You write for the *LA Times*—so I hope you read it.

Of course.

Then if you'll pardon the ham in me—or the corned beef—did you
read the letter I sent that was in the paper last week?"

I had seen it, but wanted to hear it from him.

What was it about?

You know Dick Cheney had a heart attack.
I didn't know he had a heart.
Ha! I wrote...

> *Dear Editor,*
> *I join my fellow citizens in wishing Dick Cheney good health.*
> *If anything serious happened to him, George Bush would*
> *become President.*

Well, that's only my opinion. One shared by millions of Americans. Those who are awake, anyway.

Brecher often seethes fatalistically, filling my tapes with diatribes against the government. "One of the nice things about dying," he said once, "is not having to go through what's coming, much of it their fault."

One afternoon, he explains his upset over what happened following a recent appearance by Groucho in an area high school.

Students had tacked a poster of George W. Bush on a hallway wall, and then proceeded to give the man a makeover: thick black eyebrows, glasses and cigar. Freedom of humor? The students meant only to promote the school play. The school principal had the poster removed.

Brecher has me e-mail the Los Angeles Times:

> *Dear Editor:*
> *As one who wrote two films for the Marx Brothers, and con-*
> *sidered Groucho my closest friend, I believe if he were attend-*
> *ing Woodland Hills High today, Grouch would be exercising*
> *his free expression against George Bush, too. (Nobody seems*
> *to be making Hollywood movies doing it.)*
> *Sincerely,*
> *Irv Brecher*

The Times *does not run the letter.*

These attacks of extreme worry—on subjects like politics, as well as his bronchitis, pneumonia, worsening glaucoma, loss of appetite and concern about his low weight—I came to see as a form of sport after a while. It was hard not to notice how Brecher's anxiety made everyone around him nuts.

But this was not new. Harpo Marx had nicknamed him "Irv the Nerve" in 1938.

The Angel of Death, in Yiddish

For Brecher it begins and ends with the comedians. With Jack Benny, George Burns and Milton Berle, Jan Murray, Red Buttons, Al Jolson and George Jessel. But what made them funny? Once, in my car, Brecher made me pop out a cassette of one of his "Life of Riley" radio shows in the middle. He said: "If you'll notice, so far this is basically sad. It's a sad situation. That's why it's funny."

It all begins with the comedians. And it ends with all of them dying.

In the spring of 2002, Brecher lost two of his friends: Billy Wilder and Milton Berle.

Tell me about Billy Wilder.

Billy was a complete original. A completely original, immensely talented writer and director, with a great, great acerbity.

For years, Billy and I took our regular morning walk together.

You must have talked a lot about the movies.

Nope.

Billy did bird calls, mostly. The birds just sneered at him.

Now, he's gone. Listen, you wanna know what it's like to be old? You have no peer group anymore. I used to have peers. Now I only have *disap-pears*.

The way it is these days, when I go to Hillside Cemetery? I leave the motor running. I didn't want to go to Billy's funeral. And I'm trying to arrange not to go to mine, either. I've always had kind of a disgust for funerals.

I was up much of the night thinking about it. I could not stop thinking about the way funerals are handled. It's ridiculous!

A lot of people come to a funeral and they talk about what a wonderful guy this was who just passed away. This is absolutely pointless. If they *really* liked the guy it would be nice if he could hear it. So, they should have a funeral service *before* he dies. It would also be a test for the eulogizers. How sincere they are. To see if they can really bullshit in *front* of this guy the way they would if he was *dead*.

There should be an arbitrary figure—like whatever the insurance statistics say is the longevity point—let's say 79. Then at 78, the CEO of a big company, even if he's healthy and playing golf and fucking everybody, gets together with everybody and do everything they would do at a funeral service after he croaks. Only, the guest of honor is *present*, is alive. What would be interesting is all the crap, because they'll be hoping that he rewrites his will. They're vying with the plaudits.

That's a great idea.

And if you had these funerals ahead of time, there'd be no crying. That'd be nice.

Especially if no one liked the guy.

There are certain guys who you never cared about. And those would be the difficult funerals to deal with. For financial, or social, or political reasons, they'd be *forced* to bullshit. And the non-dead guy listening would be thinking, "That cocksucker!"

We laughed. Then I introduced the subject of Irv's own mortality, something he always had new dirt to throw on, so to speak.

Irv, is the end of your own life on your mind because you went to Berle's funeral?

All of our adult life we're going to funerals.

But you said there's nobody left of your peers, so how many funerals do you even go to anymore?

Happily, there's always someone.

And most have their final resting place at Hillside?

Yeah, that's where my parents are, where Norma's father is, where my best friends are. Almost all of them.

Do you ever go there, you know, just to visit?

I visit my parents, in the ground.

A silence. And then, one of his wife's favorite stories about Irv.

Norma and I were on our way to Hillside Memorial Park for services for a friend. And we got into an argument because Norma was very critical about the way I was driving through traffic. I snapped back at her and we got into a loud, disturbing quarrel. Quite heated. As I parked near the Hillside chapel and we glared at each other, I said: "You know, you take all the fun out of a funeral." End of quarrel. She collapsed.

What do you mean?

She kissed me.

And you left the engine running.

Always. So I can get out before they grab me.

Who?

The angel of death. The *malakh ha-movess*. You know Yiddish?

No.

You should learn it before you die.

Part II

Vaudeville & Radio

OCTOBER 13 MARTINSON'S COFFEE — Clear / Cloudy / Rain / Snow

MILTON BERLE
Capitol, March '33 (50-)   20.00
Mer., April '33 (50)   20.00
Fleischman, April (50)   20.00
Speech (Jewish Guild) (10)   5.00
Chicago Palace (250.00)   125.00
Loews State, Sept. 22 (20.00)   10.00
Loew's State, 9/29/ (25.00)   12.50
Old Gold, 5th (20.00)   10.00
Old Gold, 6th (25.00)   12.50
Miscellaneous   10.00
BKLN. Papa. 12/5/33   20.00
Chi. Palace, Dec.5 (on acct.)35   5.00
Jan.17'34 Balance - $40.00   40.00
Feb. 7 - N.Y. Papa,   25.00
Mar.20 Chicago, wk of 23+30   30.00
April 5, Marbro   15.00
Apr 13 - 19   30.00
                                  30.00
August 11 (Vallee)   25.00
Sept 15 (Kenny)   15.00
October 26 (2 gags Casino)   10.00
Dec 7 (Vallee) (100.00-½)   50.00
                          (over)

OCTOBER 14 Clear / Cloudy / Rain / Snow — MARTINSON'S COFFEE
August 1933
Reiss, Irving & Reiss 6/6 (30.00)   15.00

          REISS HAMILTON REISS
Nov. 12'34 - A comedy song + gags
    Advance -   (½ of 25.00)   25.00
Nov Advance -   (30.-½)   15.00
Dec 7 "   (30.-½)   5.00

From the notebooks of Brecher, 1934: A list of performers, venues and payment for his material.

> "A sneak preview meant the feature arrived in
> a can and was unbilled. Unlike today where the
> newspaper ad gives the damn title away."
> —Irv Brecher

Do you remember how you first got hooked on the Marx Brothers?

Yes I do. I was about fifteen. A senior at Roosevelt High School that was—I wonder if it still is, in Yonkers, a little city north of the Bronx. My homeland...

A senior at fifteen?

Yes. I graduated at sixteen.

How come so early?

I finished the courses, that's how come. Sixteen-and-a-half. But at fifteen I was writing about high school sports for the *Yonkers Statesman* newspaper for six bucks a week. One night I handed in my copy to Mr. Brennan, the night editor, an amiable old guy who reeked of Irish whiskey but never seemed drunk. I enjoyed getting close to him.

"Tell me my Hebrew lad," he said. With no malice. "Do you ever go to the motion pictures?"

This was 1930.

"Yes sir," I said. "Whenever I can afford it. You know tickets have gone up to 25 cents."

"Well, the man from the Strand, who bought this ad for us to run tomorrow, gave me a pass and it's good for any time. Would you like it?"

"Would I? I sure would, sir. I love the movies."

And as things turned out, I still love Mr. Brennan, because when a friend and I went to the Strand Theatre the following night for what the marquee hailed as a "Sneak Preview," I met the Marx Brothers. In **Animal Crackers**.

I was really into comedy. On the rare occasion I could buy a ticket, I preferred to see Buster Keaton or Larry Seemon or Ben Turpin or Charley Chase or Harold Lloyd, rather than the dramatic features. At fifteen I was really more interested in some brilliant comedy shtick that Buster Keaton would do than whether or not Rudolph Valentino would get into Greta Garbo's pants.

And this time I was on the floor. I'll never forget watching four wildly funny men getting howls so loud I couldn't hear myself laughing. But I couldn't get it out of my head. That night in bed I ran scenes from the movie over and over in my mind. Seeing **Animal Crackers** made me an instant fan. When I told friends about my discovery, one of them said they'd seen them a year earlier in a movie called **The Cocoanuts**. Obviously I had missed this major event in my life! But now that I'd found these wonderful clowns, I vowed I would see every movie they would ever make. Even if tickets went up to 50 cents.

You see to the general public, Groucho was absolutely new in terms of style. No movie comedian before him had done throwaway lines aimed at sticking pins in human gasbags that way. The anti-authority. He seemed to be the spokesman for every moviegoer who ever wished they'd "said that" when the boss or the wife or the bill collector or the cop had given them a bad time. What a job he could've done on George W. Bush.

Is that when it hit you to do comedy yourself?

Kids decide what they're gonna be when they grow up, and generally change their plans every few hours...

And you decided that night to become a comedian?

Not really. I had no idea how I could do that. I wanted to be a journalist. I knew I enjoyed making people laugh. And I even went so far as doing my own version of my idol Groucho for the amusement—I hoped—of my friends. I made up my face, using a burnt cork to blacken my eyebrows and paint on a black mustache. I had dark, kinky hair that I could part down the middle. I got the wire eyeglass frames at the ten-cent store. And I would do his material at parties. (Our parties might be three people.) Jokes that Groucho had done in the movie. And a few of my own. But it happened that my natural delivery had a remarkable resemblance to that of Groucho; I seemed to have no trouble copying his timing of a punchline. I was somewhat taller and leaner than him but I really looked like a sixteen year-old clone of Groucho Marx.

What about the cigar?

Plus, a rubber cigar. Yes. That did the job. Try inhaling a rubber cigar.

The Difference Between
a Comedian and a Comic

Irv shakes his head in disbelief.

Who could imagine that eight years after I saw "Animal Crackers," I would be writing a movie for the Marx Brothers?

In researching that period I found out the Marx Brothers also did a radio show. In 1932 and 1933—

Not The Marx Brothers. Just Groucho and Chico. Harpo didn't speak, which didn't make for good radio. And Zeppo was nowhere to be heard. The show was called, "Flywheel, Shyster & Flywheel." They played shifty lawyers. The show was soon canceled. It died on the radio because you had to see these funnymen, not just hear them. At the beginning of the '30s you also had the first radio shows from comedians like Jack Benny and Eddie Cantor...

Irv, I hope you don't mind my taking advantage of your elder wisdom, by asking an age-old question.

Go ahead kid.

What is the difference between a comic and a comedian?

The comedian says funny things, the comic says things funny.

Thank you.

You're welcome.

Funny. I always thought it was the opposite.

No. Milton Berle was more of a comic. He did funny things. He walked funny, he put on dresses. Although Berle would rather be called a co-median probably. A guy who says something funny is like Joe Penner: "You wanna buy a dooooog?" That's a comic, he says something in a funny way. Jim Carrey wags his tongue. That's not a comedian, that's already a comic.

Something I've always wondered about: Is one considered higher on the clown-as-abstruse-image-of-the-deity scale?

I don't understand you, but both take skill. Ed Wynn was a comic. He would talk in a shrill voice and giggle.

And he looked hilarious.

Bob Hope would go, "The broom said to the cat," and people laughed.

The broom said to the cat?

Whatever.

And Jack Benny then, is a comic?

No, he was a comedian. Phyllis Diller was more of a comic. Abbott and Costello were comics.

Because of their style, their delivery. But when you said, "that's already a comic," it makes me think a comic is farther along.

I think it's an old bromide.

So a comedian is just different in that way.

Yes, because it's more acting. Cary Grant was a comedian.

Really. Not a comic actor?

He's a comedian. He could play drama and get you to laugh. Much different. I wouldn't call William Powell, the Thin Man, a comedian, because he played all kinds of drama.

Ernie Kovacs?

He was a comic.

Zero Mostel?

Comedian.

So Gleason is a comedian.

A comic.

Damn.

On his variety show, when you saw "Joe the Bartender," that's a comic. Or "Reginald van Gleason."

Got it.

Dangerfield's a comic, I would say. There's a narrow line. It flips over. When they're doing all kinds of shtick, they're comics. When they're just doing reactions, they're comedians. Dangerfield could be both. Jack E. Leonard. They'd bring him on. "Welcome, Opponents." That's the way he'd start. Don't you love him?

Here, let me explain why it's confusing: In discussing these people, we always called them comedians. Someone who elicits laughter. That much we do know. Comedians are different than humorists. A comedian is insecure on stage, while the humorist who sits at the typewriter may have his own miseries and complaints but he can get some relief by writing down his attitudes. They are melancholy men as opposed to some neurotic comedians. Some.

So, Sid Caesar, because of all the funny accents—Comic or comedian?

Sid Caesar is.

Is what?

Just *is*.

You're a standup comedian, Irv. Know any good jokes?

I remember some old ones. First time father takes his little son on the subway up to Van Cortland Park in the Bronx. And the little boy says, "Papa, what's the name of that flower?" Father says, "How should *I* know? Am I a milliner?"

Know the one about the two toddlers in the sandbox? The one who is circumcised says to the other—

"I couldn't walk for a year."

Right.

You're not a joke teller. If you're not a joke teller, don't tell jokes. If you like telling jokes, practice it. But if you don't really like it, don't tell them. And most of all, don't tell them to someone who *does* know how to tell jokes.

Whoops.

It's like cholesterol, you either have it, or you don't.

Got it. How about gags? How do you define them?

Gags are essentially one-liners, or a short joke, or whatever.

And how do you write them? I mean, do they just come into your head?

When writing a Marx Brothers film, I tried to write lines within the context of the story and with the incidents that were happening. Like say, in *Go West* where Groucho falls down the saloon steps and Chico slaps him and offers water to bring him back around. Groucho says, "Forget the water, force *brandy* down my throat."

My favorite line.

I wouldn't call that a gag because it doesn't stand alone. That's a bit with a topper at the end.

A bit with a topper at the end.

Yeah.

I'm not sure that's how Freud's "Analysis of Humor" put it... But isn't "Force brandy down my throat," another of Groucho's non-sequiturs?

It's the cap on the action. On a piece of business. I'll tell you what a gag is. I'll quote Red Buttons: "Never buy *gribbenes* from a *mohel.*" They scream at it. It's a stand alone, amusing line.

Gribbenes?

It's Yiddish. For the cracklings; the crisp bits of poultry skin and browned onion left from rendering *schmaltz*–chicken fat. If I have to explain, then, for the record, a *mohel* is the guy who does a *bris.* Which is a circumcision.

I confuse bits with gags, I guess.

After Larry Gelbart gave me a compliment, I wrote him: "It worked like Viagra of a different kind—I got a swelled head."

That's a stand alone. Classic gag construction. Do you consider yourself a Laughrican-American?

What?

You're a gagmaster, Irv.

It's hard to define wit. I only know that a spontaneous retort tearing down some pompous person is a very valuable tool to keep you happy.

Is a spontaneous retort like a gag line?

Retorts that are funny, I wouldn't call them gags. Listen. Louis Nye told me a joke about a new diet where he eats three bananas, and the next day eats three strawberries, and the next day three cheeses, and the next day he shits a mural. I added "mural." Louis used "painting." That's what I do, find the right word to make it funnier.

So that's a gag…

There's no difference between a gag and a joke, really. A joke can also be a long story that ends in a punch line, an anecdote that can take two minutes. A gag is a short thing. Listen, Darryl Zanuck co-founded 20th Century and was in charge of production at Fox after they merged in 1935. He produced some great movies. But one time Zanuck got mad at me because of a gag.

What happened?

He put a movie out and I told him it hadn't been released, "it *escaped.*"

The Thief of Bad Gags

> "Wonderful, Red, wonderful. Red? You said some
> of the funniest things I'll ever use."
> —Milton Berle 1983, to Buttons at Irv & Norma's
> wedding

Let's get to the nitty-gritty. When did you actually think show business would be your life's work?

In 1931, I became a part-time usher and ticket-taker at a small theatre called the Little Carnegie Playhouse on 57th Street. A few feet east of Carnegie Hall, near the Russian Tea Room. The theatre was owned by my father's cousin, Leo Brecher. I quit the Yonkers newspaper to take this job and really rake it in—$18 a week—on which my mother, father, sister, brother and grandmother tried to survive. The six of us lived in a two-bedroom, third-rate apartment next to the elevated tracks in the Bronx. I worked six days a week, ten hours a day, and using the subway added two hours travel. That was my life at the time. I didn't think it was exactly "show business." That came later, in 1933, and it took a freakish happening that started me in the direction that got me here.

Hollywood.

No. With you, near the end of the line.

The Little Carnegie Playhouse was the first movie theatre in America to show foreign talkies. We were known as an "arthouse" and our biggest customers were Germans who lived in the Yorkville section on the east side of Manhattan. I knew this because one of my jobs was working the Address-o-graph. This was a machine using plates with names and addresses embossed on them, punching out envelopes into which I stuffed the weekly programs. In the early 1930's, the beginning of Hitler's rise to power, I remember the FBI coming in and taking the plates. They didn't tell us why. This was in '31 or '32. Almost all the names on the Address-o-graph were German. There was some suspicion. (Around the same time or a little later, a prizefighter named Barney Ross went up to Yorkville with a couple of guys and baseball bats and brained a bunch of anti-Semites. He was great.)

Anyway, one afternoon in '33, after I'd punched out envelopes to my thousands of personal enemies, the reviewer from the weekly newspaper *Variety* ("The Bible of Show Business") came in. Wolf Kaufman was there to see our newest import, starring Emil Jannings and titled, *Sturme der Liedenschaft.*

I knew Wolf. He always stopped by the ticket stand.

This time he said: "I heard some of your gags last night, kiddo."

I said: "What are you talking about?"

"Well, I know you occasionally have a gag in Winchell's column and I heard Bob Hope do a couple of them in his monologue at the Loew's State."

"You're kidding!"

Quite often I mailed in topical gags—one-liners—on a penny postcard, and was always thrilled if Walter Winchell in the *Mirror* or Ed Sullivan in the *Daily News* printed them with my name. I had millions of readers. And my friends were very impressed.

"Did the people laugh?" I asked Wolf about what he heard at the Hope show.

"Yeah, they laughed," said Kaufman. "Loud and a lot. That's why he's using them." Then came something startling. Wolf said: "Did you know people get *paid* for writing those things?"

I said, "Really?"

"Yep," Wolf said. "If you can come up with more gags, take an ad in *Variety* and maybe you can sell 'em."

"But I can't afford an ad in *Variety.*"

He said they were $15 an inch.

"That's practically a week's salary," I said. "I only make 18 a week."

"Tell you what. Make up a one-inch ad and I'll get it in print. The newspaper can afford your owing 15 bucks. Pay for it when you sell your first jokes."

A real good guy. (I've been subscribing to *Variety* ever since. Only 75 years.)

Well, I got very excited and saw myself depositing checks from all the comedians whose names I knew in a bank inside my head. On my lunch break I called Al Schwartz. He also sent gags to the newspapers, but his mother insisted he go to law school. I told him I was gonna write an ad, would he wannna go in for half—$7.50—which we would eventually have to pay *Variety.*

As a constant reader of anything about show business, I knew of the rising popularity of a young, very brash comedian named Milton Berle.

I'd never seen him. I'd never heard him on the radio. But I knew that he was getting a kind of notoriety by bragging on stage that he stole material from other comedians. And got laughs with it. And other comedians, who were not kidding, were really angry at him.

I sat down to write a one-inch ad—something I'd never done—as wide as a column in Variety. But what to say? Then it hit me: as close to a miracle as I've ever been. And truthfully, I feel if any one moment changes your life, it was that moment. The ad read:

```
"Positively Berle-proof gags.
So bad, not even Milton will steal them.
The House that Joke Built
Schwartz and Brecher, Circle 7-1294."
```

After work that night, I ran ten blocks down to 47th Street and, as Kaufman instructed, dropped an envelope off at the newspaper office. And for the days leading to the next issue of Variety, I combined ushering, living, and breathing, with hoping. By the following Wednesday, I had been distracted by problems at home—basically a shortage of rent money. It was only when the mailman delivered the weekly Variety that I remembered the business with the ad. I quickly started riffling through the paper... and finally, there it was. Just one of a dozen different ads. Mine was the smallest. I was staring at it when the telephone rang. I answered it and this is what turned my life around.

"Little Carnegie Playhouse. How can I help you?"

A man's voice, in a bad German accent said: "*Vass time der farshtunkener movie es playeenk dis nacht?*"

I said, "Lee, get lost!"

I thought it was my friend Lee Geier. He was always trying to be comic on the phone. So I hung up.

The phone rang again.

"Little Carnegie Playhouse."

"Lemme talk to Schwartz or Bretsher."

Bretsher?

"Cut it out Lee, I'm working." Another half-assed hoax. I hung up.

A moment later, it rang again. And this time the voice was loud and mean.

"No son-of-a-bitch hangs up on Milton Berle! Who the hell do you think you are?"

Now it hit me and I began to shake.

"Who is it?" I stammered back.

"I told you. This is Milton Berle. Are you the wise guy who ran the ad or not?"

"Yes, but I was really only kidding—-"

"Never mind the apology, you shit. If you think you're that funny, be at the Capital Theatre tonight at eleven. Go to the stage door and ask for me. Bring some topical gags. And they better be funny!"

"Yeah, sure. Eleven o'clock." I barely got the words out.

"I'm being held over for a third week. I need some jokes about Bing Crosby and Kate Smith and George Givot. They're on the bill starting tomorrow. Listen, just be at the stage door at eleven. They'll send you up."

I hung up the telephone and the room seemed to be swirling around me. I couldn't believe a big vaudeville star wanted me to... had just called me to... I was terrified!

Limply, I started to try and do my day's ushering. On my lunch break, I ran out and bought all the papers.

And New York had papers then! The *New York Times*, *The Sun*, *The World-Telegram*, *Herald-Tribune*, *The Mail*, *The Journal*, the *Daily Mirror* and *Daily News*. It was possible to get the *news* from those papers, unlike today where the only news you get is what Dick Cheney and Karl "Robin Hoodwink" Rove approve.

Things were happening in America to write about in March of 1933. We were still in a deep Depression. Roosevelt had been installed as the President a couple of months before and he had just closed the banks. People couldn't get their own money out to buy food. A gorgeous actress named Marlene Dietrich was making news by wearing trousers. It was the beginning of a style. What a sexy beauty she was.

I thought, I strained, I felt the pressure of a novice heading for an executioner—a comedian. I typed out about a dozen lines on various subjects and called Al Schwartz and took down some funny stuff he thought of: "Things are so bad that doctors are using borscht for blood transfusions." I know. Doesn't stand the test of time, seventy years later...

When the Little Carnegie closed I went to the Capitol a few blocks away on Broadway. I was terribly nervous. I had never been backstage in a theatre. I had never met anyone in show business, except some other movie ushers. I had never spoken to anybody who was a name, and when the stage doorman sent me upstairs to Milton Berle's dressing room, I was frozen with fear. I was alone. Al Schwartz said he couldn't come with me. His mother insisted he study for a law exam and wouldn't let him stay out that late.

The door had a big star on it. I held the cards with the jokes. Trying to breathe, with my heart pounding, I knocked on the door and dropped all the cards. I was on my knees picking them up when the door opened.

What I saw was the bottom half of a man, stark naked. Being new to show business, I did not recognize him until I looked up. I knew of course that this was Milton Berle because I'd seen his photo in the papers, but I'd never seen him in such detail. I saw the reason for his great reputation among the friendly young women in show business, that earned him the envy of some of his contemporaries in the field of fornication. His cock. It was tremendous, the size of a salami chub. It was like another little person there. Big star.

"Oh," he said. "I was expecting my mother."

I guessed they were a very close family.

Berle continued: "So who are you, Schwartz or Bricker?"

I was so punchy, I said: "I think I'm Bricker. I'm Bricker. Irving Brecher!"

"Whaddya got for me?"

I handed over the cards. He grabbed them and closed the door, and I stood there waiting for the governor to call. A few moments later he opened the door and said, "Some of this looks pretty good."

Then I exhaled.

"I'll tell you what to do, kid. You go up to the Park Central Hotel and go to the office of my agent, Charlie Morrison. He's on the second floor. He'll give you a check. And then you come back here because we're going to have to work all night."

"W-What?"

"I have to get a new monologue for tomorrow's show, and you're gonna help me."

"All night?"

"I can use some of this stuff, but I need a hell of a lot more."

I ran the five blocks to the Park Central, found the agent's office on the second floor, and knocked on the door. A handsome, white-haired man opened it and when I told him Berle sent me, he handed me an envelope.

When the door closed, I pulled out a check. It was the biggest amount of money I'd ever held in my hand at one time: Fifty dollars.

What a cinch this was, I thought. I'm going to be rich!

On the way back to the Capitol, I stopped at a pay phone, splurged a nickel and dialed my home, anxious to announce that I was now in show business. I recall rattling off the news, which my mother couldn't really understand, but when I told her I was going to stay out all night and go to a hotel with an actor—she sounded worried.

"You don't have pajamas?"

"It's okay," I said. "I'm not taking my clothes off. I'm just gonna sit at a typewriter and do whatever Mr. Berle says. This could mean we'll be able to pay the rent every month. Maybe even eat."

I don't remember her response to that, or if she even had one.

I told her not worry and I'd be home tomorrow.

Berle had finished dressing when I got back to the Capitol and we went by taxicab to his office at the Edison Hotel on 47th. We worked all night, this twenty-five year-old new sensation prodding me into making up more lines based on items in the newspapers. I kept offering gags, some of which I strongly liked even if he didn't, and some of which I wasn't that proud of. And he would reword a few of them and then be satisfied. Looking back, it was an eerie experience. It was like I was standing there, watching me at the typewriter, while he paced and mouthed the lines he liked over and over. It was an all-night education.

The next morning, Berle said: "I'm going back to the theatre. My first show is at 11. You can order some breakfast and come later. I'll leave word for them to let you in."

Long before 11, I was sitting in the Capitol Theater orchestra, having a breakfast of fingernails. My heart was doing a crazy dance. I had never been that nervous.

And then it was finally time. The first show of a four-show-a-day program starring Milton Berle, with guest stars and a feature film. My heart was coming out. The orchestra played its opening salute to the star and out from the wings exploded this slim, dynamic funnyman, my new mealticket. Berle raced to center stage as the audience applauded and he beckoned them with an arm out asking for more. Then, like a six-foot-long machine gun, he started firing. Rapid firing. And to my incredible joy, each was greeted by a laugh, some small, others big.

Milton Berle's memory was amazing. The man had learned, word for word, all the new material we'd come up with the night before. When he got to some of the lines I'd written and the audience laughed—sometimes roaring and even one time applauding—I went into ecstasy.

I thought, no question, my future is a given.

After the monologue, he did his job as emcee for the others on the bill and I sat, barely watching. The show ended and I expected to get a pat on the back after I climbed the stairs backstage. I heard a shouting, angry voice behind Berle's dressing room door. Then the door flew open and a big, red-faced man burst out, and turning back, wagged a finger at Berle: "Remember what I'm telling you. Leave out that crap or you'll never work in a Loew's theater again. You got it?"

He rushed past me, his bulk nearly knocking me back down the stairs. When I made it into Berle's room, he was livid, cursing the man for forcing out some of new gags. The man was Louis K. Sidney, manager of the theatre. He told Berle some of the gags were too blue and could not be repeated.

Berle was furious. Like all comedians, he hated to give up on laughs. But he recognized that if he repeated particular gags, he wouldn't be working.

These were the days when vaudeville was very tough on comedians in terms of what they could and could not say. Blue material could end a career.

What were the lines that Berle wanted to hold onto? (I never knew one comedian who willingly cut out a laugh unless his job was in danger.) What was so terrible? I'll tell you. At that time the Mayor of New York was Jimmy Walker. He was famous, a sort of playboy, a bon vivant. And now he was up before the Seabury Committee, a self-righteous congressional group examining corruption in high places. The rumor prevalent among gossipy New Yorkers was that Hizzoner, a devout churchgoer and family man, had a secret mistress, a beautiful blonde named Betty Compton. Walker's defiant denial to the committee had made headlines. When the committee chairman hinted at the mayor's illicit behavior, he said: "I'll match my private life with any man."

The line I had given Berle was: "Did you hear what Jimmy Walker told the committee? When they accused him of you-know-what? He said: 'I'll match my private wife with any man!'"

The audience screamed. He followed with: "When President Roosevelt closed the banks, and nobody could get any money to spend, Marlene Dietrich was caught with her pants down."

Big scream. And whistles from the salesmen who usually saw the early show.

Berle was furious but he had to drop the material. We replaced some of the lines with several others acceptable to the powers that were.

But as a kid nineteen years old, I continued in my state of euphoria back to work at the Little Carnegie later that afternoon.

I was in show business, show business was fantastic, and I had twenty-five dollars. Having made half of fifty dollars with such ease, I now made a major career decision, worthy of a CEO at Enron. Because I was so young, exhilaratingly so, I did something utterly nuts.

I walked over to the Little Carnegie and told the manager, Manny Rosenberg,—after he demanded to know why I was late for work—I would be leaving at the end of the week.

"What?" said Mr. Rosenberg. "You're quitting?"

"Yes sir. I'm writing comedy for Milton Berle. You know, the comedian?"

He seemed startled.

"I've seen Berle a couple times," he said. "He's funny. You sure you're doing the right thing, quitting?

"I think so. Yes, I'm sure."

But now, as I shook hands and left, I wasn't so sure. In my naïveté, I assumed that since a big star such as Berle played dozens of theaters all year long, he would need me to come up with fresh material every week. I didn't realize he used the same material at the next theater. And at all of his future bookings!

And Mr. Milton Berle played a lot of theatres.

There was a circuit—with Loews Capitol Theatre on Broadway as the flagship of an entire chain of Loews theatres, dozens of them sprinkled around the East, all owned by Metro-Goldwyn-Mayer. (This was years before the U.S. Justice Department made the studios give up ownership of movie theatres.)

The Capitol ran fresh-run MGM-only motion pictures, plus an hour and a half stage show. This variety show always had a headliner and supporting acts of singers and dancers. The public thrived on this entertainment and to me it was the most wonderful form.

Vaudeville had something for everybody in the audience. It was like a big buffet of entertaining dishes. My favorite was the Keith Fordham Theater, located in the nice part of the Upper Bronx, on the west side. We'd walk down the Grand Concourse to get there. The Park Avenue of The Bronx, the first place with tall apartment houses. (Tall being six or eight stories.) That's where I'd go with one or two friends, if I had a quarter, and we'd see six acts. This was thrilling. Acrobats, a dance act, singers, and comedy.

One act was called the "Charles Withers 'Opry' House," where this performer dressed as a handyman was trying to erect a set across the whole stage showing the interior of an opera house. The results were disaster. Things fell and things whirled around and hit him. He'd cut off incipient disaster with superb timing, catching things, dropping things. For twenty minutes we'd be doubled up in laughter as he took a beating.

Sometimes on the bill was a man named Owen McGivney, a quick-change artist. He'd appear first in a business suit and then disappear behind a screen. While the orchestra played, he'd come out the other side in less than ten seconds, totally dressed in another costume. This was dazzling. He'd repeat this action again and again, coming out in a pirate costume, or as a ballplayer or a headwaiter in a tuxedo or as an undertaker. That was the act. He was incredible. Once (much later) the stage manager let me stand in the wings and watch the act. Then I was able to see what happened and how McGivney did it. He had helpers and a remarkable construction of costumes that snapped on in a moment.

An act could also just be a man and a woman dancing to romantic music. I had a cousin, Evelyn, who was part of a dance act. She was a beautiful girl. And her partner was a handsome Jewish boy. My beautiful raven-haired cousin. Her exquisite face.

The act was called "Maurice and Cordoba." They were a great pair. A showstopper every time they performed. Maurice LaPue was his real name. They posed as Latin dancers, which gave them an added air. Instead of calling themselves, "Brecher and LaPue."

It was a very sexy dance, as far as they could go in those days. You know, *Good Housekeeping* pablum. Body twists is all. I was all of twelve years old and my cousin was about twenty.

For twenty-five cents you saw the acts. Once a year an act came back to the theatre. And if you saw it again you liked it as much as the first time. Because they were classic entertainments.

But it was half a dollar to see Berle at the Capitol. (The Little Carnegie Playhouse—motion picture tickets were usually forty cents—got two dollars a ducat because it presented an exclusive kind of film. An imported film, for the very select audience. There weren't many art houses in the country.)

Anyway, I waited at home for a week, trying to get up the courage to go back to the Little Carnegie and hope to get my job back. And then the angel that hovers over dummies did his thing.

Berle started calling me every three or four weeks, from Chicago or St.

Louis, asking me to telephone him collect a few topical jokes, which I did, gratefully. Eventually, a check would come in the mail, sometimes $15, sometimes $25. I gave up my plans to buy a Rolls Royce.

One day he called and I shook in excitement and relief, as he told me he was booked on a new show.

"Rudy Vallee's Radio Show," he said. "Next week, I've gotta do five minutes with Vallee. You ever heard the program?"

"Yes sir. I like Jack Benny and Fred Allen better." (I had yearned to write for my favorite radio show, "Jack Benny's Jell-O Hour.")

"So do I," Berle said. "But Vallee is paying me. There's fifty bucks in it for you if you can come up with a few minutes of good stuff. Topical, but not like what that son-of-a-bitch at the Capitol made me cut out. The guys that run radio are even worse than the assholes who run vaudeville."

A couple of days later, after an exciting but worrisome period of concentrated brainwork, I had my next crisis: meeting Berle at his manager's office, hoping he'd like what I had written. The first time I'd gone to see Berle at the Capitol, I had butterflies. This time as I got into the elevator at the Brill Building, I had buzzards. I was dead and they were picking at my bones. Suddenly, I thought none of what I was about to hand him was funny.

But I was wrong. He actually even complimented me on a more personal basis than he'd ever done before.

At the Capitol, he'd said, "This stuff is funny." But this time he said, "I've got to hand it to you, kid. You're funny."

Milton Berle and the Buffalo Cathouse

"The nice thing about dreaming is you meet a
better class of people."
-Brecher line for Berle.

Berle was interesting to be around offstage. He couldn't just sit and chat like we do. He was the most out of place person when he wasn't performing, restless, and always seeking distraction.

One weekend in 1933, as some sort of partial payment, Berle invited me to watch him emcee a vaudeville show at Shea's Theatre in Buffalo. What I didn't know was besides getting out of town, I'd be in for another first time event in this ever enchanting world: sex.

Sex for me at 19 was still only a word.

I was picked up in a long, seven-passenger Cadillac, driven by Berle's bodyguard, a mug named Danny. I was startled to find out he carried a gun but Berle reassured me of Danny's niceness as a fellow Berle supporter. Berle's mother Sandra, a terribly domineering woman who really ran the whole Milton Berle show, insisted that her son have a bodyguard now that he was a "star."

"A gun is good when you're stealing material, Milton," I kidded him.

"I don't *have* to steal material anymore. I got *you.*"

Living with my parents in Yonkers, I had never been anywhere to speak of, and an auto trip to Buffalo was exciting because Danny made most of it at high speeds.

Berle checked us into what I thought was a pretty nice hotel and for the first time in my life, I slept alone. (At home, where my younger brother Jack and I were roommates, we were poster boys for the Depression.) And the next day, I loved sitting in the audience watching Berle perform for the locals. As always, he was a tremendous hit. One of the reasons for his success was that he wouldn't give up if an audience was tough. Berle wouldn't quit until he'd broken them down and could leave to the sound of their great applause. He was a bulldog. After watching some shows I added one or two funny lines to his monologue, which also pleased the audience and all of us along for the ride.

The night of the last show, at about nine-thirty when we usually went to have something to eat and then to bed, he told me he had to take a ride to see some of his cousins.

"You have cousins out here?"

"Yeah, they live in Tonawanda."

It was a mining town nearby.

"You might as well come along," he said. "You'll enjoy it, they're nice people."

We soon reached a suburb with darkened, low, and ugly houses, stopping in front of one that seemed completely gloomy.

"Your cousins live *there?*"

"Yeah, you're going to love them."

Berle grinned. He hadn't washed off his make-up; he was still wearing lipstick and rouge from the show. Danny was grinning, too. I wondered why.

As we got out, something bothered me but I didn't know what, not until the door of the house opened and a frowsy blonde wearing a scant bra over huge breasts said, "Hello baby." By this time I got the idea that this was the kind of place I'd read about in novels that referred to these "fun palaces" as bordellos.

Berle spoke to the woman at the door.

"Tony at Shea's Buffalo sent us," he said smoothly.

My eyes widened.

Berle looked at me.

"You're going to love my cousins," he said. "Or better yet, they're gonna love you."

We pushed forward and wound up in a small, seedy-looking room with a fireplace going. There I was with Berle and Danny and a few fairly young women, all dressed seductively in the barest of garments. I was kind of excited and terrified at the same time. While I stood there gaping, Berle was telling the madam, "This kid, he's a first timer."

He was acting like a veteran, and possibly he was. "Well, get with it, fellas," he said brightly. "Take your pick!" Then he added, "But before you entertain us, why don't I entertain *you* a little bit?"

Berle started to do what was then called, "swish," or "nance" comedy. He pulled the brim of his hat down and started to walk around with an exaggerated wiggle. In those days, it was rare on the stage for anybody to do it, and Berle would do it only for a moment. But here he was, swishing around the living room telling jokes. It was outrageously funny and he looked very feminine with the hat down and the lips and with all the makeup.

Suddenly, a big man came into our room. He wore a big smile. The owner. Until his eyes fell on Berle in all that makeup. He came closer, shouting: "What the hell? This is a queer! Get the hell outta here, ya queer pansy!"

"I'm not a queer," Berle tried to protest. He said take it easy

"Fuck you!" said the big guy. "And take your girlfriends with ya!"

And when he picked up a poker from the fireplace, we got out fast, clear out of Tonawanda—and that was the end of my first and only visit to a cathouse.

Girls! Berle! Catskills!

Paying money to a writer was not one of Milton Berle's favorite "Things To Do Today." But sometimes he would offer a bigger payoff, so long as it was at someone else's expense. In August of 1933, he said he was taking a weekend at Grossinger's. I had heard a lot about this place in the Catskills, which was famous for dozens of hotels supplying a retreat and food for fun-loving New Yorkers, primarily Jewish ones.

"It's a freebie," said Berle. "Ya wanna come along?"

I sure did. I was six-foot one-and-a-half inches tall and weighed 120 pounds. Berle said I looked like "a piece of dental floss."

He said, "You should eat more."

I wanted to say, "You should *pay* more." But I didn't dare. I was timid, afraid I might blow this windfall of the occasional ten or twenty dollars, by demanding a bigger return for the laughs I was supplying...

We got up to the Catskills in Berle's fancy Cadillac. Grossinger's was huge and throbbing with activity. Golf and tennis and a big swimming pool, and because Berle was welcomed by Jenny Grossinger, it was obvious he'd done some entertaining there before. He was also given a glad hand by a number of guests who had seen him on stage in either Manhattan or the Bronx and he clearly enjoyed the adulation. That night was the first time I ever slept in a room all by myself.

I can still conjure up the smell of dinner in that huge dining room— all those different dishes "like mother used to make." And dinner was long because Berle would not leave until a few dozen of the eaters had besieged him for his autograph. He was funny with them, until finally he decided that he needed cigars. So he led me from the hotel to the nearby village which had a general store.

When we stepped inside there was a clerk dozing at the cash register and two, young, nicely-shaped women sipping ice cream sodas, on stools at the fountain. The sound of the bell on the door made them turn for a quick look; then they returned to their drinks. The star, who had just been swarmed over, was being flatly ignored here. He tried to cure that.

"What's your best cigar?" he asked loudly.

"Roi-tan," said the clerk. "Ten cents."

"I'll take half of one. I'm just a poor comedian."

The girls looked over briefly but gave no reaction and I tried not to laugh as I saw Milton's frustration. He took another shot.

"Have you got a *Racing Form*? My horse likes to read it before he hits the hay."

The clerk said, "No."

The girls again ignored his majesty.

Berle marched to the pay phone in the corner. He dropped in a coin and then: "Long distance? How much is it to Manhattan?"

He deposited more coins and waited, staring directly at the two heretics. Then, louder than before, he said into the phone:

"HELLO MA? THIS IS MILTON BERLE."

The girls turned, got off their stools and left.

Years later, when Berle was in his late 80's, he still seemed comfortable only when performing. It could be in the biggest theater or for the smallest of audiences. He was a sure bet to work three thousand people or one lone victim for laughs.

That's why at his—I think 85th—birthday, I told a packed Friar's Club:

> Most of you know Milton likes to perform on occasion. He's a performance junkie—he's only happy when he's hitting you with a string of one-liners that you probably heard before. For example, the other day I was in the City National Bank in Beverly Hills, waiting on a long line to make a withdrawal. I can't afford to make deposits...
>
> Milton enters, noisily as usual, and many of the customers recognized him with smiles. They like him. I see him look up and spot the bank security camera, and then he moves a bit to make sure he's in range. He goes into a routine about his recent stay in the hospital. While he's doing this monologue, in walks two men wearing ski masks and carrying shotguns.
>
> "Hands up!" one of them shouts. "Everybody!"
>
> Everybody obeys but Milton. He keeps shooting one-liners.

One of the holdup men snaps: "Hell, let's get outta here. He did the same shit at Wells Fargo last week."

Milton Berle on a 1937 issue of *Radio Stars* magazine, which boasted, "The largest circulation of any radio magazine."

The Age of Hilarious

"Oh am I thrilled to be here and to be invited
to all of Irving's weddings. All I can say is
that I hope Norma and Irving will be as happy
as Ruth and I wish we were."
-Milton Berle

On March 27th, 2002, Milton Berle played his final appearance in a crowded chapel just off the 405 Freeway in Culver City, California. The place: Hillside Memorial Park, eternal retirement home of Al Jolson, Eddie Cantor, and Jack Benny and so many others. A few days after the funeral, Irv pulled a box of old audiocassettes out of his bedroom closet. One was labeled:
"HOLLYWOOD PRESS CLUB
1/19/92 FRIARS CLUB
80 YRS SHOW BIZ MILTON BERLE"

Marking Berle's "lifetime achievement dinner," Brecher entertained the appreciative Friar's Club crowd with anecdotes, concluding: "And that was the start of my longest, most rewarding friendship—with the pussycat we're lionizing tonight. Milton, tomorrow marks the beginning of a new chapter in our nation's life. President Clinton's efforts will encompass, at most, eight years, as he strives to make America happier. You've done that for eighty years. I wish the President well. But long live the king!"
Then came the king's idea of a brief thank you: He did 40 minutes.

I didn't make it to Milton Berle's funeral. But Irv, who had known Berle longer than anyone, told me about his sense of loss.

Even though it was expected—Milton was ninety-three—You're never really ready. I feel bad. Real bad. Did you see the *New York Times* writeup? The *Los Angeles Times* had a big spread, too.

In the chapel at Hillside, Red Buttons said some funny things. Something to Berle's widow, Lorna, like, "You killed him, you know. All the sex."

Norm Crosby was good. Jan Murray was eloquent and funny. If Milton had known that the other comics would get so many laughs, he wouldn't have died.

He had a great life and everyone there extolled it.

Then we all went over by invitation to Friar's for a four o'clock feast. Larry Gelbart and Sid Caesar came over to me.

"Why the hell didn't you speak?" Gelbart asked. "You're the definitive man on Berle."

That was sweet of him to say so.

"Plus, you're a helluva lot funnier than those guys," said Caesar.

What a guy!

"They didn't ask me," I told them. "I'm not offended."

But I had resented being denied a chance to express my long and mostly-warm connection and admiration for a tremendous talent who had given me the break that led to my life. Whatever you want to make of him, he was a phenomenon. The youngest of five children whose mother was a store detective who looked like a fullback, who became the number one smash of all time.

It's fair to say nobody was ever able to affect American viewers with the force that Milton Berle exhibited on "Texaco Star Theatre." Run those kinescopes today, you'll see Berle is breaking all the rules and creating a new chapter in comedy.

He taught them all. Me, too. Your life turns on not only what you do, but also what everyone else does…

"The service was more like a show," is what I told Sid and Larry. "His widow did the casting. And she figured I wasn't a big enough name." To their credit, the comedians got a lot of laughs. I'm sure if there is an afterlife for funnymen, Milton would have tried to top them.

So I'll never know how many laughs I might have gotten had I done a eulogy. But things even out. Milton won't do one for me.

Hoot Gibson's Vaudeville

> "Hey Mr. Roberts, wanna swap movies?"
> "Whaddya got?"
> "Hoot Gibson and The Sheriff's Daughter."
> -Mister Roberts (1955)

"That funeral really took me back," Brecher says the next time I come to his apartment to record stories. "Way back. I didn't sleep at all last night because I was playing those years over in my head. I kept seeing faces of vaudeville comics, guys and girls that I sold gags to for twenty dollars. And for many people in 1935, twenty dollars was a week's pay..."

While Berle was using the same jokes I wrote for him at every theater, I started doing piecemeal writing for around thirty vaudeville acts. Small names, unimportant names, it didn't matter—the idea was to keep supplying these would-be-stars-that-never-made-it with material.

Vaudevillians were notorious for their cheapness. Their idea of a fair price for anything: Free. But the biggest deal I got at that time was when an agent I knew got me signed for five hundred dollars. A fortune! Hoot Gibson, the western movie star was making a personal appearance in Philadelphia. Ever hear the name? Cowboy Hoot Gibson. He was in need of a few funny lines while he did his rope tricks. I worked all night and the next morning I was still writing with my pad on my lap as the train took me to Philly.

I'd seen Hoot in the movies. He made literally dozens of pictures. I thought he was okay. I liked his horse better, but no matter. When I got to Philadelphia, I took a bus to the theater and went upstairs to the door with a star on it. I was nervous; I'd never met a movie star. I took a breath and knocked. A voice called, "Come in!"

Hoot was not as tall as he looked on a horse. But he was pleasant enough. Kind of abrupt. There was a beautiful girl at the far end of his dressing room. She was sitting at a mirror and doing her nails. She turned around and kind of nodded.

Gibson said, "June, this kid brought me some stuff. Jokes."

(I found out later her name was June Gayle.)

Hoot started to read a couple of my pages. I could tell by the movement of his lips that he was a slow reader.

June left the room to get cigarettes. The star, whose lips by now were tired, grunted something like: "This stuff is good. Goddamn trouble is I gotta learn it. This personal appearance stuff is the shits. If it wasn't for the money, they could have it!"

Then he walked over to the sink in the room, unzipped his fly and peed. Right in the sink! I'd never seen that before. I wondered if that's what they did out west. Do cowboys *have* sinks? I knew they had *ranges*...

When he was said he'd try and work some of the jokes into his act the next day, I felt brave enough to say, "By the way sir, the agent who sent me said you would pay five hundred dollars."

"Oh damn! I left my checkbook at the hotel!" He waggled the sheets of pages at me. "I see your address here. I'll mail it to you. You did a good job, pal. Ever come to Hollywood, look me up."

He mumbled something like: "Yeah, okay, gotcha."

And I left.

What's the date today? How many days is that from 1935?

That check is still in the mail.

I never went to another of his movies, bad as they were.

The next time I saw June Gayle was years later at dinner in New York. My wife and I were at Lindy's with Fred Allen and his wife Portland Hoffa. The other couple was Oscar Levant and his wife June Gayle. She was even more gorgeous.

I never mentioned Hoot. And I had the feeling Oscar Levant never peed in the sink.

Henny at Lindy's

> Irv: Sometimes I wrote on spec, sometimes
> I wrote on salary, sometimes as a
> partnership. When I was writing for
> vaudeville, I'd pray. There were no guilds
> taking care of me when I handed material
> to Henny Youngman.
> Hank: You wrote for Henny Youngman?
> Irv: You know him.
> Hank: Henny was the king! I saw him once
> at The Bottom Line. He opened for the
> Turtles.
> Irv: The whom?

Vaudeville humor was marvelous; it was verbal talking teams, putdown, and some classic physical humor. There were dialect comics—that's where Chico Marx came up with his phony Italian–immigrant comedy, and immigrants loved going and seeing vaudeville. Sometimes I'd even get to provide lines to a monologist named Henny Youngman. Henny said he'd heard from Milton Berle that I had given him some "good stuff." And he needed some little gags, one-liners. Of course, Henny went on for the next fifty years or so to get all the bookings he could handle on stage or in TV.

Years later when I visited New York, if Henny wasn't working, he sat in his little kingdom of admirers at the Carnegie Deli where he regaled his fans with hilarious one-liners. And if I was lucky enough to find him there in my search for pastrami, we would hug each other as old friends and invariably he'd say: "For god's sake kiddo, get me my own TV series!"

I never did, nor did he. That was Henny's big frustration, even though he was a rich man due to his remarkable financial ability to never pick up a resturant check. Henny also liked to play practical jokes. I saw him do one on Leo Linderman.

Lindy's was a big place during those years. On Broadway between 52nd and 53rd Streets, it was a haven for show business people and also for the people who like show people and wanted to eat what they ate. Vaudevillians ate there for breakfast, lunch and dinner. It had the greatest food, and was a hangout for some of the Broadway characters who would spend a quarter for a delicious cup of coffee and use a dollar's worth of napkins and sugar and cream. Thick, heavy cream. One of the characters was a big, unhousebroken ticket scalper named Broadway Sam. Broadway Sam could, for a price, get you into anything. I remember once I asked if he could get me two seats for the Last Supper and he said, "Where's it playing?"

Henny always had the same lunch there: a decent portion of delicious corned beef on two small, seeded Kaiser rolls, perhaps a good quarter of a pound of meat. One day, on his way to Lindy's, Henny Youngman stopped at the Stage Delicatessen a block away and bought a pound of hot corned beef and stowed it in his coat pocket. Smuggling it into Lindy's, he sat down at his regular table with his cronies. While they watched deadpan, he ordered his usual lunch and the waiter brought him the two rolls with the beef. Henny pulled out his package and deftly piled a good extra half-pound of corned beef onto each Kaiser. The sandwiches sat there, loaded with four or five inches of hot meat: the sandwich was so high that if a fly sat down on one he'd have gotten a nosebleed. That's when Leo Lindy, the master restaurateur, strolled by to greet his comedian friend. He stopped and stared at the giant corned beef sandwich and was convinced that he was heading for bankruptcy. He said some curse words in Austrian, and ran into the kitchen. As we watched, the sandwich chef came running out in terror, heading for the exit, with Leo, nearly apoplectic, brandishing a skillet hoping to brain the saboteur.

But the laughter of the audience of comics finally saved the poor guy. That's a funny picture. Henny was an imp!

"Relax, Leo," said Henny. "It was worth four dollars to get your attention."

"Yah, very funny," said Leo. "Where'd you get the corned beef?"

"At the Stage."

"In that case, no charge."

Leo Linderman was short and sharp and ran a tight ship. His waiters were characters, they made jokes and tipped you off on what not to order.

What was amazing about Lindy's was, when I was on my ass I would hang out in front there, hoping to see a comedian who needed some gags. And once or twice, Leo came out with a : "Whaddya want, kid?" He was sorry for me and occasionally he would buy me a sandwich. And when

I made it and was doing okay, he couldn't have been happier. He was a really decent man. And he also invented or created the greatest fucking single piece of food. The famous Lindy's Cheesecake. What was so great? I can't explain it. And piled on top were either cherries, or blueberries or strawberries. It was not sloppy creamy. You talk to Norma about it, her eyes light up.

Henny was the one comedian who I've always thought of with great fondness for how he treated me. I loved his style. It was totally wild, a fusillade of words and punch lines.

One joke had no connection to the rest; more a concept expressed briefly, a picture painted. Like a lady asks the trash collector, "Am I too late for the garbage?"

And the man says, "No, jump in."

When Youngman told me that the most he could spend for my material was two hundred, I could not believe it. I had never seen two hundred dollars in one place. I think I had trouble clutching the bills. I floated back to my apartment.

I got a telephone call a short while later from Henny: "Pretty good stuff, kid. Only a couple I don't go for. The rest sound good."

I gasped out thanks and was happily at work writing whatever I thought would meet his style and approval.

I can still see it, I'm walking down Broadway to meet Youngman, nervously churning about whether he would like what I had to offer and would I get paid or would I get stalled as happened so many times before. Henny was much loved and cared for by other comedians. Milton Berle, Jan Murray and Shecky Greene all loved Henny, and all could do hilarious impersonations of him, the funniest impressions that I've ever seen. Henny Youngman was one of a kind—and kind.

But times changed. Broadway became a place you couldn't walk. Somebody'd jostle you and pick your pocket. It got very tough. Leo Lindy died and his nephew took over and messed up. He was a nice shmuck and he couldn't deal with it.

How to tell the Toothpick Joke

> Irv: I ought to spank you! You can't
> stretch it out to a whole Megillah. Leave
> it alone.

Lindy had a jaded, elderly and raspy-voiced woman at the cash register who dealt with the toughest and slickest from early morning 'til 2 a.m. She was my fondest character. She was always short and to the point and she had a delightful venom. Broadway Sam came up to the counter, laid down his bill for twenty-five cents and reached into the open bowl containing several thousand toothpicks. With his big hand, he grabbed a fistful. And as he did, Miss Checkout eyed him narrowly and said, "Are you building a house?"

Irv, my father told me that story, only it was about Ratner's down on Delancey.

I don't know where he got that. I saw it in Lindy's. I heard it from Broadway Sam. I *saw* that. Ratner's didn't have characters like that.

On his way out, the guy goes to take a toothpick. Then he takes another one. The woman working the register says, "Whaddya' gonna do, build a house?" That's a classic.

It's not much of a joke if you only take a second toothpick. It's only a joke if you take a fucking handful! You don't make a joke about a second toothpick.

Don't you?

It's a bad joke!

Why? It shows her chintziness. We laughed and laughed.

No. It's a poor telling of the joke. Because it's not graphic enough. You could leap to the conclusion that the toothpick breaks, so he takes a second one. This is not a *gruber yingl*. Know what that is? You better learn some Yiddish. It may enrich you as a writer.

Gruber yingl?

A *yingl* is a youth. A *gruber* is a slob.

What a word. Anyway, I'm saying if you take one extra....

That's no joke!

It's about HER.

I'm telling you it's a bad joke.

You say it's about HIM. It's a visual.

Here's the joke. Put it in Groucho's mouth. The guy does this: he takes a handful, maybe two hundred toothpicks. She says, "What are you building, a *house?*" If he takes one toothpick that comment is silly. There's a conceivability that if he takes two hundred…you can't conceive that with one toothpick.

Why would he take two hundred?

Because he's a fucking pig! Because it's free. She's sarcastic: "What the fuck are you doing, building a house?"

From my angle it's the other way.

Okay, fine. I can see I'm gonna have to watch the jokes very carefully in this book.

I agree that her response was quite a retort. There. Tell me more about retorts.

Retorts usually require someone to feed you the line. Or like Hope used to do in his monologue. Seaman Jacobs wrote a lot of those. And then he wrote for George Burns. Seaman's ninety-three and still writing them.

Were you ever friends with Bob Hope?

Only once did I deal with him, early on. He was going to be the star of the "Ziegfeld Follies" one year. The head of the Shuberts signed me to write a couple sketches for the revue. So they sent me over to him and he was all for me to do the sketches, and I said, "How about some money up front?" He turned white. So I said, "Forget it." I never did them. I was going to the coast anyway to write movies. I remember I was surprised to hear that Bob Hope died, because there's no money in it. That was his main motivation. He got paid for benefits, too. Charities. Tough guy. The people generally want a performer to work for free to help raise funds, but they had a situation when Hope was involved—they slipped it to him under the table. So it reduced the fundraising, but it had the benefit of his presence there. His public persona was wonderful.

Do you remember when he turned 100?

When Hope turned 100, did I send him something? Shit. Fuck him. If I could fax shit I would have.

You're talking about *Bob Hope.*

He's a prick. He drew the crowds, he was an icon, no question about it. His character was not a good one, but his ability was good. He was a spry showman and he deserved what he got, the attention of the world. The most popular comedian America ever produced. What he did, he did very well. And here's something: Bob Hope—misanthrope though he was—did something good for me. In business, he was a killer. But he was actually responsible for my getting into show business. The moment was when Wolf Kaufman from *Variety* came into the Little Carnegie and told me that Hope used a couple of my lines in his Loews State show. Wolf had recognized them as my material from Walter Winchell's newspaper column. So oddly enough, Hope was the instrument that started me. "No man is an island," wrote Donne. That's the way life is. When Hope died, everybody was talking about his experiences, and I didn't step up.

Mickey Mouse Magazine

> Brecher: I think Mickey is homosexual.
> Editor: What?
> Brecher: He's been living with Minnie all
> this time.
> Editor: So?
> Brecher: She's never gotten pregnant!

I was getting frustrated selling gags to the cheapest form of human life, small-time vaudevillians. But one day in 1935, a press agent I knew tipped me off about a new magazine published by a man named Hal Horne. Horne was head of advertising and publicity for United Artists Pictures which distributed one-reeler Mickey Mouse cartoons. Now Disney gave him a license to start a Mickey Mouse magazine.

At that time, the only thing Walt Disney did for movie houses was Mickey. The cartoons were a sensation! Very popular, they were in color and made people laugh, although you couldn't imagine from that beginning that Walt Disney would become a giant.

I got in to see Horne after a number of tries. He was an affable fellow in his forties. He said he was looking for writers to supply stories for what would be a monthly, 'aimed at kids and it has to be funny.' I tried to impress him with my credentials, unimpressive as they were—mentioning Berle and Youngman and Hoot Gibson.

"What college did you go to?" he asked.

I said I went to Columbia, NYU, CCNY and Fordham.

"Waitaminnit. Why did you keep changing schools?"

"I went to see football games. If you'll pardon the language, I never matriculated."

He started to laugh and said, "You're hired. Fifty dollars a week. Temporary, you understand. Until we see how it goes."

The next day, I reported to the magazine offices at 545 Fifth Avenue. The French Building. It was a whole new experience. There was some guy in charge, Mr. Pugh, but I don't know what he seemed to be in charge of. There were a couple people drawing cartoons featuring Mickey and Minnie. I met Kay Kamen. He was to make history by developing a whole new industry, merchandising the Disney character, starting with the Mickey Mouse magazine, Mickey Mouse watches, toothbrushes, dog bowls, wallpaper for the nursery, God-knows-what. Kamen's expertise spread, beyond making millions for Disney, he did it for a host of companies. Kay and I became close friends and it broke my heart when he died with his wife in a plane crash in the Azores. Kay was a genius.

Then came the fellow Hal Horne told me I'd be collaborating with: a man who in a very short time became my closest friend. He was a short, totally bald and myopic writer from Philadelphia named Abe Lipshultz. One of the first writings I did at Horne's request was to rewrite the man's name into Alan Lipscott. (Horne refused to admit what we knew to be true: Disney was no fan of the Jews.) Lipscott and I wrote stories, movie satires of actors like "Clark Bagel" and things like that, items from college humor magazines—stories with wit in them that were amusing only to grown-ups. The kids didn't know what the hell it was about. And their parents weren't buying it.

So the magazine had a short life, but during that life, my own changed radically. I was living with my family in the north Bronx in a dump of an apartment. Lipscott was living in the Mayflower Hotel on Central Park West. He had one room and a bath for thirty-five dollars a month. Once when I complained about the amount of travel I spent on the subway from the Bronx, he offered to let me share his hovel. I paid fifteen dollars a month. It was a treat. I could walk to the magazine office and have a feast for thirty-five cents at the Automat, where I would still like to go today if there were one.

Lipscott was in his late thirties and I was twenty-one. And because he'd given me a chance to live in style, I tried to be as accomodating as possible. This meant that two or three times a week, I couldn't go to the apartment until 11 or 12 o'clock, tired as I was, because my friend, though homely as hell, was an expert at attracting women who appreciated certain attention in the right places. If you asked Lippy why he liked living at the Mayflower, he'd say: "Because that's where they come across."

Another thing the Mayflower was famous for was Joe DiMaggio lived there. He was at the peak of his fame, the biggest Yankee star since Babe Ruth, and from the few times I'd see him in the hotel, his head matched his batting average. Unless there was press around, he was gruff and demanding of special attention from the front desk.

It was poverty time all across America. People like Joe DiMaggio were not suffering. They were enjoying a popularity that great athletes are, of course, entitled to. I thought it was nice, living in the same building with a big star even though we were living like mutts

I saw the definitive DiMaggio one rainy afternoon. I took a shortcut into the hotel to avoid the downpour, through the flower shop inside the building. I said hello to the little Italian lady, who I knew to be a widow struggling to raise four kids. I suddenly realized she was drying her eyes. She had been crying. When I asked what was wrong, she shrugged and said, "Oh nothing. It's okay..."

But I persisted. She had always been nice. Occasionally she'd give me a leftover wilted flower or something. I felt sorry for her. I never bought any flowers from her; I had no one to buy 'em for.

Finally she said, "I tell you, you tell no one?"

"I promise."

"Mr. DiMaggio, he come here. He say he want dozen best roses. So I'm happy. One dozen. And I say, 'thank you.' And he take a card and pen. I say, 'thank you very much. Is three dollars.' But he take pen and write. This is what he give me."

It was his autograph on the card. He told her it would be better than money. I stopped being a DiMaggio fan at that moment. He was a foul ball.

Who was your favorite ballplayer?

Mel Ott of the Giants. He was great home-run hitter and center fielder.

And the Mickey Mouse Magazine went bust?

The rat let us down. I didn't like writing about Mickey and Minnie, so one day I went in to see Hal Horne. I was wearing my best deadpan and I said, "Hal, I'm not really comfortable writing about these characters. I think Mickey is homosexual. He's living with this female mouse and he isn't doing anything! She's never gotten pregnant. Shouldn't we have them screwing around? Maybe have some baby mice?"

Horne jumped up, livid. He said, "Are you crazy? You want me to destroy Walt Disney! Get out of here!"

I started to leave but stopped and said: "I got another idea, Hal. Why don't they adopt a cat?"

Nobody was buying the magazine anyway. So Mickey Mouse was a disaster and Hal Horne was a complete flop as a publisher.

But I owe Horne something. Once, when he bought me lunch at Lindy's, he introduced me to Goodman Ace, who was the star of his own radio show, "The Easy Aces."

The fifteen-minute show consisted of a couple that liked to play bridge while making amusing comments. This was a show! It was immensely popular because Goodman was very witty. The show proved popular enough that a studio named Educational Films signed the Aces on to do a series of one-reel shorts, but Goodman was too busy with his radio show to do the writing, so he hired Alan Lipscott and me to write thirteen shorts.

This was the big time. This consisted of Goodie and Jane watching a travelogue and making funny remarks. He played the long-suffering husband, Jane playing the dumb Dora of the birdbrain Gracie Allen School, making funny comments which Goodie with great dry humor would deal with in his gifted way. They played in theaters before the feature and happily, Alan and I got $250 for each ten to twelve minute short. That was my first time writing for the movies and more lucrative than anything I'd ever done before.

Goodie was at one time the drama critic for the *Kansas City Star*. Once he wrote a piece that said: "I reviewed this play under unfavorable conditions. The curtain was up." About the play, "I am a Camera," he wrote: "No Leica."

So I guess Mickey led to something better. You know, if I had those *Mickey Mouse* magazines today, they'd be worth a fuckin' fortune.

Eve

In early 1936, when *Mickey Mouse Magazine* was still on life support, Horne, obviously no William Randolph Hearst, decided that a fashion section with articles on children's clothes could attract more readers. He told me to conduct a job interview with the fashion editor of *Parents Magazine*.

It wasn't easy. The woman who entered our tiny office was stunning. Tall and lovely, I guessed in her mid-thirties, with beautiful white hair. I was so struck by her I stammered introducing myself. Her name was Eve Bennett, she said. And I believed her. I would believe anything this beauty would ever tell me. She was high-class sexy in a long mink coat and a voice like velvet, with a southern tinge.

I made a few vapid remarks that were hardly questions. But I did say some things that made her laugh.

She was clearly not overwhelmed with the possibility of working for Mickey Mouse.

But I was overwhelmed and fell in love. When she got up to leave and gave me her business card, I was tempted to follow her anywhere.

I couldn't get her out of my mind. For weeks I kept wondering about the beauty in the mink coat who I thought was either married or the kept mistress of some tycoon.

I would lie awake at night, imagining her beside me, but not in the Mayflower, because Lippy would be in the other bed. No, I imagined her with me on the sand of some tropical island or the deck of an ocean liner—and to save you the trouble of wondering, all of that happened.

After a couple of more mundane *Mickey Mouse* months, I was eating breakfast one Saturday in the Automat; just the right place for someone earning fifty dollars a week. I could stand it no longer. So I overcame a basic shyness I've always had about females and used the pay phone.

The nickel I dropped in worked. Miss Bennett answered the ring in the same dulcet voice I had been hearing in my head for months.

"Hello?"

"Hello," I said. "This is Irv Brecher. We met at the *Mickey Mouse Magazine*."

"Oh yes, I recall."

I managed to say something to the effect that there had been no decision about using a style section in the magazine. She thanked me and then I dared to say, "I would like to take you to dinner if there is no jealous husband."

I remember it like it was a minute ago.

I was by now in a sweat.

There was a pause and then she said: "There is no jealous husband."

That was the beginning. People couldn't believe it when I got involved, because of the age difference. She was thirty-six, I was twenty-one. I was madly in love. She had never been married; a couple of affairs had left her dissatisfied. But I'll tell you this much: I had trouble convincing her to marry me. Eve found me very entertaining. But she had a great job at *Parents* and was making much more money than I was, knocking down $700 with her job at *Parents* and another style advisory business on the side. This was a time when most women were grossly underpaid.

Meeting Eve brought me luck. She had a strong belief in astrology and numerology, of which I knew nothing. The first time I took her to dinner we talked about theater, movies and she drew me out as to my goals. I said I had two: one was to write movies and the other was "to one day marry someone like you—but it must be *you*."

She laughed. She was not a giggler who will nervously laugh at anything the date says. With Eve, unless it was funny, no laugh. Then she predicted my future using numerology. With every letter in your name having a different number, however she figured it out right there on a piece of paper—mine came to the digit 9.

"That's a perfect number for success," she said, smiling at me.

We dated as often as she would permit and I would brush away her gentle reminders that this could never work. It happened to work for forty-two and a half years of a marriage that had wonderful moments and trying times until I found her one morning with that beautiful smile, asleep forever.

Here's a woman who in 1943 was told she had five years to live and she lived thirty-seven-and-a half years. She just willed it—not to die of breast cancer. She just acted like she didn't have it. And she comforted and supported other women with the disease for years. And she died of a heart failure. What's the best way to deal with sadness, *tsuris*, in life? I'm one of the best worriers that you'll ever find. I've found that it has never solved one problem. Things you worry about the most, happen the least.

But the surprise will *really* fuck you.

I still have that piece of paper with the number 9. I'm still waiting for success.

Irv Dreaming of Success

Irving Brecher

Radio Milton

"He's a very rare person. As a writer he really
has no equals. Superiors, yes..."
-Berle at Brecher's 75th birthday

*In January 2005 at the age of 91, Brecher got a stand-up booking. The Oasis
Center in the Westside Pavilion mall invited him to give one of their seminars
for seniors.*

"It's on top of the shopping center where Nordstrom's is," he tells Norma.

"I know where it is."

*"They're mainly women between sixty and ninety," says Irv. "They have a big
hall. They said there's even a few bucks in it. Fifty dollars. I told them, 'I'll use
it to take out one of the women.'"*

Norma laughs.

"It's run by the National Jewish Fund."

"Jewish Family Services," says Norma.

*"Jewish Family Services. I thought it would be fun to do more stand-up. Now
I have to live until March."*

*Two months later, in front of about forty folks gathered inside the Westside
Pavilion Community Room, on the third floor just off the luggage department
of Robinsons-May, Irving S. Brecher (how Oasis listed him in their program)
performed two hours of anecdotes, gags and improvisationals about the different
golden ages he lived through in Hollywood. He did a mocking Samuel Goldwyn
impersonation, a sneering Groucho crouch, a Jackie Gleason's through-the-teeth
whistle, and a re-enactment of Herman Mankiewicz throwing up at a dinner
party in 1940-something. He kills, in other words.*

*A post-show dine at Junior's Deli across the street is cut short in favor of the
closer Food Court where over coffee he treats Norma, his friend Eddie Marx,
another friend and me, to forty-five more minutes about Robert Wagner, Ernie
Kovacs, Carole Lombard, Spencer Tracy and Edward G. Robinson.*

*A few days later, back in his office, I asked him if he learned how to do his
standup act by watching Milton Berle in the 1930s.*

"No," he answered. *"I just started fucking around at the club."* He meant Hillcrest.

As I told you, Eve brought me luck. A few months after we met, I got my big break.

By 1936, Berle had been going around the country doing the same jokes in every theater for two years. Alan Lipscott and I finished the one-reelers for Goodman Ace and were doing small jobs writing gags. For instance, we were hired to to a radio show called "Follies de Bergere." The star was Fifi D'Orsay, who had once played a vixen in a 1929 movie directed by Raoul Walsh called *Hot for Paris.* On radio she became "Mademoiselle Fifi." The show featured Willie and Eugene Howard, brothers who were very popular in Broadway revues. "George White's Scandals." Names like that.

I loved Willie, a little sad-faced, hawk-nosed comedian, who was in my book the funniest of the comics I either wrote for or watched perform, with the exception of Charlie Chaplin. Eugene was lucky to have Willie as a brother because he was no talent. But Willie, I had heard, refused offers to dump Eugene. He was a sweet little guy and it was a joy to write for him. I still have some of his records of hilarious songs. Willie Howard had a classic routine called "The French Lesson." Teaching French, only using Yiddish. Lippy and I wrote a French lesson for each Fifi radio show. But the program attracted few listeners and I'm probably the only one alive who remembers how funny Willie Howard was...

Then came a phone call from Berle. We had been on the outs because he refused to pay me anything reasonable for the few times he'd call on me to write him a guest spot when he appeared on somebody's radio show, like Rudy Vallee or Fred Waring.

He said, "You read about David Freedman, right?"

I certainly did. David Freedman was the top radio gag writer at the time. He wrote all of Eddie Cantor's shows and was now suing Cantor for a lot of money. I've forgotten all the details, but Freedman dropped dead in court in the middle of the trial. It was a shocker.

"Yes," I said to Berle. "It's terrible."

"Yes," he said. "He was supposed to write a pilot for me. If it clicks, I get thirteen weeks on the Yankee Network—that's out of Boston—and if that works I get fifty-two weeks on CBS. National. Big. You wanna do the pilot?"

I played coy, but when he mentioned $250 a week, I said, "I've got a partner. You know him, Alan Lipscott."

"I only want you."

I said I'd have to speak with Alan, which I did, and it wasn't easy. Alan reassured me that it would be okay. (He was a very generous and decent man. And the nice part—in the 1940s we were reunited because I employed him as a writer on "The Life of Riley" radio show.)

I called Berle. "Milton," I said. "I'll do the pilot, but before I hand it to you I want a contract guaranteed that I go all the way with what you told me, your deal with the sponsor. By the way, who is it?"

"Gillette Razor. Good Irv. The first show is Sunday."

"Next Sunday?"

"This Sunday. We're flying to Boston Friday so start writing for God's sake."

This was Tuesday.

I said I wasn't worried about the script. What bothered me was the flying. I had never flown.

"I don't even like taking an elevator," I told him.

"There's nothing to it," Berle said. "You'll love it."

"I'd prefer to wait until they've repealed the law of gravity."

I spent the next two days thinking of some ideas, but I wasn't getting anywhere because the idea of getting into an airplane was making me a wreck. And I couldn't confess to Eve that I was what I was—a coward. When I told her I had this big deal, she was thrilled for me. Then when I told her I had to fly all the way from New York to Boston, she said "Oh that's great! I love to fly."

Here's the woman I'm in love with making me feel like a schmuck.

Then came the time to bite the bullet.

The planes at Idlewild Airport in 1936 didn't look like the planes now. The one for Boston was very small and had twin propellers. The Wright Brothers lent it to us for the trip. Milton tried to soothe me because, egocentric as he was, he still could see from the way I looked—pale as a ghost, obviously in a panic—that I was about ready to say, "I'm not going. Screw the deal."

Somehow I wound up climbing the steps to board this deadly trap. Did I mention it was raining? Certainly the rain would make the pilot unable to see. Well, at least when we crashed I wouldn't have to think of what to write.

I sort of collapsed in a seat, facing Berle. In those days the seats weren't all facing forward. For sociability, they were set like in a train, some facing the rear, some the front. I guess that was so when we crashed we could land on each other, which reduced the impact. As the stewardess gently buckled my seat belt, I steeled myself by reviewing in my mind those guys I knew, my friends, wondering which would be my pallbearers.

There I am in my raincoat quivering. I heard the engine cough and finally settle down and felt the plane start rolling. They called it, "taxi-ing." The stewardess gushing over Berle—she was rattling on about seeing him when he worked some Broadway nightclub—asked if he or I would like some lunch. I nodded no and Milton said: "No thanks, honey. I had a big breakfast!" (They didn't serve drinks on planes then; they gave you chewing gum because your ears popped. They didn't even charge anything for it, which I thought was sporting of American Airlines.)

Suddenly my stomach dropped as I felt the plane lift off the runway and head for disaster.

Comedians can be very solicitous when they need material. Berle was very concerned about my terrified look. He leaned forward and patted my knee as the plane bumped up and down frighteningly.

"Take it easy," he said. "Just take deep breaths. I'm telling you, I fly all the time. It's the only way to go."

Then we hit a series of breath-taking sudden drops, followed by sudden climbs.

Then Berle threw up on me.

Luckily, I was wearing the raincoat.

Somehow I sweated out the rest of the trip. As I recall, we did not crash. Instead we wound up in Boston at the Parker House hotel. I can't remember much about the pilot except that I sweated out a script and sat nervously in a radio studio that Sunday night, listening as a studio audience laughed at Berle in all the right places.

The program was called, "The Gillette Community Sing." A lousy title, a terrible title. My part was about twenty-five minutes of the forty-five minute show. The rest was a musical performance by Wendell Hall and the Happiness Boys. Wendell Hall was a guitar-playing country singer. The Boys were famous in vaudeville—Billy Jones and Ernie Hare—and boring as hell.

After the show, the head of advertising for Gillette, a fatherly type named Charles Pritzger, clapped me on the back and said some very complimentary things. We did twelve additional programs and boom, we went on the CBS network on a Sunday night in October. Pritzger became a supporter, going so far as arranging an increase in pay. He had Gillette pay me for writing a comedic station break at the thirty-minute mark of each show. It was something of a first for radio. For example, there was a cute girl singer on the show, Eileen Barton, who grew up into a good career, including singing with Frank Sinatra. I named her "Jolly Gillette," the sponsor's seven year-old daughter who heckled Berle. Eileen played this precocious kid giving the star a bad name for big laughs.

The show emanated from the old CBS Hammerstein Theatre in midtown Manhattan. The marquee read: "Milton Berle and the Gillette Community Sing," and every Sunday night people were allowed to come in, for free of course.

When the show went out on the air, I think at 7 P.M. across the country, we recorded it in the studio on a huge 33-RPM acetate platter. For posterity, or to listen to the following day. Whichever came first.

But the show never became the kind of hit that we had naturally hoped for. Then again, who can explain an audience's taste? I think, great as he was as a stand-up comedian, Berle worked a little too fast on the radio for the folks out there listening in the heartland. Or it may have been that he came across as too New Yorkish. Meaning Jewish. But I wrote the show for fifty-two weeks, part of the time in California, which I'll get to.

In those days, programs were usually written by one or perhaps two or three writers. And Gillette was only allowed three minutes per half hour for commercials. Today I find it amusing when I look at a half-hour television program which because of commercials is about twenty-two minutes. I see the credits and after four or five writers' names starts a parade: a co-producer, associate to the producer, producer's associate, co-co producer's associate—in other words, a lot of co-cos and cuckoos.

The reason TV and radio are so fucked up with numbing commercials is because President Fuck-Up Reagan, a friend of "big corporations," deregulated what the FCC had established: strict rules limiting the amount of commercials to three minutes because all the peddlers and hustlers selling their goods were using publicly-owned air. You know what Art Buchwald wrote about Reaganomics? He took a very dim view of Reagan as president, saying something to the effect: "He would never have become president if Jack Warner, just once, had let Reagan get the girl."

Going West

> "I no like-a this west. All people do in is kill
> each other. I'd like-a the west much better if
> it was in the east."
> - Chico Marx as Joe Panello in *Go West*

*I wish Brecher and I could do our own radio show full of funny monologues
and music. We both love the magic of the medium as much as we do the movies.
After all, "the pictures are better" on radio. The closest we get is a piece for the
National Public Radio program, "All Things Considered," in which we attend
a screening of one of his MGM musicals, **Du Barry was a Lady.** Our radio
debut captures Brecher's reactions on watching his film sixty years after writing
it. You can listen yourself; follow the link at IrvBrecher.com.*

*It was writing that Gillette show for Milton Berle that first got Brecher to
go West. Berle was signed by RKO to be the lead in a film called **New Faces of
1937**, so the entire cast of "The Gillette Community Sing" came by train to do
the radio show in Hollywood until the end of Milton's big movie shoot.*

A three-night train trip from New York to California was memorable
for a kid used to nickel rides on the IRT in the Bronx. We took the
famous Twentieth Century train from New York to Chicago and then
switched to the Santa Fe Super Chief. One night after feasting on fresh-
caught mountain trout they brought aboard in Colorado, Milton gathered
everyone together. He said he wanted to sing us a song. His lyrics were
from the words seen in every train bathroom above the sink: "Please Do
Not Flush the Toilet While the Train is Standing in the Station." This
was Pullman's gallant attempt, in large type on a plaque, to keep the
depots smelling sweet as possible, because whatever you crapped came
out on the tracks.

Berle sat us down in the club car and sang: "Passengers will please
refrain... from flushing toilets while the train... is standing in the station.
I love you...."

A song headed right for the Shit Parade. But since Berle had a reputation for stealing material, he may not have actually composed the lyric.
And I doubt that Cole Porter or Irving Berlin did either. But that song
became the reason why fifteen years later I made a serious enemy of the

head of Paramount Studios.

[Brecher tells his next story as if we're passing time on that train until we get to California when we'll return to those thrilling days of yesteryear...]

In 1952, I was at Paramount writing and directing a movie musical starring Betty Hutton called **Somebody Loves Me**. The head of the studio was Y. Frank Freeman, which was a good question. He was a prim fellow from the deep South, a bloodless number cruncher chosen by the lenders to which Paramount was in deep debt. They owed millions. Freeman's favorite movie was probably **Birth of a Nation** and I'm sure he rooted for the Klan. He had no talent for producing movies, but that didn't stop him. His accent and courtly manner lent him an air of authority and naturally, we employees gave him full respect. My big mistake was trying to be funny with a cold fish like Freeman.

I was in the commissary having lunch, at a table with Dinah Shore and Robert Merrill. Surprisingly, Freeman came by and politely asked if he might join us.

"Of course," we all said, and kiss-assed an overly hardy welcome. I love Dinah, she was a wonderful Jewish girl. And Merrill, such an amazing opera singer. Freeman sat down and the conversation from then on concerned the weather, the stock market, and the crop failure down South which had seriously affected a plantation he owned, I think in Alabama, I'm not sure.

Everything was fine and dull and then Dinah Shore said something that led to disaster. Dinah said she was leaving that night to do a variety show in New York next Sunday.

Freeman said, "I envy you. I find it very rewarding to ride the train."

"I like it, but I'm flying TWA," Dinah said.

Freeman went on in his heavy drawl, "I find it indeed sad that the railways are beginning to disappear. I enjoy nothing better than dining on that marvelous food aboard the Twentieth Century or the Super Chief. And the service. Oh my. Nothing compares to those waiters. Those coloreds sure do their job."

I seized the opening like an idiot.

"I agree, Mr. Freeman," I said. "They're great waiters. As a matter of fact, a few months ago my wife and I were coming back from New York on the Super Chief. And while in the dining car she mentioned that as soon as we got back she had to start looking for a maid because ours had retired and gone home to Mexico. A waiter, having heard this, very very politely said his name was Eddie Dauzet and he was wondering, 'Begging your pardon, I just heard you folks talking about looking for a maid. Well, my wife Stella is looking for a job and she might be just right for you.'

So when we got home, my wife interviewed this Stella. She said she'd love the job. And we said fine. But she could only take it, she said, if we gave permission for her husband to sleep in the maid's room on the nights he was not working on the railroad. That was fine with us."

Freeman said, "You were very fortunate. Did he serve you dinner?"

"Yes," I said. "But it didn't work out. We had to let them go."

"What happened?"

"There was a problem. Eddie was a creature of habit: He never flushed the toilet while the house was standing still."

Dinah and Merrill exploded. Freeman, sensing he had been a patsy, resented being a straight man, promptly quit his meal, got up and left. But not before he looked at me icily and said, "Glad I was able to be of help. That was *very* funny."

The thing that wasn't funny was that Paramount, which had an option for me to do another picture, didn't pick it up.

Anyway, I flushed toilets all the way across the country when Berle took his radio troupe to Hollywood, from where we did the Sunday broadcast and he was able to do his movie. I'll never forget how the orange blossom scent knocked me down when I got off the train. You got drunk on the aroma.

We had a couple of free days before the movie was due to start shooting, and I had finished the next radio script on the train, so Berle invited me to go to Palm Springs. The studio gave us a car and driver and I found myself in a dream world. This place was nothing like the Bronx. And Palm Springs was nothing like Coney Island, except it did have plenty of sand. We spent a couple of dull days sunning and watching lizards making love. Milton and I played gin rummy and swam and couldn't wait to leave.

Berle lived in a hotel in Hollywood and his secretary had arranged a paid room for me with a bath at the Rossmore-Clinton, an old residential hotel on the south end of Vine Street. It was very serene in that part of Hollywood and you could get a fabulous breakfast at Musso & Frank's for a dollar.

Hollywood Boulevard at that time was just a collection of small shops.

Open and pleasant like a village. There was a great ice cream parlor called Brown's and a few doors away, Grauman's Chinese Theatre, which was the top movie house. Sid Grauman, a little guy with white hair held all the premieres there and its where the stars, including the Marx Brothers, left impressions of their shoes or bare feet in cement.

I wrote my radio scripts in my hotel room. Then Berle read them and we went into rehearsal and broadcast the show from a former vaudeville theater above Hollywood Boulevard. Afterward, we'd go to the Brown Derby, my favorite restaurant and the most popular place in town. Not just because of the good food, but it was the "in" place for celebrities, and the gapers and gawkers from out-of-town who would wet their pants when they saw Clark Cable or Gary Cooper or Joan Crawford. I did a lot of gaping. I was a diehard movie fan. (I still am. My kind of movies were always more dialogue and less "Die Hard.") I still remember the first time I saw Ingrid Bergman walk in with some lucky man and sit at a table not too far from mine. I don't think I finished my meal. I just stared covertly at the most beautiful sight I'd ever seen. That includes mountains, rivers, paintings in the Louvre...

While I'm name-dropping, once Berle took me to some kind of pool party at what I knew to be a famous hotel where movie stars lived, The Garden of Allah. I recognized some of the faces. I was sure some were producers, maybe directors, a lot of character actors, some on the old side. And quite a few pretty young things dressed in what at the time were daring bathing suits.

I've done a few practical jokes on friends, but not mean ones. But at this Garden of Allah party, Berle did his thing. He took a plastic cup and filled it with champagne. Then he took out a little packet, tore it open—only I was aware of it—and poured some kind of powder into the champagne.

"What are you doing?" I said. "Trying to drug somebody?"

"Noooo... trying to have some laughs." He pointed to a young woman a few yards away. "I asked her if she wanted to have dinner and she turned me down. She said, 'Who are you?' I said, 'You don't know me, where've you been?' I'm Milton Berle.' She said, 'Good for you.' Then she dropped me like a hot rock and went to kiss some producer's ass."

I looked over and saw the girl pointing in our direction while talking to the producer. She kind of blanched and swallowed and sidled over to where we were sitting. This was a sharp cookie.

"Milton," she said. "Of course I know who you are. I was only kidding.

I love your radio show. And I know you're going to star in a movie at RKO." Then she went into baby talk. "Do you suppose there'd be a part for little me?"

"Could be," Milton said.

"How'd you like me to," she winked, "audition?"

"Where you staying, honey?" Berle said, handing her the cup of champagne. "Let's drink to that." (He never drank. He lifted a lemonade and toasted.)

About an hour later, the warm sun was out and a few of the women dove into the pool, swam a few laps and climbed out to be dried off by attentive men with big towels and small erections. Then Berle poked me.

"Watch."

He watched, and so did I, trying not to crack up.

Miss Private Audition was posing on the diving board, displaying her damn good figure for whomever was watching. Then she completed an expert dive into the water. Coming up for air, she started doing a sidestroke to the opposite end, when suddenly a streak, a stream, blue water appeared behind her. It came from between her legs and as people spotted what happened they screamed with laughter. When she turned to swim back and saw the blue water, the poor thing wanted to drown herself. But instead she jumped out, ran out of sight and has probably not been seen since.

It was funny, but it was cruel. And I had to assume she would not be in Berle's movie. Berle's movie was no classic. But it was the first one I ever did any writing on. Here's how it happened:

RKO was the first movie studio I ever saw. RKO stood for "Radio Keith Orpheum," a corporation formed when radio first came in. Keith Orpheum was a vaudeville circuit that got into making movies. So they called them RKO Radio Pictures. Radio City Music Hall was their big outlet in New York and that's where **New Faces of 1937** would open. RKO was on Gower Street, not far from another of Sid Grauman's theaters, The Egyptian. The studio was right next to a cemetery where I later learned you could bury bad pictures. They didn't have to travel far.

Edward Small, producer of **New Faces**, called me in. He said Berle insisted on having me rewrite his part. The original script was by two men who later became close friends of mine: Nat Perrin and Philip Epstein. It came from a Broadway show which ran a year earlier and the picture brought to the screen a lot of theater people who had never been in movies before, like Harriet Hilliard, who went on to fame as Harriet Nelson in "Ozzie and Harriet." Another character was the Mad Russian, played by a New York comedian named Bert Gordon. He greeted you this way: "How have you are?"

Like that. Joe Penner ("Wanna buy a duck?") was in it, and another character was "Parkyerkarkus," which was the creation of Harry Einstein, a vaudevillian. (Einstein had a son who would change his name to become the comedian Albert Brooks.)

And Berle was the star.

The best thing about being asked to write the movie was the fact that I was suddenly paid what to me was an immense salary: $750 a week. I was also being paid $650 a week to do the radio show. My parents thought we were the richest family in the Bronx.

I had butterflies working on the movie script but soon I got over it. It was new of course to be writing comedy and visualizing some actor later speaking the lines or doing some physical shtick on the big movie screen I keep seeing in my mind. But the biggest thing that happened was just before we were to head back to New York with the radio show, my new agent, Walter Meyers took me to Warner Brothers Studio out in Burbank. (At that time in Burbank, there were deer walking around.) Meyers said a producer named Mervyn Leroy had asked to see me. Leroy had directed tremendous pictures like **Little Caesar** and **Fugitive from a Chain Gang**, so I was excited to meet him.

Now this is so weird. It's hard to believe. When we stepped into his office, Leroy was on the telephone. He put his hand over the phone for a second to tell us he was talking to his wife. They'd just had a baby a few days earlier. We offered our congratulations and he went back to the phone, but just for a second.

"Excuse me, dear?" he said. "I'll call you right back." He hung up and looked hard and long across his desk at me. Then he swirled around to look behind him where on the wall hung a very large framed photograph of a man I recognized immediately: Irving Thalberg. I knew his picture from seeing it in papers and magazines. Thalberg had died a few months earlier, at just 37 years old, which was a shocker to the movie business because he was the biggest, the best and the most powerful, and had made MGM far and away the major studio in motion pictures.

Leroy turned back and saw me looking at the picture, too. "Irving Thalberg was my best friend," he said. He stood up and reached his hand out. "Irving," he said shaking my hand. "I think that Irving would sign you. So I will."

And that's the way Mervyn Leroy hired me at Warner Brothers. How do you like that? All on a hunch because he thought I looked like Irving Thalberg. He made a deal with Walter Meyers and that night took me to a dinner party at his father-in-law's house.

His father-in-law was Harry Warner.

First dinner party in my life! Imagine a 23 year old in a place like this, at one of the owners of Warner Brothers. own palaces! There I met Jack Warner, one of Harry's brothers.

"Attention everybody!" he shouted. Jack goes over to a lamp, pulls the switch off, pulls it back on, and says, "I'm a light comedian."

Everybody laughed politely, but I don't think *you're* laughing, are you? Jack Warner thought he was funny and he was not funny. He was hoping to be comedian, but he was a pain in the can, actually.

Meanwhile, I was 23 and hoping that if I had to talk to this tycoon everything would just come out all right.

LeRoy introduced me. "Jack, this is a new writer I just hired, Irving Brecher. Irv, this is Mister Warner, the head of the studio."

"How do you do, Mister Warner," I said in a shaking voice.

He took a paper clip out of his vest pocket, held it up and said, 'If you don't write good, I'll clip you.'

Nothing that anybody would steal, I'm sure. Executives are the acne of perfection. Pimples.

Part III

At the Movies

Going over the script for *Fools For Scandal*, **1937. That's Carole Lombard on the left, Mervyn LeRoy in the middle. I'm on the right making believe I'm looking at the script while secretly fantasizing I'm Clark Gable, Lombard's hubby.**

Spiking Oz

"I got one eye that's red and another that's
green, I never know when to stop or go!"
—Frank Morgan, in "MGM Good News"

Irv: When I returned to Hollywood in '37 with a six-month contract with Mervyn LeRoy, he put me to work putting additional dialogue into a movie he was directing called *Fools for Scandal*. It featured Carole Lombard. More on her later, but meanwhile I got a new place at The Fontenoy on Whitley, a block north of Hollywood Boulevard and Musso & Frank's was even closer now, so I had bacon and eggs there for eighty-five cents every morning. Lunch was at the Warner Brothers commissary.

Fools for Scandal stopped shooting right after Christmas and LeRoy told me that he was about to announce a major move from Warner to MGM to produce and direct. He said Louis B. Mayer gave him a great deal, which was confirmed in the trade papers the next day—an unheard of contract: six thousand dollars per week, the biggest ever given by MGM—more even than Gable or Garbo were getting. The wise guys figured, and I think they were right, that Mayer was pissing on Jack Warner, who was not only head of the studio but the brother of Leroy's father-in-law, Harry Warner. Jack and L.B. Mayer hated each other, so it was an example of Mayer's one-upsmanship. LeRoy was good. But nobody was that good.

The day after New Year's, LeRoy moved to MGM, and so did his flock: those of us under personal contract, Kenny Baker, Lana Turner and me. Kenny Baker was a singer used in *At the Circus* where he stunk and that was the end of him. He was actually very good on the Jack Benny radio show, but even Jack called Kenny a nebbish. But you know what happened to Lana Turner. A voluptuous starlet. She appeared briefly as a teenager in LeRoy's movie *They Won't Forget*. It was based on the lynching of Leo Frank, a Jew accused of rape—I never forgot it, it moved me so much. Lana was LeRoy's discovery and she became a major star. The columnists called her "The Sweater Girl," deservedly so. They didn't use words like "boobs" in 1938. She looked like she was smuggling cantaloupes.

A couple days after we all wound up in Culver City, where I had my usual butterflies about where I was going and how bad it could get, I got assigned an office on the 2nd floor of the Irving Thalberg Building, Number 242. It was hard to believe that I was actually there at MGM when I was out in the actual studio with its huge soundstages and dozens of famous faces—actors who I had paid to see back in the Bronx starting with the Nickelodeon when I was a kid. I was 24, I had a weekly pay check of 650 bucks for six months at least, and while I didn't pinch myself, I was constantly in a state of nervous excitement. Metro had most of the top stars: Garbo, Garland, Hepburn, Tracy, the Barrymores and my idols, the Marx Brothers.

I was sitting in my office typing a letter to my sweetheart back in New York when the phone rang. LeRoy's secretary said he wanted to see me. Mervyn was this little guy behind a big desk in a big, plush office. He picked up a thick script. The cover was blue. And he told me: "L.B. wants me to produce this. It's a finished script, ready to go. Except it could use more laughs."

"What is it?" I asked.

"It's *The Wizard of Oz*. It's from a book. Read it. I marked the parts for the comedy characters... what the heck were their names? Punch them up," Mervyn said. "As fast as you can. Got to shoot in ten days."

So that's what I did. I read the script after first reading the book. LeRoy had been right. It needed laughs. The three comic characters were Bert Lahr as a cowardly lion, the straw man played by Ray Bolger, and the tin man, Jack Haley. My favorite was Bert Lahr. I had spent a little social time back in New York with Bert. He was a cute guy, and I'd also seen him on the Broadway stage in revues where he was the star, one of my favorite comedians and always knocked me out. He was *funny*.

I did the punching up, adding lines and bits that I thought would increase the laughs. After Mervyn read it, he seemed pleased. Florence Ryerson and Noel Langley wrote the original script. The myth is that many writers were called in to help punch up *The Wizard of Oz*. The practice was known as "spiking" or "hyping" a scene or a line. But once LeRoy took over, I am unaware of anything that was done to the script except the polishing that I did for the three characters. And for the Wizard I did some revisions. I didn't contribute enough in terms of footage onscreen to be entitled to a co-screenplay credit. Actually, LeRoy wasn't entitled to full credit either. But I'll tell you this: I don't think anybody expected it to be the kind of hit it became.

Then I did nothing for a few days and was kind of a lost soul until I got a call from a producer named Louis K. Sidney. I couldn't believe it. This was the same man I had seen five years earlier at the Capitol Theatre who'd cut out my blue jokes! The manager who threatened to cancel Berle. Here he was now, in charge of some short subject productions. It sounded to me like a demotion, but I reported to his office down the hall. L.K. was a tall fatherly type (he had a son George who was directing shorts), he greeted me warmly, and I craftily failed to mention that I'd hated him more than anyone in or out of show business. Instead I listened as he told me the studio was putting on a radio show once a week called, "MGM Good News." An hour of variety using MGM stars in guest shots, scenes from motion pictures, and music from a conductor named Meredith Willson, who years later composed the music and lyrics for **The Music Man**. Sidney said Fanny Brice would do a few minutes as her "Baby Snooks" character, "and then that's where you come in. A weekly spot with Frank Morgan. You know him?"

"Actually I did a little writing for him as the wizard of Oz," I said.

"They're gonna start shooting that in a few days," Sidney said. "They'll shoot around him when he does the radio."

He said Meredith Willson would play the straight. So I created a character for Frank Morgan who was a dirty old man with an eye for young women and a love affair with booze. I knew the last part was for real, because on the day of the broadcast I'd have to sit with him at the bar of the Roosevelt Hotel on Hollywood Boulevard. He'd drink four Stingers and I'd cajole him into leaving on unsteady legs for the studio around the corner. The amazing thing was, on the air, his timing and delivery were perfect. And he injected his own giggle which helped his punch lines.

"MGM Good News" was the show where I first wrote for Jack Benny who came on as a guest. Eventually, Frank Morgan got his own radio show which ran for years. Another character involved in the show was the writer and producer, Ed Gardner. He was a rough-voiced man who went on to create the "Duffy's Tavern" radio series and play Archie in that show. He was married at the time to Shirley Booth, the famous actress who had starred in **Come Back, Little Sheba**. One of the writers at "Duffy's Tavern" told me how once while they were doing the show, Gardner called a meeting to come up with storylines. After a couple of hours they'd gotten nowhere. Nothing. Really frustrated, Gardner finally said, "Well, we might as well knock off. We seem to be lacking inspiration. I guess what we need is some blowjobs."

One of the writers said, "Great, Ed! Where could we go?"

Gardner said, "I don't know about you guys—I'm going home."

Doing the "Good News" Metro show for several months was okay, but not what I wanted. What I wanted came right after the show went off for the summer and I was cut loose. Then came a telephone call even more unexpected than the one five years before from Berle which called me into the wonderful world in which I now found myself.

Marx Brothers at the Circus

> "The only good thing about making *At The Circus* was beginning my friendship with Irving Brecher."
> - Groucho Marx

It was LeRoy on the phone and like his physical stature, he was short.

"Irv, you feeling funny?"

"Not particularly."

"You better be. L.B. wants me to produce the next Marx Brothers picture and you're going to write it."

"What?"

I couldn't believe it. But that's what he said. I had a flash way back to Yonkers, watching the Marx Brothers on a movie screen that old Mr. Brennan had given me the pass for. How I had become so hooked.

This was so strange. Almost like a dream. Or maybe a strange interlude... I had never really thought about writing for them, much as I loved them. I was still new to the game. But I was aging fast.

"I want you to meet Groucho," LeRoy said. "He speaks for the brothers. He's the only one who reads anything. Chico's busy at the races and I'm not sure Harpo can read. Anyway, Groucho is the man you have to deal with. He deals with the script and when he's satisfied, the picture goes."

"Well then I guess I'd like to meet him," I think I must have said.

The next day walking up to LeRoy's office, I was terrified that I was going to face and, as I'd been told, actually write for, my idols. That is, until I was sure I couldn't measure up and was fired for not being funny enough. And how do you talk to a star? Berle was not that kind of star. I had talked to Carole Lombard, but she was not sitting in judgement of me. I'm sure as I think back that my knees were shaking, and my voice too.

Groucho was sitting with his feet on LeRoy's desk, smoking a long cigar. Mervyn did the honors.

"Groucho, this is Irv Brecher. He's a very funny writer. He's going to do your script."

Groucho nodded.

Extending my hand, I said, "Hello Mister Marx." He shook my hand and shot LeRoy that famous arched-eyebrow look.

He said, "This is the funny writer you're gonna put on the picture, a guy whose idea of an ad-lib is 'hello'?"

Mervyn giggled. I nearly choked. But I fought back.

"I said hello, because I wanted to flatter you. I heard you ad-lib it in one of your movies."

Groucho smiled, showing that he was human, and then in a kind of big brother way—he was twenty years or so older than I was—he said, "If you won't talk movies, I'll take you to lunch."

"I like politics and baseball," he continued, as we got into the elevator. There was one other person in there, a tall woman with a huge wide-brimmed hat. Even with the brim down, I got a glance. It was Greta Garbo. What a thrill!

But here was Groucho, ducking down and looking up under her brim. He said politely, "Excuse me sir, but aren't you a guy I met in a hotel in Cleveland?"

All I heard from the great Garbo was a grunt. When the elevator opened, she fled. She was gorgeous, but I have to report she had very big feet.

I told you when I was a kid the fun I had making up like Groucho. I told that to Groucho during lunch in the commissary.

"Stop doing that," he said. "There's a law against impersonating an officer."

"You're an officer?"

"My brothers and I have a corporation to evade income taxes. I'm one of the officers."

I had the famous chicken soup that L.B. Mayer's sister created. I don't remember what Groucho ate. I was still on a cloud and starting to worry about what in the hell could I possibly write for a movie he told me was about, "some horseshit circus."

Only someone who does it can know what it's like to make up out of the blue or his own head, ninety minutes of what is supposed to be a load of laughs. With nothing to go on, not a play nor a book, you're really flying blind. Yet somehow, like so many other victims, you manage to get the work done. Or so you hope.

After I finally settled on a rather simple plot, designed primarily to allow five or six lengthy sequences of Marxian craziness, I sweated out the script, which kept me awake most nights. Finally it wound up being okayed for production. But not before the material satisfied, and to my delight, actually seemed to meet with genuine approval from Groucho. It took me eight or nine weeks and I think if Groucho had his way, it would have been much longer, because Groucho had a basic insecurity about acting. He hated it. Although he eventually wrote at least one very readable book, "Grouch and Me," he was stuck with performing. All that did was make him world famous.

And he would do anything rather than go forward with shooting until it became absolutely necessary from a financial standpoint. So he would find reasons not to do it. But since no other writer ever got solo credit on a Marx Brothers picture—and it happened that I had two, **At the Circus** and **Go West**—I suppose it demonstrated his satisfaction with what I wrote. It sounds self-serving, but it just happened to be that way. Sometimes they had more than three writers. Sometimes they had platoons. I did the two and when I was doing them, Groucho and I grew closer and closer. And after doing them I was exhausted. I'd had it. I assume for most writers, it is not that much fun sweating out what you hope will be an original comedy scene. But it is great fun when you see it happen on the screen.

If it works.

For example, a line that audiences seemed to love in **At the Circus**, is spoken by J. Cheever Loophole to Mrs. Dukesbury. Dukesbury was played by that classic straight woman, Margaret Dumont. Dumont always did her high society schmuckette: stiff, stuffy, opaque, pompous, and endearing. Always a victim of Groucho's amusing larceny.

So Dukesbury is hosting a huge banquet, a fundraiser at her palace in Newport. Society's richest 400 were expected and Dumont is giving orders regarding seating arrangements at the head table. She is expecting an important guest. And she's been won over by the lies that Loophole—that is, Groucho—has fed her. As she beams, she says: "Judge Channock will sit on my left hand. And you Cheever dear, will sit on my right hand."

Groucho says: "How will you eat, through a tube?"

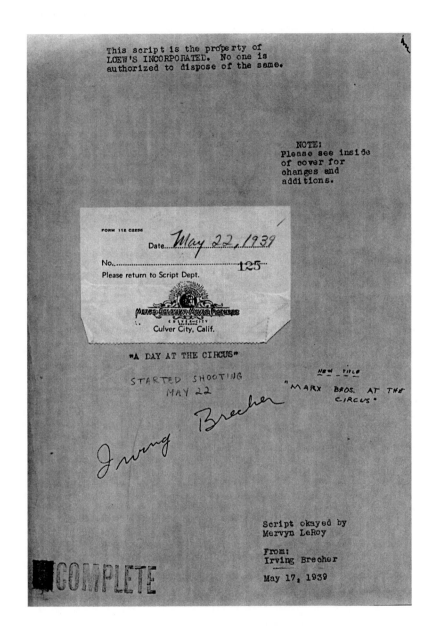

My script from the originally titled, *A DAY AT THE CIRCUS* **in 1939.**

That's a line not even a second-rate director could ruin. I say that because though I liked him personally, I had problems with Eddie Buzzell who shot both of my pictures with the Brothers.

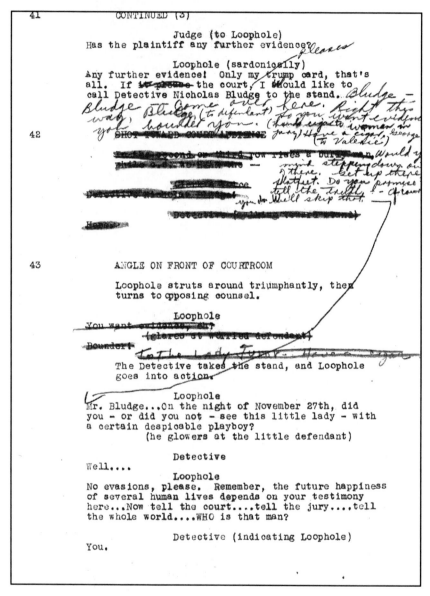

Working on the courtroom scene which was cut from *AT THE CIRCUS.*
"Your Honor, I move for an adjournment," said J. Cheever Loophole. "And I'm gonna keep moving!"

Irving Brecher

Before coming west, Edward Buzzell was a leading man, essentially a light comedian in musicals on Broadway. He'd actually been on some vaudeville bills with the Marx Brothers. He had done a lot of little movies at Universal and at MGM and was far from an "important" director, but L.B. Mayer did not like the Marx Brothers kind of comedy, and had signed Buzzell as a bottom-line director known for the fact that he would shoot fast. He saved money. I know the Brothers were not happy under Buzzell after their great experience with Sam Wood in **Night at the Opera**. He inhibited them, they weren't as free, he had them do too much mincing. But with Thalberg gone, just two years before, Mayer could indulge his likes and dislikes regarding product and personnel.

But in one way, Buzzell did me a favor. His request for one line in Circus made it possible for me to come up with what turned out to be a blockbuster in a comedic sense.

The circus of the picture stars "Peerless Pauline." She is played by Eve Arden in a sexy leotard. Her act is walking on the ceiling and in one scene she is in her dressing room, wearing the suction soles that keep her hanging upside down. Groucho, claiming mad passion, joins her on the ceiling, saying things like, "I'm heels over head in love," which is an easy line—you see the scene and it's obvious Loophole would say that. He is really there trying to retrieve a wallet containing ten grand which has been stolen from Kenny Baker and if not gotten back, it will bankrupt the circus. (Loophole shows up looking to save the day for the leading man and leading lady, the ingenues of our story—that kind of simple plot.) Groucho suspects that Eve Arden is an accomplice of the thieves and is sure she has the wallet. So he's doing his familiar phony romantic.

It was at this point that I was called to go down to the set, because Buzzell needed a line from Groucho, a response that would smooth out a bit of the action, rather than just having him catching with his eye: Eve Arden slipping the stolen wallet down her cleavage.

First, Loophole tells her: "The thing I like about you, is that money doesn't go to your head."

Then I thought for a moment and suggested that Groucho walk to the camera and say directly to the audience: "There must be some way I can get that money back without getting in trouble with the Hays Office."

Today nobody would know what that means.

The Hays Office was a censor, a watchdog of the movie business from the 1920s (It was finally abolished in 1968 by Jack Valenti and the ratings system came in), paid for by the industry to please itself because of a groundswell of anti-Hollywood feeling in the country. It was like a religious institution, brutal on any suggestion of sexuality. Anything. A husband and wife couldn't be shown sleeping in the same bed. You couldn't say "hell" or "damn." W.C. Fields invented curse words to get around the censor: "Godfrey Daniel!" "Mother of Pearl!"

The question about any script was: "Will this pass the Hays Office?" Some movies had offended the Bible belt. A man and a woman kissing with their mouths with any show of passion was upsetting to millions of God-fearing good folks who would stop masturbating to write in and complain. All it did was make Westerns clean and self-censorship rampant.

Meanwhile, Peerless Pauline put the money down her tits and a writer gave a line to a director...

Buzzell looked at me like I was an idiot.

Groucho said he liked the line.

"Are you kidding?" Buzzell asked. "What kind of shit is this? Nobody knows the Hays Office."

Groucho said, "I still like it."

"I'm directing this movie," Buzzell said. "And I'm not gonna shoot it."

"LeRoy asked me to get you a line and that's the best I could come up with," I said.

Buzzell must have felt his oats. Maybe he had it in for LeRoy, who was at least one inch taller.

"Then let LeRoy shoot it."

And he walked off the set.

All I could do was call LeRoy.

"Do you want me to shoot it?" I asked him.

"Irv, you're not a member of the Guild. Maybe someday. But meanwhile, fuck him."

He sent down S. Sylvan Simon, who had done some pictures at MGM. Simon loved the line and quickly shot Groucho saying it. A month later at the sneak preview, it got the biggest, longest laugh in the movie. I felt sorry for Buzzell, he seemed to slink down in his theater seat watching.

They laughed so long that after the screening, MGM had to take the film back and put footage in that was innocuous to cover the time of the audience's uproar. To take care of the laugh.

Groucho said later, "It was the biggest laugh I ever got in my life."

But what it really did was prove that the moviegoing public was alive and well aware of the behavior of the Hays Office and the censorship they practiced in what was supposed to be a free country.

At the Circus company: I'm behind Groucho and Margaret Dumont, Harpo, and next to Eve Arden, Kenny Baker and Florence Rice. Chico, not pictured, is out trying to make some trapeze artist.

How Chico Saved the Marx Brothers

Chico in the saloon sitting on a sexy gal's lap:
All my life I wanted to meet a girl just like
you. (He switches to the next gal's lap) And
you're the girl!
- *Go West*

The Hays Office joke happened in 1939. Sixty-five years later, Marx Brothers movies are still playing at festivals and all over cable TV. They constantly run in Europe, too; Brecher says there's one place in Paris they show a Marx movie every day.

Meanwhile in Westwood, I'm watching a Warner film crew shoot Irv for a feature being added to a new DVD of A Night at the Opera, the Marx's biggest hit. (I had rushed over to document the documentarians after he called to say he was breaking our lunch date because he got the gig.) This commentary track, "Remarks on Marx" includes Larry Gelbart, who praises the boys for a "durability that doesn't diminish" and how there will always be an "Establishment" so, "as long as you have three people trying to tear down authority or make fun of it or embarrass it, that's gonna remain constant and will attract newer fans." And director Robert S. Weide calls them "film comedy's first anarchists," relating the famous anecdote about Night at the Opera and A Day at the Races director Sam Wood's frustration with Groucho. Wood was used to directing dramas and not comedies. And he said regarding Groucho: "Well, you can't make an actor out of clay." So Groucho said: "And you can't make a director out of wood."

After 33 minutes of quips from actors and writers like Kitty Carlisle, Carl Reiner, Dom DeLouise, and Ann Beatts, it's left up to Brecher to supply the punch line. Shown tilting his head back in his living room chair, a row of bound scripts on the bookshelf behind him, he buttons it up with, "I know they're gonna be around forever. That's long after a lot of us are gone. And as Groucho said, 'Hello I must be going.'"

During the taping, he tells the Taylor Made Films folks (outsourced by Warner), "It's amazing how popular the brothers were. Everybody is an expert on them. Of all the names you mentioned on this, I think only two of them worked with them, other than me, Bob Weide and Carlisle. Too many people who would have loved to be on your DVD have made the mistake of dying."

*He says **Opera** is "the greatest Marx Brothers movie because opera is so serious, so pompous and ceremonial that of all their subjects it was the best to have fun with. It was an ideal opportunity to go wild against the characters associated with the stuffiness of opera, particularly the egocentric star, Rudolfo Lassperri, played by Walter King." He said **Duck Soup** was his next favorite, "because war would be better fought as satire."*

*The film crew is fawning and then respectful and then workmanlike, and then after they leave, Brecher shows me a check for a thousand bucks and tells a tale not in the doc, a classic of very unusual Chico chicanery that took place about a year after Paramount dropped the Marx Brothers in 1934. They'd done five pictures there: **Cocoanuts**, **Animal Crackers** ("very primitive, the first two, they pretty much photographed their stage shows"), **Monkey Business**, **Horsefeathers** and **Duck Soup**.*

*Irv says even though he greatly admires filmmakers like Weide who had directed Lenny Bruce, Mort Sahl and Larry David, and enjoyed his movie, **The Unknown Marx Brothers**, everybody but everybody gets the following story wrong... that critical turning point in the history of American comedy... the unheard-of legend herewith embellished I'm figuring, in Brecher's telling version:*

It wasn't until we went out on the road to Chicago, Joliet and Detroit to break in comedy scenes for **Go West** that I learned just how the public felt about the three brothers individually. I had assumed because Groucho was the one quoted by movie fans that he would be the most popular. But on the stage, Chico got the bulk of applause. Groucho got the most laughs, wearing that painted moustache and taped-on eyebrows and wiggling a cigar. And Harpo got his laughs, he was an elf in a funny wig and a constant grin and big, buggy eyes.

Chico, he didn't get as many laughs. But while their overall impact as a team was tremendous, it was Chico who, for some remarkable, down-to-earth reason, got the most approval in the theatre. As the three comedians discovered how to block scenes to find the most laughs, more applause came for Chico's weird piano playing and his idea of an Italian accent: whatever Chico said, he added an "a" as in, "It's-a-fine. Who's-a-fine? That's-a-fine, I tell-a you."

I'll never forget the day Groucho told me: "It was Chico who did it. He saved our lives. We've always had headaches with Chico when we were doing well because he can't stop gambling. And even though he's a great card player, he never seems to quit until he loses. And if he should win something at cards, he'll blow it at the track or on a ballgame. He's always in hock. But he's a genius at some things."

The last couple of pictures they did at Paramount had been big losers. They were idle, no offers from the studio, which was very disturbing for actors with egos. Harpo spent most of his time practicing his harp and playing with his adopted children on whom he doted. Groucho, who was basically withdrawn, spent his time reading and writing letters to correspondents who admired him, like George Bernard Shaw, T.S. Eliot, George Kaufman and others. In those days, you wrote; phoning long distance was too costly.

And Chico, the eldest, indulged his penchant for the higher pursuits: going to the racetrack every day, stopping at Hillcrest or somebody's home to play gin rummy, and then capping off the evening with a roll in the hay with some young lady who I imagine had his promise, "You're gonna be in our next picture, honey."

But there was no next picture. So Chico resorted to his best friend, a deck of cards. He performed a card trick of sorts. The executive at MGM in charge of distribution was also a member at Hillcrest. Al Lichtman was a powerful, highly-regarded member of MGM's top brass. He also considered himself a great gin rummy player. One day after lunch at the club, he challenged Chico.

"Everybody says you're the best at the club. Me, I don't think so."

It was said with a smile and Chico responded with modesty.

"I'm lucky. I win, I lose..."

Lichtman suggested they play two-hand and Chico complied. In a few hours, Chico had lost a few hundred bucks and got up and apologized. He had no cash and no checks with him and Lichtman with the victory said, "No problem. See you tomorrow, Chico."

And they played the next day and Chico lost again, almost a thousand dollars. Afterwards he confessed privately to Lichtman that he was short of cash. Lichtman, proud of his ability to beat Chico, particularly with the many kibbitzers watching, was magnanimous and said not to worry.

The next day, Chico asked if he could double the stakes: "Make it ten cents a point, give me a chance to get even."

Lichtman agreed with enthusiasm. And this time Chico never won a single sheet. He lost about two thousand dollars. When it was over,

Lichtman, like a gentleman, informed him: "You're down about sixty-eight hundred, Chico."

"I know, Al."

Lichtman politely asked for payment and Chico admitted—almost tearfully, Groucho told me—that he couldn't come across with it. In fact, he was headed for bankruptcy. He said sadly, "If we were doing a movie, I'd have the money. God knows when that's going to happen. Then I could pay you, of course."

Lichtman tapped him on the shoulder, told him it was okay, and added with a big grin, "Just remember to tell everybody who's the best gin player in the club."

Chico gave him a bear hug.

A couple of days later, Chico got a phone call from their agent, their brother Zeppo. "Big news, Chic! Out of the blue, I got a call from MGM. They want to sign us. Can you believe it?"

"Who called you?"

"Al Lichtman. He said he recommended it to Thalberg who okay'd it."

The Brothers were back in business. In a few days they had a contract for a five-picture deal at 150-thousand dollars per. Chico went to the club and quietly thanked Lichtman for his part in the deal and Lichtman said modestly, "We'll make some money for you guys. Wanna celebrate? Let's play some gin."

And they did. Except now, the best card player in the club was no patsy. For the next three hours, Al Lichtman never won a sheet. Chico beat the pants off him. While gin rummy is partially luck, a great player like Chico had the edge. And after winning back the $6800, and a few bucks more, Chico quit, not wishing to do harm to his naïve savior, and, I think, genuinely grateful.

"Force Brandy Down My Throat!"

> "We were young, gay, reckless! That night I
> drank champagne from your slipper. Two quarts.
> It would have been more, but they were open-
> toed. Ah, Hildegard!"
> "My name is Susannah."
> - Groucho Marx and Margaret Dumont

A letter of correction to the editor of The Greater Los Angeles Jewish Journal:

> *Dear Rob,*
>
> *Re my story on Irving Brecher—please print corrections.*
>
> *The opening line, quoting Groucho Marx's character J. Cheever Loophole, romancing Margaret Dumont in* At The Circus, *should NOT be: "That night I drank champagne from your slipper. Two quarts. It would have been more, but you were wearing inner soles." This was taken from "The Marx Brothers At the Movies" by Paul Zimmerman and Burt Goldblatt (Berkeley Books, 1968).*
>
> *But it is wrong.*
>
> *The correct line, from Mr. Brecher's original script, is: "It would have been more, but* they were **open-toed.**"
>
> **Not** *"inner soles."*
>
> *"Inner soles," the screenwriter explained to me, "is not funny and makes no sense!"*
>
> *Also, the headline for the story shows Brecher mentioned with Zeppo, Groucho, Harpo, and Chico Marx. Zeppo did not make Marx Brothers movies with Brecher, nor did Brecher ever write anything for Zeppo.*
>
> *Also, "Irving S. Brecher" should not have appeared. Mr. Brecher finds the "S." pompous and has never used it in his life. Not since he was Irving Sidney Brecher in the Bronx as a four-year-old in 1918.*
>
> *Thank you for your attention to these. There will probably be more TK.*

Yipes! Clearly, I hadn't grilled Irv closely enough about our Jewish idols. I set out to correct ***that*** *error at my earliest opportunity....*

May I ask you more about the Marx Brothers?

Of course! I'm glad. There never has been anything like them. But Buzzell's poor direction of their movies left me with some bitter feelings.

You don't appear bitter.

I'm not bitter about my years in Hollywood. I knew a lot of shitheads. They amused me. They entertained me while I entertained the audience.

You never worked with Zeppo Marx and I see you have Gummo Marx in your 1937 address book, but no phone number—

What's the difference? I knew how to reach him.

Let's talk about Go West. The great actress, Margaret Dumont—

She was in *At the Circus*.

But not in Go West.

There was no part for her.

Hard to believe.

Believe it. The poor pathetic creature...

Pathetic? Wasn't she the doyenne of the dumbfounded? The foil of frivolity and—

She wasn't in *Monkey Business* either. They cast Thelma Todd.

What did you think of Ms. Dumont?

She was the oldest virgin at MGM. Margaret Dumont came to me one day and said, "You know, Mr. Brecher, I've been in a number of movies with the boys and I never do anything but play straight for Groucho. Is there something you could write that would make me more, successful, you might say, in my career, and not *type* me so much?

So I said, "Well, I'll give it some thought."

In a moment of recklessness, I wrote a scene in which she tried to seduce a gorilla, and I submitted it to the producer.

He said, "You gotta be crazy. You want a gorilla making love with Margaret Dumont? The S.P.C.A would fight it. Cruelty to animals."

Good one.

That was it. It was never shot.

Back to Go West. One reviewer wrote: "The majority of the sequences are ones that the Marx Brothers have tried out and timed in recent vaudeville tours. The movie begins with the business in the railroad station with Chico and Harpo hornswoggling Groucho..."

What does that mean? "Hornswoggling."

You don't know?

Some of the readers might not.

That's a swindle. They swindled Groucho in the station.

You just don't hear the word anymore.

No.

Can we talk about anarchy? Is that what you would say they brought to motion pictures? A sweet-scented anarchy set loose—

Not a *sweetness*! Nobody ever threw lines away like Groucho. What he created long before on stage, he transferred to pictures, this new kind of comedy technique, tossing off lines.

A kind of standing "out of time" technique.

A style that soon other comedians tried. Carole Lombard, Eve Arden, William Powell and others began to work like that. What a great compliment to Groucho.

Have you seen *Brazil*? Terry Gilliam includes a clip from *The Cocoanuts* in there. There's this wild black-and-white Marx Brothers fight on TV in the middle of the scene, surrounded by lurid, exploding Terry Gilliam mayhem. It's like two surreal visions combined, Groucho's and Gilliam's.

Special effects were used with great result in **Go West**. Especially during the final train sequence. A week before shooting, the head of the unit, Bernard Hyman, one of the more respected executives at MGM, called me in. He said, "You know I love the script, but I've got bad news. The budget just came in and we've got to cut a hundred-and-fifty thousand dollars out of the script."

The budget was over a million dollars.

"The only place I can see to make major cuts," Hyman said, "is in the last couple reels with the action on the train."

The famous chase scene where the bad guys go after them.

I moaned because in my opinion, cutting big hunks of the sight gags would water down the laughs. This was typical of a writer clinging to what he bled onto paper. Bernie Hyman commiserated but he said he had no choice. So with a sense of despair, I cut and rewrote enough of the last chase sequence to add up to the amount he needed. With a sense of foreboding—always ready at the worry—I turned in the revisions.

Two days before shooting, I was bowled over.

Hyman called me and said, "Put back in what you cut. I told them upstairs they better not do it at all unless we do it right. So we'll spend a little more and take a shot."

That was the attitude that prevailed at MGM in the years I worked there. One of the biggest laughs is when the train goes through the barn and there's a guy hammering on the roof who doesn't even notice it. Then down the tracks, Harpo leans out of the train and gets snared by the mailbag trap. The catcher. Now he's hanging in the grasp of the steel arms of the mail thing and as the last boxcars come by, the steel arms throw Harpo into the open door of a train car and he slams into the conductor, knocking him flying so the conductor goes spinning around and out into outer space. Fucking scream.

The second unit did that scene in pieces. They had such amazing skills. And everything took time to construct and execute and cost hard dollars. That was a good hunk.

"Hunk?" You mean "stunt?"

By that I mean, a good piece of film.

That train madness was on a list of the Ten Best Sequences in motion pictures, right?

Of course this is back scratching, but—yes. This from the critic in the *New York Times*, Bosley Crowther. Think of all the antics of the brothers. Now think of them being chased by villains on a train full of passengers . They run out of coal so the boys have to burn up the freight cars to make steam in the engine. They have to burn the train to keep it going, chopping up all the wood they can find. That includes the seats and the ceilings of the club car. Turned out to be a hell of a couple reels. The special effects stuff was reminiscent of Buster Keaton, who was actually on set working with Harpo. We shot it in the San Fernando Valley and that train... well, it took liberties.

Chico, Harpo and Groucho, they weren't really running on the top of the train were they?

I think they were, but the train was not moving. They were running but the background was moving.

How's that?

The train only looks like it's moving. It's film in the back of them showing movement. That's called a process shot. Same thing in the scene with the stagecoach almost tipping over. In the theater it was a riot. That's the good part of writing. The money is to pay the rent but an audience's approval is the candy. Ego being what writers live on. Because, just imagine: I'm young and I'm ambitious and I'm pressured. I was pressuring myself to make up stuff all the time.

Is that how Harpo came to call you, "Irv the Nerve?"

He called me that because I was a type A, always high and moving around a lot.

You actually developed a tic, right? Some kind of physical twitch while

writing for them?

Well, at a certain point I had this thing going on. But I got over it. Like a crick in my neck. The stress of getting it off, getting it right, and doing it alone had become intense. The pressure was on to be funny every second.

Nat Perrin, who had written some Marx Brothers movies at Paramount, said to me one day: "Irv, what do you weigh?"

I was 135 pounds dripping wet. And six feet one-and-a-half inches tall.

"Nat," I said, angling myself against him. "Why do you wanna know my weight?"

"Because," he said. "You must be the strongest writer in town."

I didn't know about that, but I did wind up with insomnia for a long period.

Wow. What kind of approach did you take, trying to create scenes and gags for performers who were clearly beyond, and brilliant? I'm trying to conjure up an image of you, finding your comic voice at the age of 24 writing for the Marx Brothers.

Luck. I was not a hardened pro.

The fact is, if I hadn't gotten lucky, those pictures wouldn't be there. When I wrote, I would talk to myself out loud in the voice of Groucho. I also had long moments where I would sit at my desk, lean back and shut my eyes. Not sleeping, but as a kind of self-hypnosis or meditation. At home in bed, too, just before going to sleep. Just thinking of say, "purple." Trying not to think of anything except the color purple. And thoughts, ideas, would come to me. The five blocked comedy scenes they required. Or just images. Occasionally I would close the blinds of my office at the studio and lie down. An image… and I'd make a note… something about a thousand-dollar bill on a string, and Groucho getting taken for it. That became part of **Go West**'s opening scene in the railroad station.

The hornswogglers!

Yeah. Groucho was a great straight and as S. Quentin Quale played with it magnificently.

What about the opening with the pioneers heading west. "The Time: 1870. The Jokes: 1860."

That's what we call "The Forward." The station scene is right after that.

What about the scene in the saloon where Harpo sticks up a bad guy with a brush instead of—

A whiskbroom. A whiskbroom instead of a gun. That's no big trick to make up. But what's interesting is if you write something like that for Harpo Marx—and his cowboy hat business—nobody believes it could be written because of all Harpo does with it. He would embroider it. Or he would have an idea and I would embroider that. Inside the saloon, all those extras were really laughing! Like where Harpo is so dry at the bar that he strikes a match off his tongue.

How did they do that?

What they did was put some sandpaper on his tongue. They pasted it onto his gums, and he lit it up.

That's pretty dry.

Sure is.

That's Harpo's character, "Rusty." But what about the name you gave Groucho?

"S. Quentin Quale." That was a play on a name from way back. It referred to the name that wise guys used when they talked about screwing with underage girls. The penalty for which was a long term in prison, in San Quentin Penitentiary.

Yikes.

The term "quail" didn't mean that in real life Groucho was taking advantage of teen-aged girls. He was above that. His second wife was in her early twenties.

Ha! You seem to enjoy playing with cliches in your dialogue. Can you explain some of these lines? Didn't one of them because a catch phrase back then?

Particularly among men who went to bars. The line is from Groucho when he gets into a confrontation in the saloon with Robert Barrat, who played "Red Baxter," the villain. Baxter knocks Quale down a flight of stairs and he lands at the bottom, presumably unconscious. Chico runs over, slaps his cheek and offers water to revive him. Groucho opens his eyes and says. "Forget the water. Force brandy down my throat."

I love that.

Guys would say it to the bartender: "Say Joe, force brandy down my throat."

A catch phrase in the early 1940s. Amazing. Like the "cheeseburger, cheeseburger" that John Belushi and Dan Ackroyd made famous on "Saturday Night Live," maybe two comedy generations later.

Whatever. It pleases a writer.

To become part of the cultural currency.

The line came from a stock phrase in movies where some miner or mountain climber is rescued and he's so frozen as to be near death. One of the rescue party would quickly command: "Force brandy down his throat!"

What a kick that must be, hearing a stranger use a line from your script.

I liked it. But don't forget the tremendously difficult work that leads up to it. Michael Kanin, husband to Fay Kanin—they wrote some great films together—he said something I've always remembered: "Writing is tough, just sittin' and sittin'. I hate writing, but love having written."

So true. And that would make a great title for the book.

What, the Kanin?

No, "Force Brandy Down My Throat and other lines I wrote for..."

"Force brandy down my throat?" That doesn't say anything!

Well, it's only the most famously repeated line you say you ever wrote. I picture it covering the entire front, all in caps. FORCE BRANDY DOWN MY THROAT. Very McSweeney's.

Huh?

That's a hip publishing house, created by Dave Eggers who wrote _A Heartbreaking Work of Staggering Genius_. They go in for the odd non sequitur, self-reflexive ironical humor the kids dig today.

Well, I don't know about them. I got a title for you: The Age of Hilarious.

Yeah! Also great.

Or the one I thought of the other day: Don't Rain on My Tirade.

Let's shake on that.

We can shake on it. I'm shaking all the time. Ever since I first met Groucho.

How about Chico? You always pronounce his name "Chick-o." I thought it was "Cheek-o."

No. Mine's the correct way. He got that name because he was always chasing chicks.

But he had a wife. What about _her_?

Betty. Chico was really tough on his wife. She was long-suffering in terms of neglect, because almost every night Chico was out playing cards or womanizing. Groucho told me of one time Chico came home late in the morning to find a trail of playing cards leading from the entrance of the house through the hallway, up the stairs and into Betty's bed.

She was saying "Fuck you," to Chico?

No. She was saying, "Fuck *me!*" It's a funny picture. Betty had a sense of humor. Maybe that's why, despite his misbehavior, the marriage lasted as long as it did.

In the *L.A. Times* obituary of Harpo's wife Susan, it said:, "The Marx Brothers, famous for such films as, *Animal Crackers, Monkey Business, Go West, Duck Soup,* and *A Night at the Opera.*

That's not bad. I feel pretty good that some people liked the work. I wish I could do more. I have a feeling of unfinished business.

I want to ask you more about Harpo.

Harpo was such a cute devil.

In Alan Pale's study, *Comedy is a Man in Trouble: Slapstick in American Movies,* you're quoted as saying Harpo worried only about his solo scenes and he left the overall structure to Groucho.

Harpo I never worried about.

He's been described as the "silly" Marx brother. I looked up the derivation of the word and silly originally meant "blessed" in the Bible and then developed into "innocent," then "simple," to today meaning "foolish."

That's quite interesting. Harpo had a child-like innocence. And he seemed to be having a very good time screwing up people. Surprising them. Like in **Go West** where he outdraws the villain but instead of shooting him he brushes the guy's shoulder with the whiskbroom. He was off the wall and mischievous, when he thought there was reason to be.

During the filming of **Go West**, he decided to give Eddie Buzzell a special kind of birthday party. It was the most unusual one I'd ever attended. The partygoers were ordered onto a rented bus which drove us to the front of the Brown Derby in Hollywood. Harpo had promised a great dinner so we were salivating as we got out of the bus.

But we weren't permitted to go inside the restaurant. Instead, a hot dog wagon wheeled up in front of us. It had an umbrella that read, "Happy Birthday Eddie" and the hot dog man started dispensing frankfurters. The celebrants were too busy laughing to really eat.

When the joke was over, we actually *did* have dinner at the Derby. Then afterwards the bus took us to the Olympic Arena, where they held prizefights every Friday night. Since this was Saturday night, the place was empty, except for two wrestlers we saw hurtling each other around the ring. Two huge fat over-the-hill wrestlers. When they finished a wild series of attempts at mayhem, they suddenly stopped, turned around, and arm-in-arm sang happy birthday to Buzzell.

Harpo liked doing such amusements. And he was never hurtful. A wonderful man with a kind of interesting chutzpah. Harpo was lovable. We didn't sit around holding hands and singing. But you could touch him. You could get a little closer to him than to Groucho.

That's nice, Irv. I want to read you one more review, from London, of Go West.

"The story is very well told. Groucho, tying a muffler over the mouth of an engineer driver, looks at the audience and asserts, 'This is the best gag in the picture.' He is wrong. The climax... is a race between a railway train and a horse, beautifully done... the train arriving in triumph rather like a half-plucked goose... [after] a nightmare journey during which the timber of the coaches is used as fuel... For the first time in their careers, the Marx Brothers have risen to slapstick." **I don't get that.**

I don't either. What the hell, you wanna go get half a sandwich?

I also love in your script where S. Quentin Quale looks out at the audience and says, "Hey you up in the projection booth, would you mind running the film backwards to I can get the deed back?"

I think Buzzell had that cut.

Another Groucho Marx catch phrase came from Go West: "Time wounds all heels," he says in the saloon. That's a line I once heard John Lennon use.

Is that right?

I'm telling you! That's why I'm asking. Was your movie the first time it was used?

I'm not sure I came up with that.

I'm just saying, forget about "Force brandy down my throat." "Time wounds all heels" is still so familiar...

I don't want to take credit for it. Let's go get a sandwich.

MARX'S 'GO WEST' THEIR BEST;

Buzzell, Brecher Set Up Big Laugh Fest

"GO WEST"
(MGM)

Producer	Jack Cummings
Director	Eddie Buzzell
Original screenplay	Irving Brecher
Photography	Leonard Smith
Edited by	Blanche Sewell

The players: Harpo, Groucho and Chico Marx, Diana Lewis, John Carroll, Walter Woolf King, Robert Barrat, June MacCloy, George Lessey.

"Go West" should prove to be the best picture the Marxes have made in quite a while. It's screamingly funny in spots and has a running finish that's hilarious, together with just enough plot to not overburden or slow up the comedy. It's a good show and should please all the customers, as it did the preview gathering last night.

Main credit for the success of the picture must go to Irving Brecher for the swell screenplay of his original yarn and to Eddie Buzzell for his slap-hang direction. The combination working under the supervision of Jack Cummings clicked, and it seems the answer to MGM's Marx Bros. problem.

Some of the best gags the Marx boys have ever had are in this picture, and there are lots of them—both gags and dialogue, and the finish with almost the entire troupe on and off a train, of the early American period, all trying to get to New York before the others in an effort to sell the railroad some property, is one of the funniest series of sequences photographed in a picture for a long time.

The plot centers around the deed to a piece of property for the building of a railroad. Chico and Harpo get the deed as a security for a $10 loan to a prospector on the desert and, in turn, put it up as a 10-cent collateral for a glass of beer in the saloon owned by the heavy of the picture (Robert Barrat). The discovery by Harpo of the importance of the deed, its recovery from the saloon, only to be snatched back by the heavy and finally its return to the Marxes, furnishes a good stage for the play of the gags and the recitation of the funny dialogue.

In addition to the Marxes the cast includes Diana Lewis, doing a swell job as the chief feminine interest, John Carroll, okay as the romantic lead; June MacCloy who has been away from the screen too long; Walter Woolf King, Robert Barrat and George Lessey, who all fit well into the show.

There are a couple of song numbers well placed and sung and Chico's piano and Harpo's harp, both of which came in for good applause.

Marx Bros 'Go West' Riot of Zaney Fun

MGM

Good reviews from Hollywood Reporter (above) and Variety (below). Archer Winsten in the NY Post wrote: "The Marxes are in their own peculiar groove. They are nuts, professionally & profitably."

Marx Bros 'Go West' Riot of Zaney Fun

MGM

Producer	Jack Cummings
Director	Edward Buzzell
Original Screenplay	Irving Brecher
Stars	Groucho Chico, Harpo Marx
Featured:	John Carroll, Diana Lewis, Walter Woolf King, Robert Barrat, June MacCloy, George Lessey.
Photography	Leonard Smith
Time	70 minutes

The Marx Brothers, after a few recent irritations with vehicles that labored more or less with plot, have returned to first principles 'Go West.' The result is an elongated vaudeville show, a riot if you are a Marx Brothers addict, and plenty of good fun no matter what you are.

Several times as zaney as any of the zaney Marx offerings, "Go West" would seem to be geared for present audience tastes. It...

one through, gag by gag. Because, aside from a few brief moments in the opening reel or so when time must be lost to establish some semblance of plot, the picture moves on scene by scene as a studied and proven succession of laugh scenes. The timing of gags is perfection, the sequence of situations such that they start at moderate tempo, and gradually build to a hell, wide, and handsome shoot the chutes climax of action.

The picture should ride to top Marx money in these troublesome days.

Chico, Groucho and Harpo all run currently through the action, from the moment in Grand Central Station when we discover that they have taken Horace Greeley's advice to heart and have decided to "Go West." But, without forcing, the picture

self as a standard on the MG his first chance to sing since Monogram days, and his cont picture is worth while. Dian William Powell, to you, give mantic interest to the alleged

The majority of the seque that the Marx Brothers have timed in recent vaudeville tou with the business in the ra which finds Chico and Harp ling Groucho, then take a bi to the stage coach sequence meets up again, and on to scene when the boys are try the "papers" from the heavy's save the day for honesty as r the gal and boy of the roman

Did I tell you that when I was a kid, the greatest thing in life was making up like Groucho?

Well, Harpo called me very early one morning in the summer of 1939. The brothers, a director, some actors and myself were scheduled to leave Hollywood by train for Joliet, Illinois to put on a live version of **Go West** in a vaudeville house. Before shooting the movie, we broke it in on stage, road-testing material for laughs. The plan, previously used by MGM to sharpen the comedy scenes in **Night At The Opera**, made sense. The stage show would have a narrator spouting a sketchy storyline which tied together the four of five "block" comedy scenes, separated by songs sung by the romantic leads, musical numbers by Harpo with his beautiful harp solos and Chico, who was always a big hit with his odd way of fingering the keyboard, as he played more for laughter than what the composer had in mind. For each show I was in the wings or at the back of the house making notes as to how the jokes played. If something didn't play well, I'd replace it for the next show. There was pressure on them to learn it. Chico never really learned most of his lines, he was always somewhere else. But Groucho was a responsible person and Harpo you never worried about—he didn't have any lines.

We couldn't use this method—returning to their vaudeville theater roots—with **At The Circus** because the scenes required too many variables, like a trapeze, a bear, a few elephants. You know?

So Harpo called to tell me that a photographer was waiting at the studio to make photos which were urgently needed for posters and billboards for **Go West**.

"Get over to MGM," he said, "because they're gonna make you up to look like Groucho."

"What are you talking about, Harpo?"

"They've got a deadline to shoot us today and Groucho won't get out of bed."

"Why?" I asked. "Who is he with?"

"He should be so lucky. He thinks he's got a cold. He sneezed and that's like having the bubonic plague."

Groucho was a hypochondriac. If he had as much as a sniffle, he would cancel any social or business activity.

"They wanna shoot *me?*" I said to Harpo. "You're kidding."

Harpo said, "Irv, I've seen you doing Groucho with the burnt cork at parties. Don't worry, when they make you up, you'll look okay,' "

So I hurried over to the studio to see Jack Dawn, the famous make-up artist—he did Greta Garbo, Joan Crawford, Myrna Loy and all the other beauties. Now he did me! And when Jack Dawn got finished dyeing my wavy locks and parting them a la Groucho, and did my eyebrows and upper lip with shoe polish, all I needed was a long cigar.

When I looked in the mirror, there I was: Groucho a.k.a. Julius Marx.

The impact of being a famous figure didn't really hit me until I arrived in Illinois three days later with the rest of the crew. Walking out of the train depot, I had the sudden sensation of seeing a billboard announcing the impending appearance of the three Marx Brothers. Only there I was, in between Harpo and Chico, a fraud attempting to deceive the good people of Joliet. The only tip-off was on the finger of "Groucho:" a tiger's eye ring that my Uncle Paul, a diamond broker from 47th Street, gave me. Get out your magnifying glass. It's in there.

When we got to Detroit, Groucho was busy with four live shows a day in the Fox Theater, so he asked me to do him a favor. His young daughter Miriam had arrived from Los Angeles and he wanted me to bring her to the show. I picked her up at her hotel and as we walked downtown we passed a wall covered with the 24-sheet promotional posters announcing **Go West** at the Fox. Big as a billboard.

Miriam looked up at the picture—Harpo and Chico on either side of Groucho—and with a note of puzzlement she said, "I never saw that ring on Daddy's finger before!"

I lifted my hand and showed her. I was wearing the ring.

She couldn't believe it. Me up there. *That* was fun. I think that now, even as an adult, the greatest thing in my entertainment life was making up like Groucho.

But the most memorable part of that trip was the moment that Grouch and I, in between shows, were walking to our hotel and heard a newsboy shouting: "Nazis Invade Poland!"

"The only thing good that could come out of this," said Groucho, "is it may be the end of Polish jokes."

Chico and Harpo wondering about the man in the middle. "It is I, Brecho!"

Irving Brecher

Harpo Loses His Mezuzah

Harpo Speaks!
That's the name of a book Adolph Marx wrote with Rowland Barber in 1961.
It's on Irv's bookshelf in the living room and he insists that I read it because it
is packed with wonderful stories of the Marx Brothers on the road after mother
Minnie pushed her five boys into performing.

Harpo says the first thing he did on stage was wet his pants. He subsequently
traveled twenty-five thousand miles to three hundred different towns in the
next twelve years. He stopped speaking forever in 1964 at the age of 76, a huge
loss says Brecher.

Susan Marx and Brecher remained friends and in December 2002, I called
to read him her obituary from the L.A. Times.

"She was 94," he said, knowing all about it. "Lovely. She took an activist's
role in Palm Springs where they lived. She was sweet and beautiful and her
heart was in the right place. They adopted four kids. Bill Marx is now in his
sixties and we talk often. He just wrote a book about his father and called me
to write an introduction for it. Susan Marx.... God, I loved her..."

Then he said sharply in his next breath, "Listen, kid, come on over and let
me give these stories to you before I croak. That's a grim kind of thing I realize.
I'm not particularly thrilled about it myself."

HARPO TAKES A TAXI FROM TIFFANY'S

One day walking in New York, unrecognized without the wig, Harpo
strolled past Tiffany's on Fifth Avenue where there was a line of taxicabs
waiting for fares. A tall doorman working for Tiffany's was shouting, "Hey
you fucking Jew boy, move your Jew cab!"

Harpo walking by hears this so he walks until he gets to a Woolworth's
Ten Cent store. In the novelty section, he buys a bag of diamonds and
rubies for a nickel and walks back to Tiffany's and goes inside.

When he comes back out—the doorman with the purple veins in his
nose guy is still saying, "Hey Kike, move it!"—Harpo bumps up against
him and drops the bags of jewels all over the sidewalk.

The doorman bends down to help gather the spilled items and Harpo
hands a jewel to the guy and says, "This is for *you*, my good man. I can
afford it."

The guy almost faints at the diamond.

"And would you please get me a taxi?" Harpo adds, "I'm late for the synagogue."

Now that was a great fucking piece of revenge. When the guy goes home and has it appraised, he'll have a heart attack.

HARPO'S MEZUZAH

Harpo Marx loved his mezuzah, that metal piece of jewelry with a small scroll inside with God's name on it. He wore it on a little gold chain around his neck. Every time I saw him he had it on. For years.

He came home from a trip to New York and when I talked to him he said, "I'm so annoyed. I lost my mezuzah and it's kind of a good luck charm. I'm sure I left it on the airplane."

I said, "Did you have them look for it?"

Harpo said, "Well I left my name and described what it was. I don't think I'll ever see it again."

But when I ran into him a few days later he said, "Can you believe it? They found my mezuzah. No kidding, yeah. They called me: 'Mr. Marx, we have good news for you. We found your whistle. But somebody had stuffed it full of paper, which we dug out so you can blow it.'"

HARPO GOES ON UNEMPLOYMENT

In the late 1960s, Harpo was retired, except when he played one-nighters out of town. One day he said he went to the Unemployment Insurance Office. (We all did in between jobs—you got sixty dollars for a week for thirteen weeks. I once saw Adolph Monjou drive up in a Rolls Royce, get out, go in, and come back out with sixty dollars.)

Harpo goes to the window clerk.

"Name?"

"Harpo Marx."

"How long have you been unemployed?"

"About two weeks."

"What was your last job?"

"I played the harp in the Toronto Opera House."

"And what was your salary?"

"Fourteen thousand dollars."

The clerk reacted nervously. She thought she was dealing with a nut until the man in back of Harpo said, "He's Harpo Marx, the comedian. They make a lotta money when they work."

The clerk gathered herself together. "Okay," she murmured. "Do you still want the sixty dollars?"

Harpo said, "If I don't take it, the Treasury Department couldn't balance their books."

He took it. The rest of the line behind him fell down and peed in their pants.

HARPO'S BIRDIE

Harpo Marx loved the game of golf and we used to play together. One afternoon at the Hillcrest Country Club, it was hot as I recall, and Harpo decided to shed his shirt, which was wet with sweat. He played the rest of the round in his shorts. When we got in the clubhouse, he was informed, "One is not allowed to golf without a shirt."

The chairman of the house committee dressed him down.

"Playing without a shirt is absolutely a violation. If it happens again, you will be suspended for six months."

Harpo dutifully apologized.

"No more no shirt," he said. "I really didn't know what I was doing. I must have had sun stroke."

The next time we played the ninth hole, after teeing off, in full view of the clubhouse, Harpo took off his pants. He played the rest of the way in his jock strap.

When the rest of us stopped laughing, I pointed to his covered crotch and told him, "No fair, you got an extra club!"

HENRICI'S OF CHICAGO

Of the three brothers, Chico was the black sheep. But he was so sweet, so charming. He also loved mugs and goons, so he takes me to lunch in between shows at a famous restaurant called Henrici's. We're in Chicago and all of a sudden I see three guys come in the door all wearing plaid mackinaws, and all of them have broken noses.

And they see Chico and they swoop down and in their kind of poor English they say: "Hey Chikky boy, what are you doing here in Chicago?"

And one picks him up and hugs him. They're tough.

Chico tells them and then adds, "This is the fellow who's writing the movie."

Guy whacks me, almost dislocates my collarbone.

And finally one of them says, "Chico, how long you gonna be here?"

"We're working," Chico says.

He says, "We got a ranch. Right outside town. In Wheaton. Big ranch."

"Mazel tov."

"No, you gotta come out there, Chico, for old time's sake. We hunt. You like to hunt?"

"Well I haven't done a hell of a lot of hunting."

"We hunt," he says.

"What do you shoot?"

"Chickens, cats, dogs."

Sportsmen.

HARPO'S FAVORITE THORNTON WILDER STORY

A little girl comes up and asks him what a war was. Wilder tells her, "It's where a million men with guns go out and meet another million men with guns and they all shoot and try to kill each other." The little girl says, "But suppose nobody shows up?" Wilder had no answer for this.

THE UNCIVIL TONGUE

Groucho called me "Brech." Harpo called me "Irv the Nerve" because I was high all the time. Not high on drugs. Active. I moved around a lot. I named Groucho's character in **At The Circus**, "J. Cheever Loophole, Legal Eagle." It was a play on the name J. Cheever Cowdin, a hatchet man slashing the payroll on behalf of an eastern bank that had lent too much money to a then-drowning Universal Studios. A thin-nosed, thin-lipped, Yankee banker. I thought the name would be an affront to anybody who reads. So pompous. I never met him, but a writer at Universal told me he'd heard someone in the commissary talking to Cowdin about the derogatory character name.

"Whoever did that," Cowdin vowed, "will never work here."

Actually, he was long gone when I did work at Universal, writing and directing **The Life of Riley** feature in 1948.

BEDTIME WITH ARCH & GROUCH

During the war, Groucho and I were meeting with Arch Obler at his office. Obler was a great radio producer of scary shows like "Lights Out," and we went in to pitch him ideas. He was supposed to produce a radio show for the Armed Services and I was there to discuss a ten-minute spot for Groucho. (I wrote a number of radio shots for Groucho back then, but that's another war.) Obler kept referring to himself in the third person.

For fifteen minutes, I suggested one idea, then another, and all the while Obler kept saying: "Uh-uh. Obler doesn't like that. Anything else?"

I think I tried six or seven times, but we got, "Obler doesn't think that's funny," or "Obler doesn't buy that."

That was it.

Groucho knocked a long ash off his cigar, which landed in the middle of the man's desk. Then he smiled and said: "When Obler shows up, tell him he can go fuck himself."

And we walked out.

NATIONAL PASTTIME

In 1948, I went with Groucho and Julius Epstein to a baseball game, semi-pro, at Gilmore Stadium, which is now the Grove shopping mall on Third and Fairfax. We're sitting there watching the game when some fellow comes up and he says: "Did you hear on the radio? The state of Palestine has just announced they have a new name: 'Israel.'"

Julie says: "In another six months, they'll change it to Irving."

THE LAST GROUCHO

Groucho was over at the house once and I was showing off my dog, Toulouse-Lautrec, a little black cornice poodle who went about a pound heavier than a miniature. My daughter Joanna gave him that name. I bought him for her after she'd broken up with some boy and was depressed. He was a terrific, brilliant, little dog. Toulouse-Lautrec went over and did what most dogs do to visiting men's trousers. He sniffed the cuffs. Groucho said, "He must be smelling my son." (Most people would have said "He's smelling my *dog*.")

TO IRVING BRECHER

New York, December 16, 1940

Dear Brech,

This is either a day for writing, the early stages of a honeymoon, or fifteen grains of opium. It's raining, a very pretty rain; not the spasmodic kind that we get in California, but a long steady one, the kind they show in the newsreels with the natives sitting on the rooftops with their cattle, wives and chickens.

I know nothing about the radio situation, and I presume you know about as much. I thought the show we gave that night was good, but I have a hunch there is deepseated aversion to accepting me in any role other than the one I have always played.

Our tour east was uneventful and fairly strenuous. We stopped off in Washington to see President Roosevelt and the Spewack show. Roosevelt was out of town. It would have been just as well if the Spewack show had also been out of town, although it had a lot of very funny stuff in it.

Wednesday night I saw "George Washington Slept Here." Very amusing, and the critics ought to be ashamed of themselves for the knifing they gave it. Thursday night I saw "Hellzapoppin'," second time for me. I found it just as dirty and unfunny as I did last year. However, they are still selling out, and I'm sure they're not interested in my opinion. Friday night, the Ed Wynn show. Utterly delightful, a master comic, not a dirty line or joke in the entire two and a half hours. Saturday night, Al Lewis's "Cabin in the Sky." Good singing, dancing, Ethel Waters in top form, and a quaint story. Sunday night at the Garden with Morris Ernst. Rangers and Americans, ice hockey, tickets two-twenty, ice fine, track fast. Met Ira Gershwin this morning in the coffee shop at the Essex. He had three newspapers under his arm, and four bags under each eye. He told me he hadn't slept all night. Not worry, just keyed up. I'm sure you know the condition by now. I understand the show "Lady in the Dark" is great. It's the story of Moss Hart's psychoanalytical career, and I probably will go to Boston for the opening.

A letter from Groucho in December 1940: "We stopped off...to see President Roosevelt and the Spewack show. Roosevelt was out of town. It would have been just as well if the Spewack show had also been out of town..."

Turning Groucho onto Woody

> "Suppose I brought you to our country place at
> Drooling-On-The-Lapel? What would my people say?
> (A drunk belches.) Well, they'd phrase it more
> delicately."
> – S. Quentin Quale, *Go West*, in Crystal Palace
> Saloon to the glamorous Lulubelle, Red Baxter's
> girl

We're heading out to Label's Table, Brecher's favorite deli, driving east on Wilshire, south on Beverly Glen, east on Pico, passing Fox Studios and Hillcrest C.C., passing the Simon Wiesenthal Center/Museum of Tolerance, joining the parade into Pico-Robertson, the old Jewish neighborhood. But Label's is easy to miss. The joint's just a hole-in-the-wall with a wide window that says "Sandwich special" across from Chick 'N Chew Glatt Hut ("Kosher Chinese") and Doheny Strictly Kosher Meats & Poultry ("Prime & Choice Only—Personal Service"). We can park on Pico, right in front, using Irv's blue handicapped placard, and I guide him and his walker inside.

His face creases into a crooked smile. "I can smell the Jews," he says, and the great Catskills comedian Jack Carter is in there with his wife, both in sweat suits. They come over to say hello, and Bruce, who runs Label's, is always lovely to Irv—they'll get into a good jawing sometimes about garlic; Irv's theory is that garlic lost its punch when China took over the world and began exporting it...

At the counter we order a pastrami sandwich to split, with coleslaw and extra mustard, and he tells me to make sure to grab him a bunch of toothpicks, and after maneuvering him into one of Label's slippery plastic, curvy uncomfortable, orange tables (sticking the walker somewhere*) set my recorder and microphone down, not too close to the thimble-full of extra mustard sitting there on the side of his half-a-sandwich.*

Whew. Okay. Vee may perhaps to begin?

Ha!

You've said that Groucho was your alter ego, a complainer, a dissenter, that you were a putdown artist like Groucho. But what if you'd been shy? Would you have been a success?

I doubt it. The putdown didn't make me a success. It's what I put down on paper. I was shy about standing up.

Ha. And how's that comedy thang working out for ya?

Like in comedies, I want to end high and funnier and not peter out.

How would you critique your Marx Brothers movies?

If I were a critic, I'd suggest cutting out out all of the scenes with the two lovers. They're annoying. They get in the way. **Night at the Opera** and **Day at the Races** were made under Thalberg, and he cast lovers with real talent. Alan Jones with Kitty Carlisle and Maureen Sullivan. Classy performers.

I read that Roland Barthes showed his university students scenes from Night at the Opera when he was trying to illustrate semiotic theory.

That's interesting. But I'd still like to fast-forward through the lover scenes in **At the Circus** and **Go West**. And Groucho agreed with me. He thought the "love teams" should be better than good. One night we went to a movie together called, **Samson and Delilah** [1949]. The leading man was Victor Mature in a loincloth—he looked like a smaller version of Schwarzenegger. Chest! And the leading lady was a gorgeous woman named Hedy Lamarr, walking around in a little slip. Beautiful of face, but the rest of her body was like a boy. Afterwards, I asked Grouch what he thought and he said, "I don't like any movie where the leading man's tits are bigger than the leading lady's."

Ha! Is it true you turned Groucho onto Woody Allen?

Well, I called him up the first time I saw Woody Allen on TV. Woody was on the Jack Paar Tonight Show. He was nothing then, he was new. One of his gags knocked me out: "I'm not supposed to over extend my time." He pulled out a pocket watch on a chain. Opened the cover. Glanced at the face. "This watch is a family heirloom," he said. "My grandfather sold it to me on his deathbed."

That was the line I called Groucho about.

Wow.

All I did was make a phone call.

To me that's like Allen Ginsberg turning Bob Dylan onto the Beatles..

[Silence]

Or Paul Krassner turning Groucho onto LSD.

[Silence]

Woody took a lot from Groucho, especially in *Annie Hall*. Is that one reason you love him?

No. He doesn't take from Groucho. He's his own.

In *Take the Money and Run,* Virgil Starkwell's parents are wearing Groucho disguises.

Ha. Yeah. He may mention him and admire him greatly. One curmudgeon resembles another.

Did you turn Groucho onto any of his wives?

No.

He had a few.

The first was Ruth Johnson, mother of their two children. A blonde beauty. Then there was the one who was married to Leo Gorcey. Kay. And his third wife was a beauty named Eden Hartford.

In the book, *Groucho: The Life and Times of Julius Henry Marx,* Stefan Kanfer wondered if perhaps Groucho was "so marked by [his mother] Minnie's dominance, by her usurpation of his childhood, that he felt compelled to tyrannize and humiliate any woman who ventured too close."

I don't think so. He was no wife beater. He kind of put them down intellectually, sometimes in front of others. They weren't as well-read or didn't have his passionate interest in music.

I just saw a line you gave to Groucho in a book called *Great Hollywood Wits* by Gene Shalit.

Gene Shalit, oh he was a pain in the ass with those movie reviews of his...

The book is a compilation of witticisms, and he quotes from your script for *Go West:* "Lulubelle, it's you! I didn't recognize you standing up."

Oh yeah, funny line. Groucho in the stagecoach.

His first entrance into the saloon. I love this, Groucho says, "Sweep 'em outta the gutter." Somebody says, "There's nobody out there." So Groucho, more sweetly, says, "Well then, sweep out the gutter." Then he sees Lulubelle at the bar.

And he says he doesn't recognize her standing up?

Yeah. That's kind of risqué, isn't it?

Well, if that's what I meant. I don't know why the censors passed it.

And Lulubelle says to Groucho, "Vamoose, you goose."

Ha!

Another I like is where Groucho is trying to get the deed to Dry Gulch and says, "I'll have that deed pronto, whatever *that* means."

Ha ha!

So anyway, Irv, in attribution for the *Go West* line, Shalit wrote: "Screenplay by Jack Jevne, Charles Rogers, James Parrot, Felix Adler."

That's outrageous! He's out of his fucking mind. I wish I could find out how I can contact Shalit and tell him. Goddamn, I wish there was a way to sue for damages.

Don't people edit these books?

Most of the books about Groucho are full of inaccuracies about me. The worst piece of shit was that one you mentioned by Kanfer. Another was a book called *Monkey Business*, by some cocksucker. He had me teamed with a guy and I didn't even know the man! It infuriated me, this fucking book. I don't think it sold ten copies. I do have a memory, you know.

Yes, I remember.

Yes, now you do.

So are you saying all the books are rotten?

No. I said most.

I've been reading one I like, *Groucho, Harpo, Chico and Sometimes Zeppo*, by Joe Adamson.

Yeah? I think I have that one.

Not only are there twenty-five pages referencing you...

Oh?

He has this quote from Groucho: "The first thing which disappears when men are turning a country into a totalitarian state is comedy and comics. Because we are laughed at, I don't think people really understand how essential we are to their sanity."

It has merit.

I found a tiny little book written in 1966 called *The Marx Brothers: Their World of Comedy*, by Allen Eyles. It comes from England. He calls them, "the most heroic of all film comedians."

Oh really?

He says they translated the art of commedia dell'Arte into vaudeville and film...

Yeah.

And "tackle a world that obstructs them and bring it to submission as capably as a cowboy hero disposes of the villain."

That's what I enjoy the most. Fucking the big shots.

But then this fellow Eyles goes on to say he doesn't care for the two movies you wrote.

That's too bad. I apologize.

Yeah... for instance, he calls *Go West*, "an insipid potpourri of misunderstanding."

What the hell is he talking about? What a pretentious comment...

insipid potpourri. Who cares? Fuck him!

I can see why some of these Marx Brothers books describe you as quite brash back then.

No. I was scared.

Scared? You really ask a lot of yourself, and still do, don't you?

I'm all I got. Why not get the most out of it? Life teaches that if you can give out love and get some in return, your life has been full. But if I said that to Buddy Hackett, he would be derisive...

Too corny?

Yeah. But I'm not a comedian, so I can say it.

Can I ask you, do you ever pray, as a way of dealing with being scared?

I do one prayer every night before bed, "*Sh'ma Yisroel Adonoi Elohenu Adonoi Echod. Baruch Shem K'vod Malchuso Le-olam Vaw-ed.*" That's saying to me, I'm a Jew. Good night.

Movies Don't Just Happen

```
Rags Ragland: We'll slip him a Rooney.
Red Skelton: A Rooney? What's that?
Rags Ragland: It's a high-powered Mickey.
- Du Barry was a Lady, 1942
```

MGM was known as the "dream factory," but Brecher just calls it "Metro," where he says he "spent a miserable but happy ten years." I asked him if his happiest moments were spent with fellow screenwriters around the studio's famous Round Table of wits.

*"It **may** have been round," he snapped. "We didn't **call** it that. We just said, 'I'll meet you for lunch at the table.' People don't talk that way: 'I'll meet you at the Round Table...'"*

One afternoon we're in Brecher's study because I want to see a musical he wrote starring Fred Astaire and directed by Vicente Minnelli in 1945 called **Yolanda and the Thief.** *Norma is here, attempting to thin their video collection. She says she is running out of room because of all the DVDs the Academy sends during awards season that he can no longer see.*

*"Here's one," she tells him. "**Royal Wedding.**"*

"Oh we don't need that one," says Brecher.

"Yes we do!" Norma chirps. "There's that wonderful scene when Fred Astaire dances on the ceiling and the wall."

"Okay."

"When you're sick and you can't do anything, read or whatever," she continues. "It stays!"

She told me once that when Irv took her to the movies, he never let her eat or drink anything because he said the noise disturbed his concentration. That's why, she said, they saw most of their movies at the DGA or the Academy of Motion Pictures because you couldn't take food in there.

"That one," she's back on **Royal Wedding.** *"And* **The Band Wagon** *where Astaire and Jack Buchanan do the dance," she begins to sing, "'I guess we'll have to change—'"*

He joins in and now they're both singing. "I guess we'll have to change our plans..."

I love this couple. They remind me of how sweet my parents get when they talk about old movies.

"That's by my friend Arthur Schwartz," Irv says. "It's one of the magic, magic things ever on film."

*"**Royal Wedding** is a terrible movie," says Norma. "But I'll watch it over and over just for that scene."*

"Yeah," says Irv.

"Okay," she pipes up. "I won't bother you anymore. I just want to hang out with the guys, like a little sister. I'm the kid!"

*"Do it!" he shouts. "Stay! And we'd all like **Royal Wedding**... but it could turn out terrible, you follow?"*

Watching them I'm thinking life could be terrible but you'd listen to Irv over and over again, just to laugh in one of his scenes.

Norma bugs him to show me a video he keeps in his closet among a collection of 78-RPM records. I find it. It's a tape of an annual lunch put on by the women's division of his country club: "Movies Don't Just Happen: Women's Committee Panel, May 1992."

"Go forward," Brecher instructs as I slip the video into the console. "Can you do that?"

"Sure."

"And pass a lot of this shit with the greeting from the chairman and the introduction and all that crap."

"Okay."

Fast-forwarding, we see a panning shot of the audience at the event, a couple of hundred women finishing lunch. Then a shot of the panel on a slightly-raised stage, and sitting alongside Brecher are: Howard Koch, a producer; Robert Wise, a director; Fay Kanin, a screenwriter; Ralph Winters, an editor; and Sidney Poitier, a star. Brecher is 78 in the video, looking like a very young old man, very tall and in a light gray suit. And here, in a deadpan delivery, pausing during the women's laughter to wet his finger and turn a page on the podium, is what he said: (A rare, small smile tips off how pleasurable he finds happily talking to an audience, especially ladies, and keeping them roaring)

[Brecher appears on the video, speaking at the podium. Laughter throughout.]

Hello ladies... I see there's a few husbands here. I'll have to keep it clean. Thank you Barry [Merkin]… Your introduction was a lot to live up to, but I prefer it to how I was introduced some time ago when I spoke to a group at a college. The man who introduced me said, too generously, "And here he is… the Dean Emeritus of comedy."

I never got past high school but I know that emeritus means you're out of work. An unemployed dean is someone who's lost his faculties.

Your attendance today in such large numbers might be attributed to your desire to know more about the techniques of moviemaking. Your curiosity about what goes on behind the screens in understandable, but I think there's another reason you're here. I think the magnet that has drawn you here is a shining star. Sydney Poitier. It's always the handsome leading man that pulls them in. The charm and sex appeal that women have imaginary affairs with. In their secret hearts. It's always the actor. You show me one girl who collects pin-up photos of a producer. Or a director. Or a writer? God forbid! The blame for this big crowd goes to you, Mr. Poitier. I don't mean to embarrass you. I know you're modest. That is, for an actor. But it's true. Because you are extremely talented and very attractive. And it requires that sort of man to make these dedicated homemakers tear themselves away from their ironing, washing windows, and then go out and eat food that some stranger cooked. Hillcrest women are happiest when they're home, in that little cozy nest. I dare say, 90% of these women have not been to a restaurant since last night.

Fay, I'm not being sexist, believe me. I'm
really part of the feminist movement and I love
the feminist movement.

Up or down, sideways.

No, actually, Fay, I'm not chauvinistic. I was
part of the group that forced this club to stop
gender discrimination. Now the once-restricted
men's grill is open with full equality to women,
and I think it's great. Hardly a day that I
don't hear some wonderful new filthy joke.

Now, about writing films, specifically the
screenplay, which is the blueprint as Mr. Wise
said, that writers feel will make or break a
movie. I'm not going to speak of the how-to
because frankly I don't know of any special
process, tricks, rules, systems that get the job
done. I don't mean to oversimplify it, but the
creative writers I've known, all seem to have
an inborn instinct. Call it a gift. Maybe it's
genetic. You either have it or you don't. Like
high cholesterol.

But I do think you might want to hear about
some of the witticisms that were coined by the
wonderful writers that I knew back there in
what was, or what is, I should say, now called
"the golden age of the movies." And that was
long before MGM was a hotel in Las Vegas and
before Columbia Pictures began producing frozen
sushi.

Even though some of us were highly paid, we
writers never forgot that we were considered
expendable. You milk 'em, when they're dry,
you get somebody else. Writers were always
considered a necessary evil by most of the
studio chieftains. It was a rare producer or
director who valued our contribution. A case
in point is something that Fay touched on
regarding Ann Sothern. I saw another review,
Fay, of an Ann Sothern movie which also said

something like you reported. This time it was by Louella Parsons who said, "The script was dreadful but the movie's hilarious because Ann Sothern ad-libbed some very funny cracks."

I knew Ann Sothern. She couldn't ad-lib a belch after a ten course Hungarian dinner…

So, we *schleppers* took our refuge in humor, mocking the big brass, mocking the system. We laughed at ourselves, too. The writers' table at MGM was a battleground. Our weapons were sharp tongues. Thinking back, we really had a good time while we were miserable.

One of the wittier writers was Herman Mankiewicz, who would later on write *Citizen Kane*. He was brilliant. His pet hate was the blatant stupidity of the studio. The heads. One day at lunch, Norman Krasna walked in and said, "Did you hear about Dick Scheier?" Now Scheier was an old man, nice guy, who had written some dreadful silent movies and was there, kept on through the kindness of a producer who was also his brother-in-law, as a charity case, walking around, scratching himself, doing nothing on a pension.

"Well, what about Scheier?" I asked.

Krasna said, "They just assigned him to teach the junior writers how to create screenplays."

Mankiewicz said it was a brilliant move: "The guy with the worst case of V-D is in charge of the clinic."

Another time Mankiewicz was at an elegant dinner party. Our host was Arthur Hornblow. He was a top producer, with many fine films: *The Asphalt Jungle*, *Witness for the Prosecution*. But Hornblow's greatest pride was his legendary wine cellar. With each course, we were served a different, fabulous, rare type of wine. And we got a lecture about its vineyard, its age, the vintner's name, his mother's name, his father's name, the name of his dog... Hornblow was such a wine nut that once I told a writer who worked for him, "Hornblow will not read your script unless it's at room temperature."

Anyway, this night, Herman sat drinking refills of the five fabulous wines and suddenly he got very sick. He staggered to the powder room and gave back the whole dinner.

Hornblow ran over, "You okay, Herman?"

Herman said, "Your dinner was perfect; your white wine came up with the fish."

The Hollywood yes man who lived by licking some potentate's rear was always part of the scene, but I had never known one so dedicated to brown-nosing the boss as a producer for whom I wrote several musicals. Arthur Freed was flagrant in his sycophancy toward L.B. Mayer. And this is odd because Freed actually was talented. He was a writer of lyrics for many hit songs and he had a real talent for recognizing other talents and putting together musical pictures. He didn't need to demean himself kissing Mayer's can.

Dorothy Kingswell, a new writer, said: "I've never seen L.B. Mayer without Arthur Freed; they must be very close."

I said, "They're so close, if the barber wants to shave Freed, he has to lather Mayer's ass."

I'm embarrassed to quote myself but those other fellas, they're on location—up *there*... And I miss them. Mayer, you knew a lot about him. He only liked a certain type of schmaltzy movie. He was forever talking about family values, morality, marital fidelity. Not only to us, but probably to his mistresses. Above all, Mayer was a super patriot. For an example, Laurence Stallings had written a war movie, *What Price Glory*? But that was years before. Since then, he was kept on at MGM at big money, never turning out any work. But Mayer was proud to have a war hero to show off. Big patriot, Mayer. Stallings had lost a leg in battle, so he stomped around the studio on his wooden leg. To remind you he was a hero, he would constantly rap his termite-ridden leg with a cane. That wooden leg was his job security.

Once, he had a terrible argument with Ben Hecht about politics. Finally, Stallings screamed, "You bullshitting bastard! I hope they deport you!"

Ben Hecht said, "You overpaid hero. I hope your leg grows back on!"

But some people did respect screenwriters, especially several of our late club members, who from time to time would offer to invest in the movie if I was planning one. With a slight condition: "If there's a nice part for a young, beautiful girl... Now, believe me, Irv, it's not what you think. This is just a friend of a friend of a cousin of a brother of my uncle. Believe me, I wouldn't cheat on my wife. That bitch."

I thought that was outrageous. But I respect a husband who is supportive of his wife and her career. Like the husband of Pia Zadora, who happens to be well fixed. And she's a cute little thing. She's got talent. But the movies she made were flops. And the critics didn't appreciate her acting. So finally she said to her husband, "Darling, I'm not for the movies, but I am for the stage. With a live audience, I'm a great actress."

Her husband said, "Honey, so do a play. I'll finance it."

And she did. She chose "The Diary of Anne Frank." She played Anne Frank. They tried to play out in Miami with a sympathetic Jewish

Irving Brecher

audience. In the third act, when the Nazis ran in and said, "Where is she?" four hundred Jews stood up and said: "She's in the attic!"

Sometimes, in trying to get laughs, some of us went too far. I know I did. I was about to get a plum assignment with Arthur Hornblow who I had mentioned before. Hornblow was a nice man, as I said, and talented. But very prim and proper, particularly at language and innuendo.

A group of us were at his home playing a very popular party game at the time we called "Indications" or "Charades" where you had to pantomime—I think you all know the game—where you give the other team a phrase or a title. I was captain of my team and I wrote out a song title for Hornblow to act out. It was "I'm Forever Blowing Bubbles."

I didn't know he was dating Bubbles Schinasi. I didn't get the job.

[Laughter and applause keep coming as Brecher leaves the podium and Barry Merkin takes the microphone. "Another home run, Irving," he says as the tape ends.]

I asked Irv to explain.

Bubbles Schinasi?

You were born too late. This was the 1940s. Arthur Hornblow was dating a beauty named Bubbles Schinasi. Her father was a Turkish millionaire, a tobacco king, I think he made it with Murad cigarettes. Actually it would have been a great play on words: *'I'm forever Hornblowing Bubbles...'*

And what about the incredible Pia Zadora story?

It was a joke! The greatest fucking joke I ever heard. And everything I said about that is true, except I don't know whether she actually played the play or not. She may very well have done it, but whoever came up with the fucking thing, "she's in the attic..." I didn't take credit for it, obviously.

I don't know who wrote it. This business of being quoted—it's almost impossible sometimes to find out who wrote or said what originally.

Nights at the MGM Round Table

Tell me more about being armed with the quick retort.

Apparently there's a hunger on the part of most of us to be the messenger of something funny, whether in person or by phone. It happened this way more than once. L.B. Mayer was the most powerful man in Hollywood and you didn't take his name in vain. Which I'd happened to do. I'd been at MGM a few years and had been a guest a couple times at his home at the beach in Santa Monica where he had some directors and producers and even a few writers over for a rare Sunday brunch. I fired away I guess because I'm a dedicated opponent to nepotism. Probably because I was jealous of anybody who had enough influence to get ahead without working. I liked to blow the whistle on guys who get a free ride.

Mervyn LeRoy had married Harry Warner's daughter, Doris. The Bush Administration has since perfected this kind of cronyism, but when producer Jack Cummings married Mayer's niece, I said he was a product of "nephewtism."

Anyway, what happened was one day at the studio I was having lunch with Ruth Flippen, a new writer at the time, and she was naturally curious about what went on. I filled her in best I could.

Then she got around to asking: "There's one man. I know his name because I saw him go in and out of an office. His name is Revnes."

"Bingo!" I said with glee. "You just won the nepo-prize. "That's Maurice Revnes."

"From my office window," she said, "I see him come in and go home every day about the same time. I never see him in the commissary. And I was looking at the movies being shot or planned—has he been here long? What movies has he made?"

"He's been here as long as I've been here," I told her. "Over five years. But no, no movies. He has a much more important job. As you know, his office is on the top floor of the Thalberg Building. It's in the northwest corner. On a clear day you can see the Pacific Ocean. Revnes' job is to sit there and look out toward the ocean. And if he sees a glacier heading toward the building, he's supposed to send a memo to L.B. Mayer."

She laughed it up pretty good. So did a few of the other writers at the table. After wallowing in their approval, I started getting nervous. What if it got back to Mayer? I could be in big trouble.

The next day, when I was deep enough into trying to write something, I got a call from one of Mayer's secretaries. Would I please come up? "Mr. Mayer wants to see you." My stomach dropped. I guess I must have looked like a zombie as I went up to my doom. I was sure he'd throw me out of the studio, contract notwithstanding. When I got there, Ida, his number one secretary, looked at me sternly—I figured she'd heard what I said and did not approve. She buzzed the Dictaphone and when Mayer's voice said, "Yes?" she said, "Mr. Brecher is here."

"Send him in!" Mayer barked.

I had a fleeting picture of me emptying my desk, took a deep breath and walked in. Mayer's office was huge of course, and I'd been there before, but it never seemed as if the walk from the door to his desk had been that far. I'm sure I was shaking, and finally I reached him. He looked at me with a grim face.

"Did you say something about Revnes?"

"Yes, sir, I did. And I'm sorry. I guess I shouldn't have said it. I was just kidding."

Mayer suddenly grinned.

"But you were almost right," he said. "That shnorrer is on the payroll because I got a soft heart for poor relatives. His mother is my aunt. She was good to me when I was a kid in Canada. So I let him look for glaciers. God forbid the stockholders find out."

What a relief.

"Thanks, Mr. Mayer," I said, beginning to breathe again. "I'll watch what I say."

"If it's funny, put it on paper. Comedy sells tickets!"

And I got out of there fast.

A few days after the glacier line about Revnes, I got a call from Fred Allen. Fred had been a visitor in my home whenever he came out to Hollywood and I enjoyed being with him and his wife, Portland Hoffa. She played the dumb dame on his radio show. This was the first time he'd ever telephoned me from New York. And it was typical of his grace, that instead of his acting as if he was doing me a favor, he very politely said: 'I heard what you said about the glacier. Harry Tugend phoned to tell me about it. Probably because on my show I never miss a chance to put down the cretins at the ad agencies, would it be okay with you if I pin your glacier story on one of our Madison Avenue morons?'

I told him, "Coming from you, that's high praise."

And sure enough, in his opening monologue the next Sunday night, he did the story, which got a very pleasing laugh and some applause from his studio audience.

The glacier story also shows up in anthologies with other people given credit for having said it. In an autobiography by a composer I knew named Saul Chaplin, he attributed it to Herman Mankiewicz. Mank didn't need the credit; he was witty enough on his own. The glacier story is the most wrongly attributed thing I ever said, but I got used to being mildly annoyed when something I said was attributed to someone else. Once I said something at Metro and a guy sitting at the table says, "I wish I'd said that."

And I said, "You will."

And to prove that I adhere to what I just said about not taking unearned credit, I'll tell you something and give the credit to myself.

I was very new at MGM and had just been invited to join the writers' table. A veteran screenwriter named George Oppenheimer [**The Last of Mrs. Cheyney**, a contributor to **Day At The Races**], a very talkative fellow, quite effete in speech, would often take over. He rambled on with long stories, bragging nonstop with a remarkable skill at not only name-dropping, but also at city-dropping, about his travels in Europe and about the big names. He "went with Somerset Maugham to the Cape and then we saw Noel Coward at Capri and ended up with Chevalier at a soiree at the chateau of Marquis Passardiere..."

When he paused to take a breath, I took a shot.

"Mr. Oppenheimer?"

"Yes?"

"So I take it you've been to Paris."

"Paris!" he squealed. "Paris is my second home."

"In that case, would you please pass the French bread?"

The laugh I got was enough to make an enemy of Oppenheimer for a long time.

A writer I thought was particularly sharp, was a big, charming Irishman named John McClain. Early in 1942 we were discussing the brand new war the country was in and how tough it might prove to be. McClain was the most optimistic.

"We'll win," he said. "And if we do, that'll make two in a row."

John was gone long before Vietnam and Iraq ruined our record. In fact, all those guys who were fun to hang out with at the table are gone.

Here's a story definitely credited to George Kaufman, the wonderful playwright on Broadway and a great director of plays as well. He was once in Atlantic City, breaking in a new show. Alfred Bloomingdale, son and heir to the Bloomingdale's department store family, also had a new play he was trying out in Atlantic City. And it was in trouble, so he got in touch with Kaufman, the number one play doctor in the business.

"Please come see my play," he beseeched Kaufman. "I need you to tell me what we can do to fix it. It just isn't working."

Kaufman grudgingly went and took a look at a matinee of Bloomingdale's dreadful so-called comedy. When it was over, Bloomingdale anxiously asked, "What do you think? What should I do?"

With his classic deadpan, Kaufman said, "Mr. Bloomingdale, you should close the show and keep the store open nights."

Metro was truly a haven for writers. Mayer had an instinct for talent and around that lunch table sat very bright and amusing guys, some of whom wrote films that were hits in their day and still stand up on cable. Actually television would be in big trouble if it weren't for the movies made before 1960. The movie studios made millions on those pictures leasing them to the networks, and the writers or their estates have never gotten a nickel in residuals. On the other hand, we get checks from European TV companies that have a respect for what they call, "artistic material"—I got one for a thousand dollars recently for the airing of Marx Brothers movies and **Yolanda and the Thief.**

Who were some of the writers around that round table?

The ones I felt a kind of privilege to be with? Well, there were writers like Joe Mankiewicz (**All About Eve**), his brother Herman (**Citizen Kane**) and Nat Perrin (**Hellzapoppin**). Billy Wilder was there while he worked on **Ninotchka**. Dalton Trumbo sat with us, he wrote **Thirty Seconds Over Tokyo**, a real patriotic film for which he was rewarded by being jailed as a Communist. The novelists Irving Stone (**Lust for Life**) and Charles Jackson (**The Lost Weekend**) were there. A few others. This group kept me from going crazy, because how do you sit all day and just look at pages and try and put down what people are going to laugh at months later in the theater?

The conversations were lively and the main sport was savaging the producers we worked for. The screenwriter was low on the Hollywood totem pole. Rarely was any attention paid by the director or producer. Except in the case of very few. These were the best in their trade, smart enough to listen to a writer and weigh his or her opinion.

I was lucky on one film, **Shadow of the Thin Man**, starring William

Powell and Myrna Loy. I particularly enjoyed writing it because of Hunt Stromberg, the only producer in my experience that I totally respected. He had been making movies since the 1920s and he made some of MGM's best: *The Great Ziegfeld*, *Treasure Island*, *Pride and Prejudice*, *Idiot's Delight*, and two *Thin Man* movies.

In another life, Stromberg might have been a screenwriter, or so it seemed to me, because I felt that he had, by suggestion and patience, made me write better dialogue and create better situations than I thought I was capable of. A rare experience. He was a bulldog about getting it right. He had great skill as an editor. When critical of a line of dialogue or a scene, he would give a valid reason for it, rather than: "It don't hit me." Or: "This really stinks."

Overall, even with producers lacking any particular ability, I can't really complain about being kicked around. I like to think it's because they approved of my work. But it was probably because most of them would have a lackey read the stuff first and tell the boss it was good or okay.

There was one producer at MGM who gave me a chance to get a big laugh from those around the table who understood Yiddish. Harry Rapf was universally despised because of his brutal treatment of writers, hiring and firing them with contempt and actually vilifying them in the process. This monster was considered the most inept producer on the lot... and had enough stock to protect his position. But anything he touched, or even went near, was a flop. He was such a disaster, one writer named him the angel of death.

I said, "The angel of death in Yiddish is *malkha mooves*. Rapf should be called the *malkha movies*."

Once he called in my friend Norman Krasna [*Mr. and Mrs. Smith*] and made him suffer through a screening of his latest bomb, *The Chief*, with Ed Wynn playing his "Perfect Fool" character. When it was over, Norman, not the timid type, said, "Okay, I saw it. Now what?"

Rapf, in self-delusion said, "It only needs a little work. How do you think I should cut it?"

Norman said, "Up the middle."

Irv, what about your first producer, Mervyn LeRoy, AKA Marvin Levy from San Francisco? In his book about Louis Mayer called *Lion of Hollywood*, the author Scott Eyman writes that you told him: "Mervyn was like a big brother to me."

Yes. I had a lot of big brothers. Milton Berle, certainly.

You also said the producer Isadore "Dore" Schary was a big brother.

Well, more LeRoy than him. Schary was older than I was, and a very good writer on movies like **Sunrise at Compobello, Young Tom Edison.** But he was no good on the Marx Brothers and he went behind my back on **Go West.**

How so?

When he became head of production at MGM, Schary took credit for a rewrite of a scene in **Go West** I wrote by hand and had given to a stenographer to type up. I found Schary reading it to the producer, Jack Cummings.

"Irv, you should hear this!" said Cummings.

Hear it?

I *wrote* the fucking thing! But I just left it at that.

Years later, when Schary was appointed head of production at Metro, he had somebody fuck around with the negative of **Go West** and put his name on it. It's in the frame in the middle of the picture. It said, there on the bottom of the screen: "Dore Schary contributed to this film." I never saw a credit like that. This is absolutely a first. Unheard of. (I think.) He evidently ordered this petty larceny. I thought of reporting it to the Writers Guild. They would have taken him apart. They probably would have canceled his membership, if he weren't already dead.

Good God. And you still considered him a brother?

I found out about it twenty years after he died! At one time I loved him and respected him! And he produced some good pictures, like **Crossfire** about anti-Semitism.

Here's a story:

I was a fairly good tennis player in the '30s and '40s, and I belonged to the Beverly Hills Tennis Club. I used to play with Ricardo Cortez who was a movie star, a faded movie star I guess. But I had to quit because of my eyes. My doctor said I could wind up with a detached retina from all the jouncing and jumping aspects of tennis. Around that time, Dore Schary said to me, "Bubbeleh. I'm going to do you a favor. I'm going to let you buy my membership at Hillcrest."

"I don't play golf."

"You really should. It's good for your health."

"Well thank you for thinking of me."

"And it'll be good for your wife. You'll enjoy it. I insist. It's only a thousand dollars."

"That's too expensive," I told him.

But he was a real terrific salesman. He could have sold a diaphragm to

Mother Teresa. So I let him talk me into it. I sent a check for a thousand dollars to the club and they sent me a letter back welcoming me with an announcement: They were just adding an eight hundred dollar assessment fee.

So he fucked me out of eight hundred dollars.

I went into his office, steaming.

"Caveat emptor!" he sang. "Let the buyer beware!"

A week later, Hillcrest struck oil on the property.

I was to get about thirty thousand dollars in royalties over the years. So after the oil strike I went back into Schary's office.

"Caveat Shmaveat!" I sang. "Let the seller be wary, let the shmuck be Schary!"

Did you deal much with Sam Goldwyn?

Samuel Goldwyn was unique in his character.

Goldwyn was the kind of guy who would say things like, "What a beautiful day this is to be Tuesday." He was the most self-opaque man I'd ever seen. He wasn't a snob. He had no time to be a snob. He was an ignorer.

One night Ben Hecht came over to the house for dinner. Harpo came by, and he brought Goldwyn over too, after they'd had dinner somewhere else. And Goldwyn for some reason thought it was Ben Hecht's house, not mine.

Goldwyn comes into the house and lays down on our white couch. In his black shoes.

He says to Ben, "Nice place." Ben pointed to me, but Sam refused to believe I could live in Bel Air.

After dinner, we say good night to everybody and Goldwyn says to me, "Can I drop you some place?"

My wife covered her mouth, hysterical.

I said: "Actually I live here. I own this house. I could show you the deed but I know you're in a hurry."

Best Foot Forward (1943)

Irv, one of your movies was in the news yesterday. A leading lady passed away...

I know. June Allyson. Norma read me the obituary in the Times. She had a pretty good career and *Best Foot Forward* was her first movie.

They kept mentioning Best Foot Forward in the obit. You wrote that in 1943?

I have it here. June Allyson, Lucille Ball, William Gaston—

The headline said: "June Allyson, Adoring Wife in MGM Films, is Dead at 88."

She came out here from Broadway, where she had done the stage show. We also got Nancy Walker and Gloria deHaven from the same show to come do the movie. The first time on film for all of them. I wrote a funny entrance for Nancy Walker. She was a cute, funny broad.

It also said that Allyson was "a film sweetheart that GIs pined for" and how she "arrived in Los Angeles by train with $10."

Bullshit. Ten dollars? I'm sure that's taken from her book. People tell their stories how they want to. I just told you she came from the Broadway show of "Best Foot Forward." But the actor I really enjoyed writing for was Lucille Ball. She played a movie star on the skids who comes to a military academy to get some publicity. She handled comedy lines beautifully, brilliantly, and it was never a surprise to me that she grew into a giant star.

The movie was pretty damn good and it had a great song: "Buckle Down Winsocki." [He sings] "Buckle down Winsocki/Buckle down!/ You can win Winsocki/If you knuckle down..." That's a classic and there were other good numbers like "Barrellhouse Boogie and the Blues." The movies during the war were pure escapism.

How did you come to write the screenplay?

Fred Finkelhoffe asked Arthur Freed to bring me in.

Finkelhoffe, co-credited with you and another writer on your most famous Freed Unit picture, *Meet Me In St. Louis*.

What do you mean?

That's what it said on a poster I saw at a Vincente Minnelli festival—

I didn't write it with anybody else. If the poster is in error, that's too fucking bad. If the credit shows three names, that's terrible on their part.

Okay, what was it like working with Fred Finkelhoffe?

Fred did a very cute thing. He was kind of an artful hustler. He didn't tell Freed, but after he got me in on **Best Foot Forward**, we worked a couple weeks before I found out what he was really doing. Finkelhoffe had formed a vaudeville show, a variety unit of about four or five acts which he produced. And he went away with them. It's hard to believe now, but Freed would call to see how the script was going: "Lemme talk to Fred."

And I would have to lie and then call Fred, who was in San Francisco or somewhere with his show, and he'd call Freed. I didn't mind. I felt I owed him this. Fred got me away from the fucking Marx Brothers thing.

Who would want to get away from the Marx Brothers?

After the two of them, I didn't wanna do any more pictures and they wanted me to do another one. I wanted a change of venue. I didn't want to get typecast. This was a different kind of writing. It was not just gag gag gag. This got me out of that cycle and I didn't know at the time, but it led me into something much better.

Meet Me In St. Louis?

No!

Du Barry?

Best Foot Forward! Problems with the variety show caused Finkelhoffe to leave the stuio, and me. Now at the same time I had a play going on in New York, it was planned for an opening. Anyway, when I finished **Best Foot Forward** I gave it to Freed.

To my amazement and annoyance, he said, "It's shit."

I said, "What do you mean, it's shit?"

"It's no good."

"Sorry," I said. "But I have to go to New York for the play."

He said, "You're not going anyplace, you're staying right here." Freed demanded that I go back to page one of the script. I said the least he could do was let Sam Katz hear it.

Katz was a supervisor of producers. A head. I liked Sam Katz. He was a pleasant man who had somehow gravitated to Hollywood after having been part owner of an early theater chain of movie palaces in the Middle West called, "Balaban & Katz." It was his theater in Chicago where a few years earlier we'd tested sketches and scenes for the Marx Brothers' **Go West**.

Anyway I can still remember how upset I was. He lived about four or five houses north of mine on Stone Canyon. The next morning, Freed, whom I hated by now, was sitting in Katz's backyard on the patio. Freed, damn sure of himself, smirking and smoking. Sam Katz said to me, "Why don't you go ahead and read it, son."

As I read it, I kept watching Freed. Katz was smiling on the lawn there and when it was done, Sam said he loved it.

Freed said, "Didn't I tell you, Sam?"

Imagine a prick like that. Totally reversing himself. Like a snake does.

Sam said: "I think it's very funny, Arthur. You don't?"

By now Freed was his usual slimy self.

"Oh I like it, I really do," he said. "All I meant when I sounded negative was that I felt some of the scenes were a little too long. Nothing serious."

His barefaced bullshit appalled me. But I was to get used to it.

And they shot it. Eddie Buzzell directed.

I'll tell you how Metro worked. Mayer had a lot of producers. Three or four would be under one executive. For example, Sam Katz oversaw Freed and Joe Pasternak, who produced musicals, too. Larry Weingarten. Freed was good; he didn't know about scripts, but he had a great eye for musical talent. Another was Bernie Hyman, who supervised the producer of **Go West**, Jack Cummings.

The only producer I had any dislike for was Freed. I first met him when he was an associate producer on **The Wizard of Oz** when I came to MGM in '38. After I wrote the two Marx Brothers movies and **Shadow Of The Thin Man**, I was assigned to Arthur Freed's unit. By then he had risen—or a writer might say, sunk—to the role of producer.

We had a love-hate thing. I suppose he loved the results of the pictures I wrote, but I know he hated me because I was not afraid to stand up to him. Before you get the idea that I'm bragging about being brave, let me clear that up. I could stand up to Freed because, unlike other writers who, being human, depended on their paycheck to survive, I didn't. I was the producer and owner of a successful radio series running weekly on NBC, "The Life of Riley." It paid me more than I was getting at Metro and supplied me with what every screenwriter would have loved to have: "Fuck You" money. When you had that, you could argue, contradict the producer and still keep that rare feeling of self-esteem which the average working stiff never enjoys.

What else were you able to do with this kind of nasty coinage?

Once, after **Meet Me in St. Louis** became a big hit, MGM got an offer from 20th Century Fox. Darryl Zanuck wanted MGM to lend me to Fox to write **State Fair**, a musical remake of an old Will Rogers movie.

But I begged off because I didn't want to work on a remake. Fox went on and made a decent movie with good songs.

Another movie I turned down was the sequel to *The Jolson Story*. Harry Cohn wanted me to write and direct it at Columbia.

Columbia was the Cohn brothers, right?

Harry was the owner with his brother Jack who was in New York handling distribution. But I told Harry there was no way to write anything to equal the original. Know what I mean? I politely thanked him and moved on. My agent was unhappy. They always are when they lose a commission. I told you about Jolson. He was at the Hillcrest table. Al Jolson was known as "the World's Greatest Entertainer" for his brilliant singing and storytelling that made him a giant, even in retirement. He was also the definitive egomaniac.

I'll tell you one story. At one point he married a much younger woman, a beautiful woman who adored him and wanted to be not only a loving wife, but also the mother of his children. But she couldn't seem to get pregnant. From what I heard, Jolson was very sympathetic, but that didn't help her. It was years later that she learned that Jolson had gotten a vasectomy, but never told her. This way, he said, if his young wife ever got pregnant, he would know she cheated on him. It's true. We knew he could sing. But he said this way he could also fuck freely.

So wait. What happened to the play you told Freed you had to go back east for? Did you go?

I went and worked on the play and it closed in Boston. Then I came back to MGM and a short time later, the producer of the play, Alfred Bloomingdale—

From the George S. Kaufman story.

Yes, yes, Alfred Bloomingdale inveigled one of Broadway's great comedy directors, George Abbott—he did "Room Service" and many other hit plays—Abbott agreed to restage the play. This was very encouraging, so I went east the following winter to work with Abbott on the play for Broadway.

What was it called?

"Sweet Charity."

I loved working with Abbott and after a few weeks of rewriting under his experienced hand, we opened at the Mansfield Theatre.

"Sweet Charity?" The Neil Simon play—?

No, this one was first. It was about a charity run by a group of matronly women called the Friendly Hand. Set in a small town in New England. A bunch of Yankee ladies who fuck up the lives of other people when they try to put on a fundraiser. They were good-hearted, and the Friendly Hand supported dozens of needy families, but everything, as is usually the case in a comedy, gets screwed up. Disaster looms.

Opening night, Abbot and I stood in the back, watching the audience. I was worried. I'm good at that. That night I was at my best.

I said, "George, whaddya think?"

He said, "They're laughing but I'm not sure they like it. I'm not sure they have sympathy for these ladies."

"Do you think it would work better if the fundraiser with this jazz band was put on maybe by girls at a college sorority? Maybe there's some sex going on?"

He slapped his forehead in the traditional Jewish way—even though he's not—and gave me the proverbial, "*Now* you tell me!"

The play closed after a week. The reviews said it was somewhat funny, but far from a hot ticket. And that was it. Sometimes you can get a lot of laughs but it doesn't mean anything because the audience can't take anything away from it...

Did you recall the actors in "Sweet Charity?"

I remember Philip Loeb was very funny in it. He played the band manager and when the women couldn't pay him he said, "The Friendly Hand is giving me the finger." Tremendous laugh. Philip Loeb. He committed suicide, in the 1950s, after he was blacklisted by the House UnAmerican Activities Committee. An actress named Augusta Dabney was very good as the lead, and another actor in the play, Whit Bissell, became a popular character actor in TV and movies.

And that was it for the play?

Samuel French put out the text. Other groups picked it up, I got paid a few bucks. Then later, we got a request from Neil Simon's producer, could they use the title? I don't remember if I got paid or not but I did let them use it when he wrote the book for the musical, "Sweet Charity."

Did you write anymore for the theater?

No. I should've done more. Tried some more. I kept getting involved in movies and TV. The good thing about playwrighting is that the writer is in control. The Dramatists Guild protects you. No director or producer can make any changes without your permission. When you write a movie, you're like Rodney Dangerfield. No respect.

Yes, I notice in those Leonard Maltin movie guides, he lists thousands of movies, naming the actors and directors, but there is no mention of

the screenwriter.

That's a tipoff on the arrogance of most movie maggots who feed on the work that always starts with a script. The movie couldn't be made unless there were people like us who did the work, but according to Maltin, movies were not written.

I noticed in another book, one strictly about Hollywood musicals, that writers _are_ mentioned.

Oh, good.

But the author, Ted Sennett, tended to dislike most of the writing in those MGM classics of yours.

Fuck him. I'm gonna get upset about his opinion? How many movies did _he_ make?

Du Barry Was a Lady (1942)

Gene Kelly: Ah... Rami, isn't she wonderful?
Zero Mostel: Just another female woman! Take
away her eyes, her nose, her mouth, her legs
and what have you got? A blank expression.
—*Du Barry Was A Lady*

What was your method of turning Broadway musicals into movies?

I would fly east and see the play, but I didn't take any notes. I just watched them. I would look at the libretto, fly back west and write the picture. I know. Sounds easy. Don't worry, I sweated it all out.

Irv the Nerve.

Yeah. I happen to be a Type A, which is not good. I wouldn't advise anybody to be a Type A.

Did they even have Type A back then?

What I mean by that is, I moved around a lot. There's a German word—*zitsfleisch*. When you have no *zitsfleisch*, "sitting flesh," that's part of being a Type A.

Thank you for that. *Du Barry* also featured the great Zero Mostel.

Zero Mostel played a faker named Rami the Swami. He was fun to write monologues for. *Du Barry* was a tough movie to do, trying to keep the thread going. With all the numbers. The numbers were great.

By Cole Porter! And was that really Lana Turner in there, who was under contract like you were with Mervyn Leroy in 1937?

Yeah. It was a shot of her. A cameo of her, that's all.

She looked great. And Zero is skinny as Rami the Swami. He looks so young, making that one silly face over and over. Of course it was 1943...

They play it on Turner once in a while. The stars were Lucille Ball, Red Skelton and Gene Kelly. Zero wasn't the lead, but if you saw him in *"Fiddler on the Roof,"* then you saw one of the great performances of all time.

Do you have any stories about him?

The thing I remember most about Zero Mostel was when I invited him to dinner in my home and, cocksucker, he burned a hole in the couch with a cigarette. And never apologized. That's my memory.

And Gene Kelly?

Du Barry was his first motion picture. He had been a hit on Broadway in "Pal Joey." I don't think I told you—Gene Kelly used to say I made the greatest kosher dill pickles in the world. Billy Wilder and some others, they were crazy for them. I always left a jar for Gene and Billy. I grew the cucumbers in our garden at the wonderful house on Stone Canyon. Grew the dill, grew the garlic, bought the spices. And I used kosher rock salt. I made brine in a big crock, which probably held six gallons of water, in a cool corner of the basement. Few homes had basements and this was a big one. I would make five pounds of little gherkins. Maybe ten jars. And anytime I was working under pressure, I just went out there, it was great therapy. And the dill grew so fucking fast, overnight, in the summer...

Seducing Judy: Meet Me in St. Louis (1944)

> "[The Meet Me in St. Louis] adaptation proved one the handful of truly satisfactory screenplays ever to grace the American movie musical."
> - Stephen Harvey in his book, *Directed by Minnelli*

The time: April 2004.

*The scene: The Directors Guild of America building, a coffee-colored highrise on Sunset Boulevard. Inside on the ground floor foyer, a red carpet flows between forty yards of rope line. Pressed up against the barriers, a dozen men and women poised with still cameras, video cameras, microphones and notebooks. The media gauntlet greets hundreds of guests arriving for a Hollywood happening: the 60th Anniversary celebration of **Meet Me in St. Louis**.*

June Lockhart appears, as does Liza Minnelli, and Lorna Luft, too. And then, here comes my droll model in a gray, checkered jacket, sporting a colorful tie, accompanied by his stunning wife Norma, who strolls like movieland royalty in a black Armani suit. Peppered by questions from young press people, Brecher pauses between pushes of his Invacare walker to offer an unending flow of amusing comments.

"Mr. Brecher, what's special about this movie?"

"That I'm alive!" he spits back. "That's what's special, because I wrote it when I was thirty and now I'm ninety and both the picture and I are still running."

Laughter, cut by the exploding pop of flashbulbs.

"Or rather," he continues. "I'm using this walker. I really don't need this—I could give it away, and then I'd fall down."

"Mr. Brecher!" shouts a paparazzo from behind his camera. "What would you like us to remember about the movie?"

"The fact that they constantly run it and I never get paid any residuals!"

This guy could play the Palace. Leaning forward across the top of the walker, tilting his head like he's modeling for USA Today, Extra, Inside Edition *and the other media outlets. Someone from something called Fred TV from the Worldwide Web asks: "Have you been reminiscing today with the other people from **Meet Me in St. Louis**?"*

"Aside from June Lockhart and Margaret O'Brien," Brecher tells him, "everyone from the film is dead!"

Finally, everyone adjourns the lobby and heads into the huge auditorium.
"I love your passion!" says a DGA security guard who is guiding Brecher's walker. "Straight ahead four feet..."
"I'm basically fairly angry," Brecher tells him "But I control it."
"Me too!" the guard laughs.

Inside the huge theater, halfway down the middle aisle, Irv schmoozes with Norma, his daughter Joanna, and their good friends Ursula and Tom. Then comes some agent who has to tell Brecher he just completed his memoir of working in the MCA mailroom and how he had coffee with Cary Grant. The director Arthur Hiller takes a picture of Norma and Irv, and the composer and pianist Michael Feinstein introduces himself as a fan, promising to send Irv some CDs. Up from San Diego is Hugh Martin, the living half of the songwriting team from the movie, Martin & Blane. (One of their numbers, "Have Yourself a Merry Little Christmas," has been used in two dozen movies since.) Irv greets Hugh in the aisle with a kiss. It's the first time he's seen him in forty years and they stand clutching each other as a senior V.P. from Warner Brothers takes the podium.

"Tonight," he tells the still-milling throng, "we will see a newly remastered, ultra resolution process and Dolby Digital 5.1 soundtrack print of this classic. We scanned the original 3-strip black and white Technicolor records at extremely high resolution. The records are then combined electronically to create the color images, which are also electronically re-registered, steadied and cleaned."

After this commercial, the DGA host introduces Arthur Freed's daughter, Barbara Saltzman. He praises Freed, who died in 1973, and then introduces Brecher, who despite glaucoma and other tsuris, is still making appearances all over town:

"This is a movie that has transcended the annals of time. It will be as powerful sixty years from now as it is today. The unforgettable songs, the dazzling choreography, the costumes, the beautiful performances from the stars—when stars really were stars and not just... well, what they are today... and one of the great things about Mr. Freed was that he cultivated talent from all over the place. And he brought in Lena Horne and Gene Kelly, and Vincente Minnelli and all sorts of amazing people. One of the key screenwriters in the Freed Unit created the words that you will hear tonight in the screenplay for **Meet Me in St. Louis**. At the age of twenty-five [sic], he wrote the **Marx Brothers At the**

Circus, followed by **Go West**, *and then a string of classic MGM musicals including* **Best Foot Forward**, *with a score by a songwriting team called Martin &* *Blane, I think you've heard of them... [Applause] and of course,* **Meet Me in St.** **Louis**. *Please welcome, Mr. Irving Brecher!"*

[Applause as Brecher rises from his aisle seat]

Hello... Ahem. If I may, I'll sit down, because standing you can't see me anyway.

[Laughter]

I was fascinated with the story about the resolution process.

I'm 90, can they do something for *me*?

[Laughter]

I'm really grateful to have been part of what everybody seems to like and praise, so I'm not about to knock the movie. I can only tell you it's very nice to be here. Of course it's very nice to be any place when you're 90.

[Laughter]

Of course I'm very happy and kind of proud. But I must tell you, when you talk about St. Louis, it would never have been the film that it apparently is without the tremendous contribution of a man who I saw tonight for the first time in many years, who I love and admire, the composer of those great songs: Hugh Martin.

[Applause]

I think he's sitting here.

[Shouts of "Behind you!"]

You probably all know the songs, so great, which became standards instantly, like "The Trolley Song" and "The Boy Next Door" and that wonderful, "Have Yourself a Merry Little Christmas." "Merry Little Christmas" became such a popular song that every Hanukkah they sing it at my synagogue.

[Laughter]

Well, I'll just wind up by saying I'm very
lucky and happy that I was part of a marvelous,
fascinating business, writing movies. And I had
many wonderful relationships and I made many
friends, and I think I may be bragging, but
please excuse it. Today I don't have an enemy
in the world. They all died.
    [Laughter, applause and "Bravo!"]
    Over the years, I've been very pleased at the
approbation that the movie got. And one of the
most pleasant things that I read was that among
Ronald Reagan's favorites movies that he used
to run in the White House was *Going My Way* and
Meet Me In St. Louis. President Bush's favorite
is *The Texas Chainsaw Massacre*.
    [Roars follow. This one knocked them out.]

*What Brecher didn't tell them that night at the DGA was that Judy Garland,
MGM's planned star for the film, refused to act in it. And, as he explained, a
movie that stands high among the classics of the past and has in fact, "transcended the annals of time," only really exists because of the camera. "It's an odd
story," he told me.*

A very odd story. The best movie I was ever associated with was made
for the wrong reason. Most great films are produced with enthusiasm,
even passion. **Meet Me in St. Louis** was made with reluctance. Arthur
Freed called me in. The producer and the other suits had no confidence in
the script; they said it had "no storyline and no real plot." They only reason
it was OK'd was because during the war, there were only two Technicolor
cameras available. Freed said Metro had a commitment to use one if they
had something they could shoot in color.

"But the only thing we have to shoot is this crap," he said, pointing
toward a pile of scripts. Four different scripts had been lying around but
none of them was ever pushed forward toward production because nobody
at the studio cared about them.

"I'd like you and Freddie to see if you can get something we can shoot in
color. I don't care what the hell it is." (Of course, having the movie made
in color doesn't change the way one writes it. That's only good if you do a
movie where you cut somebody's throat. Then the color is important.)

"Freddie" was Fred Finkelhoffe. He was quite talented; he once collaborated on a hit play in the '30s with a writer named John Monks, Jr. called, "Brother Rat."

Have I said that Freed and I were not exactly buddies? I was still a contract writer and I knew that I should be careful after hearing whatever it was Freed wanted. So I took my orders, trudged back down the long corridor from Freed's fancy suite and my friend Finkelhoffe and I went to work. We wrote at my house for a couple of weeks getting a rough outline out of Sally Benson's "Kensington Avenue" stories, a series about her childhood that originally ran in *The New Yorker*.

But then I was left on my own. Fred had to go back east to Bucks County, Pennsylvania, to try, as he said, to save his marriage. He was married to a popular performer, a singer named Ella Logan.

And that was the last I saw of him, until a couple days before the finished cut was to be sneak previewed out of town. When I finally finished a draft of the script, I started working with the director, Vincente Minnelli. He was a Broadway man who had done good work on his first picture, **Cabin in the Sky**, starring Ethel Waters, Lena Horne and the fellow who played Jack Benny's "Rochester"—Eddie Anderson.

I found Minnelli to be very helpful as we worked scene by scene and he constantly challenged me to improve the dialogue or to invent some pieces of action.

It was my first experience working harmoniously with a director who had a definite talent. We were nearly finished with the polishing when we got a call to come to Freed's office.

He was visibly upset. I remember he was smoking one cigarette while another was burning in his ashtray. He said Judy Garland had told them she did not want to do the movie. And there was nobody who could possibly play the lead role as required.

Freed threw up his hands. "Goddam ingrate! I was the one who pushed Mr. Mayer into using her in **The Wizard of Oz**. It *made* her!"

Minnelli and I were shocked. Why wouldn't she play it? Did she say?

Freed said he thought he knew: "Because she's been screwing Mankiewicz."

We all knew Joe Mankiewicz, the producer and writer, was influencing her. They were having an affair. Joe was a talented man and according to his advice, this was no good for her career.

"And that girl who works for Judy," Freed said, mentioning the name of a press agent whose name I forget. "She told me Mankiewicz said Tootie will steal the picture. Maybe if you cut out the character…"

"This would be a disaster," I said. Margaret O'Brien was set to play Tootie. She was a kid, maybe nine. Minnelli agreed.

"Tootie moves the action to a large degree," Minnelli said. "And if we watered it down…" He shook his head.

"I talked my lungs out," Freed said angrily. "Maybe L.B. can straighten her out."

Vincente and I went back to my office and agreed the only thing to do was finish work on my script and hope that some miracle would change things. Minnelli, not much of a talker, lit another one of his Parliament cigarettes, and with a number of carefully choice words said: "That fucking bitch! Stupid bitch with big tits!"

(I thought they were okay. You could live with them. But he continued fuming.)

"That idiot! Listening to Mankiewicz's cock… she's lucky she's alive! I'd like to kick her ass 'til her teeth fall out."

Then my phone rang. It was Ida, Mayer's secretary. He wanted me to come up right away.

I was on very good terms with L.B. On a couple of occasions he had even said to me, "One of these days you're gonna be a producer for me. Writers we can always get. But good producers…"

I was too cowardly to correct him about writers.

This time the big boss wore a worried look.

"I can't do anything with this goddam stubborn Judy," he said. "Arthur tells me he thought you and she were friendly."

"Sort of sir," I said. I liked her and thought she was sweet. "She's been to our home at parties where I had some songwriters over… she sang and even played with my little daughter."

"So maybe," said Mayer, "you could kind of convince her that your script would be perfect for her."

"I'm not sure I can."

And I wasn't.

He buzzed his Dictaphone. "Get me Garland!"

I listened to him on the phone sweet talking her like a grandfather, cooing about how much he loved her and how he understood that she has opinions and he would never do anything to hurt her career, she was his favorite star and a lot of other schmaltz. And she was telling him she couldn't face making the movie. It would finish her. All very dramatic. Then Mayer, the intelligent grandfather, asked her if he had ever done anything for her she could remember that would cause her to say yes to a favor he wanted. She said yes.

"Then this is the favor," Mayer said. "You know Irving Brecher, he wrote the script. And you know you can trust him because he thinks you are the number one actress in the business. He loves you. So I'd like you to come in tomorrow and I'd like him to read you the script, which may help you understand why you really are the starring part and I wouldn't have it any other way. Will you do this, honey?"

There was a pause.

Two Sisters: Tootie and Judy (Margaret O'Brien and Judy Garland) in Meet Me In St. Louis.

"If it doesn't change your mind," Mayer went on, "So be it. We'll junk the picture, lose almost a million in pre-production, but at least we tried. When can you come in? Is three o'clock okay? Thank you darling."

The next day when Judy arrived, the big man hugged her, kissed her, the kindly grandfather embracing her a little too long, obviously enjoying the mammary. Then he said: "Why don't you do the reading in here..." He steered us into one of his numerous side suites.

"Judy," I began, after Mayer locked the door behind us. "I think you should play it, but I'm not going to beg you to play it. It's not my business to do that. But I'll read it to you and I think you might agree. I hope you will."

"Well, you know I think a lot of you and all that," she said. "But I'm worried about it, really."

I could tell she was scared. So I sat her down to read to her, calmly as I could.

Except for one thing: the way I read it was terribly deceitful. When I got to Margaret O'Brien's lines as Tootie the child, I kind of threw them away like they weren't there. You could barely hear them, they were in the sewer, or I mumbled like it was nothing. At the same time, in every scene, I emphasized everything Judy was saying, delivered in a style that equaled the best of the actresses in MGM's stable of stars. Everything I read was the greatest line she ever heard. I acted them out. I paused in the right places. I laid them on. I sounded feminine enough to hold her attention, getting smiles, and then a few giggles. During her first scene with "the boy next door," she actually cracked up with a laugh that gave me hope.

After two hours, she had a tear in her eye when I read the last line. Esther: "At the Fair. This is where we live. Right here in St. Louis."

There was a long silence.

She sighed finally, "I don't know what to do."

"I'll tell you what to do," I said. "Decide what you're going to do *after* you make the movie."

She laughed.

"Now go tell L.B. what he wants to hear."

And she went in and told Mayer she would do it. More embraces, squeezing, and lavish promises from the man now remembered as "the Lion of Hollywood."

Well, of course it became the biggest picture she ever did. When it was released in 1944, it surpassed **The Wizard of Oz** and **The Big Parade** as the biggest box office grosser in the history of MGM. The only one to gross more was **Gone With The Wind**, which was not actually an MGM production, it was made by David Selznick and MGM distributed it.

What was really weird was when the shooting began, Minnelli had to bury his deep resentment at Judy's previous turndown. Apart from her lack of faith in the script, she had also been advised that Minnellli was not the right director for her. And during the shooting, he developed a terrible, terrible antipathy toward Judy. She came in late and she was fooling around with pills. Her diet pills screwed her up; made her nervous so she couldn't sleep. She took sleeping pills, but that made her dopey and he'd send her back home. Minnelli said things about her that were pretty awful.

The reason I make the point is, later when, to my amazement, he became romantically involved with her, he was unable to talk to me anymore. I could tell he was very uncomfortable when in the course of shooting we had to make adjustments and I was on the set. He was too embarrassed by what he'd said to me previously and he couldn't face it. That was painful because I loved his effort and learned a lot from working with him. (Of course their romance has been well discussed and written about. If it *was* a romance. I'm not sure *what* it was.)

At any rate, **Meet Me in St. Louis** was a love affair, even though there were executives at the studio that said it could never work. I remember hearing one say, "This *ferkaktah* thing has no story, but at least it will look good in color."

They didn't know what to make of this warm drama with great laughs. Laughs of joy, not shock. For instance, after the first party scene, when Judy comes down the stairs and she's putting out all the gaslights and she wants to be kissed. "The Boy Next Door," John Truett, played by Tom Drake, shakes her hand. And he follows this up with: "Esther, you've got a wonderful grip for a girl."

Then she tells him her perfume is, "essence of violet."

He says, "Just like my grandmother." And that crushes her. What a fucking square Truett is. She wants somebody to come on to her and this guy's a real putz.

She turns the lights back on. End of scene. That's right. And then she looks over the banister and we get: miles of face. That fabulous face that this idiot from next door missed kissing in the half-light of the chandelier. You'd think even an executive might discern a story going on there. I don't know. Maybe it was because Tom Drake was so stiff. But later, Judy

Garland and Tom Drake, in the snow, their conversation about getting married, and then changing their enthusiasm in mid-scene. Showing the confusion of two young people, how they may have to separate. That was the hardest scene I've ever written in movies.

The day of the first sneak preview, Minnelli comes into my office, hysterical. He was bawling.

"I can't talk to Freed! He threw me out of his office. He's crazy. The son-of-a-bitch cut the Halloween scenes. You've got to talk to him."

So I went into Freed's office and asked, "Why the cut?"

Freed said, "Who the fuck are you to tell me what to do? I'm the producer."

"I know," I said. "I also know that at the preview you can afford to show everything and then trim later. You're absolutely wrong about this."

"Get the hell out," was his comeback. (Which reminds me: Freed didn't know any Yiddish so I was able to sneak things past him, like the name on Esther's dance card: "Hugo Borvis." Borvis means barefoot.)

That night I went to the preview down in Huntington Beach by myself. There were only two limousines because of a cash shortage due to the war. Minnelli didn't make room in his car for me because we were now touch-and-go about Judy. He took Ira Gershwin and his wife.

And what a preview!

Freed had backed off and put the scenes back in. The Halloween sequence was the most memorable in the movie. The sneak was a tremendous success and two of the executives, Ed Mannix and Ben Thau, came over. They said to me on the sidewalk, "You know I never thought it would work, but it sure did. I didn't think it had a story."

Often when they talk about the best things in writing, it's character, not plot. Apparently the lack of the usual kind of story and the period setting—1904—was attractive. It's very unusual to see a film based on a series of events, not a plot. It's not truly a "Hollywood" movie of those days. Back then, if you didn't have a story that went boom-boom-boom-boom, they didn't understand it. So I felt great when that audience in Huntington Beach went through the roof. Which is all you want. That and the executives, the men who made it only grudgingly because they wanted to use a color camera, saying to me very gracefully, "We were wrong."

In 1945, the Academy Awards were not yet a television show and you could only see them by attending the ceremonies at the Biltmore Hotel in downtown Los Angeles. We were nominated for best screenplay, but I knew we wouldn't win because there was a drama nominated. Everyone knew instinctively that when it came to drama against musical comedy, drama would come out on top. So in spite of the excitement of sitting there in the Biltmore, when they opened the envelope I wasn't surprised to hear, "*Going My Way!*" (Take a look at the other movies made in 1944: *Double Indemnity, Hail the Conquering Hero, Laura, To Have and Have Not*.)

In retrospect, with all the hardship, the film remains something that I like to keep with me and think about. For one thing, nothing matches having talented people to work with. Like Minnelli, the best director I ever worked with. His eye for detailed sets and how he broke open doors for many styles made him a big contributor to the picture's success. He made me want to change certain things and I'm glad he did. I'd reached a point in the script where Esther and Truett and their bunch go out to a place called Skinker's Swamp for some kind of fun. They all jump onto a trolley. All I did at the end of the sequence was write on the script, "Instead of dialogue, might be a good place to have a song."

Simple as that.

And Martin and Blane wrote a pretty good one.

"*Clang! Clang! Clang! Goes the trolley! Zing! Zing! Zing! Went my heart-strings!*"

By 1949, or rather a little later, when color came in, **Meet Me** started playing on TV around Christmas time and has been on ever since. It so evokes the past, like no film I've ever seen, it so captures that quality. The Smith family, the whole lot of them from Leon Ames as the father all the way down, were wonderful to portray. Marjorie Main as the feisty maid, Katie, went on to a series of comedies, Ma and Pa Kettle. I enjoyed her because she threw lines like I did.

Tootie was adorable, and Margret O'Brien won a mini-Academy Award. She spoke from the heart and was so touching as she tore down those snowmen as Judy sang, devastatingly, "Have Yourself a Merry Little Christmas." This song debuted in that picture with lyrics that stood out for that year, 1944. There's a war on. People are dying. Fathers. Children are away from home. So here Judy sings: "Next year all our troubles will be out of sight. But until then, we'll have to muddle through somehow. So have yourself a merry little Christmas, now."

The picture works by showing what the audience doesn't have; most of us don't come from homes with that kind of warmth and love. During the war people longed for that sense of home, and **Meet Me in St. Louis** took them home to 1904. So while it was escapism, it had a reality, as I look at it. It's not super-sweet and there are no villains. Today, it's a relief for people used to Hollywood movies to see a movie that treats a family without any saccharin crap. In its way, it's sophisticated corn. There's a love among these people and they become funny in their frustrations. And all for ticket prices that today you wouldn't tip a person. Forty cents.

Above all, look at Judy Garland. The whole experience remains above all a wonderful memory of Judy—somebody I cared a great deal about—at her greatest as a musical performer and fine actress.

It's different today. Occasionally you see something among these actresses, but not a lasting quality that you take home with you. Nobody gets up in the middle of a snowstorm and says, "I gotta run out and see a Jennifer Lopez movie or I'll die." You know? The current crop—the ones who are around for a while—it seems the most important work they do is get married and divorced and remarried.

With Garland, it was pure talent and a kind of inner... something. She had a vulnerability that made you care for her and worry about her. She never let the audience down and I loved her. We all did. And it was right for us to worry about her. She had a tragic life from then on.

Yolanda and the Thief (1945)

*Andrea Grossman's "Writers Bloc" evenings are lively events in L.A. Gross-man gets two of her favorite writers on stage and just lets them fly. I've enjoyed seeing Norman Mailer, Gore Vidal, Frank Rich and Larry Gelbart there, and was in the audience when two writers about film, Anthony Lane and Peter Rainer, mentioned **Meet Me in St. Louis**, somewhere in their wide-ranging discussion. About the Halloween chunk of **St. Louis** that Brecher told me Arthur Freed wanted to cut, Lane said, "The Halloween sequence is one of the best child-frightened scenes ever made."*

Brecher would be pleased, I thought. So I raised my hand afterwards to ask the New Yorker *critic his opinion of my favorite screen scenarist.*

"Really quite marvelous, I must admit," Lane answered. "Rather an operetta, isn't it? A rare fusion where you can't tell where the dialogue ends and the music begins."

*Everyone seems to love **Meet Me in St. Louis**. But Irv's next assignment, **Yolanda and the Thief**, struck some critics as a not-so rarefied fusion of the surreal and the silly. I like it because it mixes Minnelli's mad dada with a fairy tale from Ludwig Bemmelmans and a gag-jammed script by Brecher. There's an extremely hep number called "Coffee Time" featuring Fred Astaire and Lucille Bremer (Johnny Riggs and Yolanda Aquavita), dancing through Bremer's mystical homeland of Patria, where the only soft drink is Aqua Vita, a romantic elixir...*

Brecher remembers it this way: "The picture was a flop."

Really? Why do you say that? Frank Morgan, the Wizard of Oz himself, plays a con man bringing Johnny Riggs to this strange place called Patria. Snowcapped mountains, wildflowers and the sea. Astaire looks around and says, "It's a cemetery with a train running through it." That's great stuff.

And I still think I was right to try and turn down the assignment. You see there was an actress who had played Judy Garland's older sister in *Meet Me in St. Louis*, a redhead named Lucille Bremer. Even Minnelli's skill at directing could not make her anything but wooden. God help the studio, Bremer got by in *St. Louis*. And more importantly, our producer Freed had the hots for her.

She was no star. She wasn't even an asterisk. I told Freed after agreeing to read the short story he'd bought by Bemmelmans, that I didn't want to write the screenplay. I didn't tell him it was because Minnelli and I were uncomfortable with each other. Having married Judy after endlessly reviling her to me during the shooting of *St. Louis*, Minnelli seemed too embarrassed in my presence to be casual, let alone friendly.

Freed was still combative with me because of the bad scene we'd had over the Halloween sequence a year earlier.

But I did enjoy telling him I didn't think Mayer had a winner in Bremer.

"As Yolanda?" I said. "No way."

Freed turned red.

"I'm casting the movie and she'll be great."

"Look," I said. "I know she's pretty. But she can't act. And she can't handle comedy, which this had better be."

"She can act and she can do comedy and you're going to write it," said Freed. "And that's it."

"Don't hold your breath."

I went back to my office, hoping that had ended it. I was feeling very secure because I had a radio show, "The Life of Riley," paying out a big number every week and I had a deal that ran for another year. Still, standing up to an MGM producer was tantamount to pissing on a king. The phone rang. It was Sam Katz's secretary, calling me up to see the head of the unit, the man Freed reported to.

Katz sat in his executive office, a small man in an oversized swivel chair. He was eating some very crisp celery when I arrived. Each bite he took sounded to me like I was on a firing range.

"I had a call from Arthur," he said smiling.

"I know," I said. "I hate Alexander Graham Bell."

Katz looked at me.

Finally he said, "He made the telephone."

"Right."

I liked fucking with guys like Katz.

"Sit down," he said. "Have some celery. He's upset. You don't want to write this thing? This... whaddya call it?"

"**The Deadass and the Thief.**"

"What?"

"**Yolanda and the Thief.** But they should call it **How to Lose a Couple Million**," I said.

Katz nodded.

"You're right about that, son. But just between us, we know we're going to lose money. You see, whether you like Freed or not—"

"Don't go that far," I said. "I despise him."

"The fact is, the studio owes him. He's made us a helluva lotta money on a lotta pictures. Letting him blow some of it on this turkey is kind of a thank you present. It's just good business."

"It may be good business for the studio, but I don't want my name to be on something doomed to fail. And this movie's got to be, with Lucille Bremer as the star."

"You're probably right," Katz said. He paused. "I wonder if she's a good lay?"

"Why don't you ask Arthur? Maybe he's not in yet and he figures this picture will help him."

Katz smirked. "The main thing is, let him be happy. Be a good boy and write the script."

"I can't do it, Sam."

Now he was chewing carrots.

He said, "By the way son, how much are we paying you?"

That seemed odd. Was he going to cut my salary?

"You're paying me seventeen-fifty," I replied.

Katz cupped his ear.

"What did you say? I can't hear you with my mouth full."

"I said seventeen-fifty."

"Twenty-five hundred did you say?"

I blinked.

"I didn't say that."

"Well, I'm saying that. Your new salary. Twenty-five hundred a week. Four years.

"What?" I was rattled.

"Four years firm. Four weeks a year paid vacation."

He smiled. I must've swallowed. A thought came to me: So if I wrote this flop, I would still eat regularly for four years.

I said, "Sam, I am thrilled at this opportunity to possibly ruin my career."

"Good. So go make Arthur Freed happy. Go and do *Yolanda and the Thief.*"

"So Freed can do Bremer..."

And I left and went to work. Bremer was a nice enough girl. I knew she could dance and that Astaire, who was a genius, could make her look better than she was. But I dreaded having to write talk scenes for her. She couldn't talk. And she couldn't move, unless she was dancing.

Did you work out your problem with Minnelli?

Not really. We were civil. He was under the influence of Salvador Dali at the time. Wearing lots of colorful eyeshade. And although the movie was a flop—deservedly—it became a cult film in Europe. I'd get residual checks from Belgium, which apparently likes this sort of thing.

It looks exotic, Patria. Did you shoot it in South America?

No. Culver City. There was one taxicab scene made to look like it was in Mexico, but we shot it in Malibu.

Ha! There's your international touch.

Anyway, I wound up with that incredible contract for more money than I thought there was in the world. But I didn't stay for the four years.

Why?

Because after *Yolanda* came a new assignment. And this time, Freed truly got out of line.

Ludwig Bemelmans: A Lust for Laughs

"It's the rarest of treats for cineastes... it is
a timeless work of art."
- Kevin Thomas in the *Los Angeles Times* on a
1976 revival of *Yolanda*

**Most people know Ludwig Bemelmans from reading his *Madeline*
books when we're children...**

Getting to know him was the one aspect of working on *Yolanda* that
made it worthwhile.

Really? What did he think of the movie you made from his story?

He liked it pretty well. He agreed with me that our leading lady was
not a star. I really enjoyed the time I spent with Bemelmans. He told me
Yolanda was an idea he wrote down on a napkin in midtown Manhattan and sold to Arthur Freed: a fantasy about an American charmer in
some banana republic who sets out to swindle a beautiful heiress out of
a fortune and, you guessed it—falls in love and goes straight. Not very
original, but I thought I could get a decent script out of it. But during
our so-called story meetings, we talked about anything except the script
I had to write.

Ludwig Bemelmans was utterly intriguing and lived like a rich bohemian. A small, red-faced man from Bavaria with a shaved head full of
fun and fascinating stories. He told me he came to America in 1914 and
started at the lowest job there was, busboy. Which he did at the ritziest
hotel there was, the Waldorf-Astoria in New York. He worked for a year
at eighteen dollars a week, then worked his way up to waiter, to maître
d' and banquet master, where New York's wealthiest welcomed him into
society as a European sophisticate with savoir-faire. Eventually he began
to write. I've got copies of all his books. Read them, you'll love them. I
think my favorite is, *My War with the United States.*

Displaying that trademark bald top that I suspected he Simonized,
Ludwig spent the last part of his delightful life as Boniface of Bemelmans
Bar in the Hotel Carlyle in Manhattan, where Bobby Short worked the
piano and the glitterati convened. Boniface means he was the *ballaboosteh.*

The boss. I got a dose of nostalgia when I went there with Norma sometime in the '90s and it was the "in spot." And it was covered with his wonderful original paintings.

But beneath the sophisticated Ludwig who loved to talk about the big names he knew, there still lurked the waiter from the Waldorf-Astoria. One day he reverted to type one day when we planned to drive to Malibu to possibly make believe we were working and discussing this dismal project. He said he'd bring a picnic lunch for the beach, but when he came to pick me up, it was pouring rain. So we stayed home and when lunchtime arrived, my wife offered to serve us whatever he'd brought in his good-sized wicker basket.

"No no," Ludwig insisted. "Let me do it."

And we watched, charmed, as the former head waiter flipped open a box and quickly dissected a roasted chicken with the speed and expertise of a master of the art. He draped a napkin over his left arm, dispensing the side dishes with style, and we had an excellent repast. And the nice part, no tip.

Ludwig and I talked for a week straight and before he left, he made this observation: "The studio I'm sure appreciates you. You've got a halo over your head there."

"The thing about this business," I told him," is one moment you have a halo and the next it drops down and becomes a noose."

I meant it. He put it in one of his books.

Of course Bemelmans had that beloved series of books about a remarkable little girl called Madeline. Children of future generations will delight in her. And in that funny, original style, he also painted watercolors about my baby daughter Joanna all over my office walls! I think everything he did with a brush was funny. If he drew an egg, he made you smile.

When I agreed to write the screenplay, Ludwig came to my office and the very first day he painted a mural on all four walls. He started with an egg, which hatched and gradually developed into small and then larger caricatures of Fred Astaire and Lucille Bremer among a cast of characters, all in a Spanish palace. He was drawing the screenplay from beginning to finale, the end of the movie done in broad sweeps across the office door. Every square inch of artwork a delight to behold. (When I left MGM later on, my biggest regret was being unable to take those walls with me. I settled for photographs.)

One of his stories of his days as a busboy, turned me into a cautious diner forever. Among the snooty clientele of New York society, there was one dowager, or spinster—or both—who lived at the Waldorf and drove the personnel to distraction with her complaints and demands from every poor slob who dealt with her. Bemelmans took quite a beating from this harridan, but not as bad as one particular waiter on one particular day.

"She had apparently abused him to an extreme," Ludwig said with his usual twinkle. "I surmised as much, anyway. And I happened to pass from the kitchen through a dark corridor, and he was standing in an alcove, masturbating into her soup. I fired him. But not until he was finished. It would not be fair to interrupt someone in his pursuit of happiness."

Isn't that a beauty. What a picture that is. What a truly unforgettable character he was. A fucking classic. I'd like to tell that on television. And as a result of his implied warning, if I ever complain to a waiter, it is only on the way out of the restaurant, never to return.

During Yolanda and the Thief, Ludwig Bemelmans in front of one of his drawings on my wall at MGM. His idea of Bavarian graffiti. ("Achieve the honorable," it says on the back of his head.)

Farewell to MGM

You told me that after all that fun you had getting to know Ludwig Bemelmans on *Yolanda and the Thief*, you had a big fight at MGM?

Ludwig did me a favor indirectly, by selling that *ferkaktah* Lucille Bremer vehicle. It led me to the incredible four-year contract that Sam Katz had bribed me with. A hundred-and-four thousand bucks a year in 1946—I don't know, it must be a couple million dollars a week in today's cheap dollars.

How did all that money change your life?

We kept going.

You didn't change at all?

No. We had a beautiful home. A couple of cars. It's hard to believe now, thinking about it. Anyway, Freed decided to do a remake of "Ah Wilderness," one of Eugene O'Neill's most popular plays, as a musical. And no surprise, he wanted me to write it. Maybe he wanted to punish me. I had no reason to dislike the project, except I didn't want to do a remake, even though I thought the play could make a good movie. Done as a musical, a young boy's coming of age story called, **Summer Holiday**. Mickey Rooney as the boy, and his first sexual experience, with a beautiful older woman. That would be Marilyn Maxwell. And there was a drunk uncle, Walter Huston, and Lionel Barrymore as Mickey's father.

Rouben Mamoulian was signed to direct. Mamoulian had a great reputation, well deserved, with Broadway hits like "Porgy and Bess" and movies I loved, like **Golden Boy** and **Dr. Jekyll and Mr. Hyde**. I was pleased when Freed said while I was there that Rouben was to act as producer and overseer and work with me on the script.

"I've got my hands full with other projects," Freed told him. "So you're in charge."

For the next few weeks we had a good time discussing changes in the original play, because a musical requires very different treatment of the story and the plot. It may have been six or eight weeks, and I was happy I had written about three-quarters of the script and Mamoulian had expressed a good deal of enthusiasm.

Then came the bad news. Mamoulian got a call.

"Mr. Freed," he said, "would like to see what we have on paper."

I went into my typical anti-Freed mode.

"Cross your fingers, Rouben. I've had experience with this guy. He's good at casting, he's good about music. But when he reads a script, *oy vey.*"

Rouben lit another of his Turkish cigarettes and said, "It's good. He'll like it." We had about eighty pages. I took them down the hall, handed to Freed's secretary, and then went home.

The moment I got in the next morning, my secretary said Freed wanted to see me. When I walked into his office, I could sense what was coming. The expression on his face was like some beast about to sink his teeth into his helpless prey.

He picked up the script.

"When it comes to shit, this is number one."

Unhappily, I said: "Most people call it number *two.*"

He went on to say how it wasn't at all funny, and the construction was all wrong, the songs misplaced...

"I don't think you're right," I said. "But I think you should tell this to Rouben. He thinks it's good."

He slammed down on his desk, turning loud and snide.

"He's not the producer. I am!"

I said, "I was standing here when you told him he was in charge—"

"That's enough!"

"Arthur, why don't you talk to him and tell him that under his supervision we developed a script that is shit."

Freed was furious.

"And," I added, "tell him you're the producer."

That was it.

"Don't tell me what to do," he said, "you sheenie bastard. Get the hell out of here!"

This was the second time I'd been thrown out of his office. And it would be the last. The self-hating prick had crossed the line.

I went back to Mamoulian and told him what Freed thought of our script. This calm, decent man shook his head, I guess in resignation. "Knowing what you said about Mr. Freed," he said, "I would be worried if he *liked* the script. But what about this name he called you?"

"Yeah, but you wouldn't know it Rouben, you're not Jewish."

Still burning, I had to tell someone else, so I went to the executive I was closest to, L.K. Sidney. We'd become good friends long since that night in 1933 I heard him at the Capitol Theater threatening to fire Milton Berle.

I knew he had no love for Freed. All the executives would badmouth Freed whenever it was safe, but they were very careful because he was L.B. Mayer's pet. Grossing big bucks on his pictures had turned Freed into a cocky know-it-all and he was universally disliked.

When I told Sidney what Freed called me, he jumped up in outrage.

"That schmuck," he said.

"Yeah," I said. "And I've got a deal here but I'm going to leave. I'm going up to Benny Thau to cancel my contract."

"Take it easy, son," said Sidney. "Don't cut your throat because of that egomaniac."

I told him I was sure I couldn't stay anywhere I'd be seeing Freed, even once in a while. So I went up to see Ben Thau, the head of Business Affairs. Thau was a quiet, serious man who listened to my story and then blinked at the "sheenie bastard."

He asked me what I wanted to do.

"I'd like you to release me from my contract."

He looked shocked. Then I took out a check I'd been given for eighteen-thousand dollars, part of the raise Katz had given me for *Yolanda* when I signed the new contract.

"Put that back in your pocket," he said. "I've got a better idea. We're going up to see L.B. He might like to know how his best friend treats a writer."

I have to admit, I loved the idea. This usually humorless man, I sensed he was eager to do Freed damage. He called ahead and then led me up to the king's suite.

I was very tense as we entered. But then surprised and pleased to see two other studio wheels there, two men I liked on a first name basis: Eddie Mannix, who ran Studio Operations, and Sam Katz.

"What is it?" Mayer asked.

Thau said, "Brecher had some disagreement with Arthur. An argument. And now he wants us to release him from his contract. I thought you might want to know about it."

Mayer was impatient.

"What argument? What disagreement?"

I rattled off for him a short version of the episode and how, "The part I really resented was when he called me... a nasty name."

"What name?"

"Sheenie bastard."

All the executives in the room were Jewish. But none quite so Jewish as

Mayer. I can still his face there—a mixture of shock and fury. He turned to his Dictaphone and barked, "Get Freed up here! Now!"

The room got quiet. But while we waited, he went on.

"Son of a bitch," he fumed. "A Jew calling another one what the Jew haters say."

It was only moments later that Freed, always in a hurry to see Mayer, came marching in with his big I-love-you-L.B. smile. Suddenly, he saw me with the other men and his jaw dropped to his shoetops. He stood speechless.

Mayer stood up and looked squarely at Freed.

"Arthur," he asked. "What temple do you belong to?"

Freed muttered the name of a synagogue.

"Is that where you learned to call another Jew a sheenie bastard?"

I could hear Freed gulp. Then he finally managed to speak.

"I'm sorry, L.B. I guess I lost my head."

Mayer sat down, folded his arms and issued a command:

"I want you to apologize to this young man."

"I..."

"Turn around and look him in the face!"

Like a robot, Freed did that. He turned to me. His chest was heaving.

"I'm sorry. I apologize."

"Okay," I said. A couple of the witnesses were trying hard to conceal their enjoyment at this public whipping.

Then Mayer said to him, curtly: "You can go now."

Freed slunk out. The other men left, too. And I started to thank Mayer.

"I really hate to leave," I told him. "Particularly, I thank you for always treating me so well..."

"You shouldn't leave. Forget about it, you don't have to work with him anymore. You belong here. You've got a big future here."

"Thank you. I appreciate what you're saying, but if I stayed here I'd keep running into him—I just don't think it would work. I think I've just had too many problems with him over the years."

He came around from behind the desk and started to walk me to the door, his arm around my shoulder. I was touched by this warmth.

"Well, it's a shame," he said. "But I know you'll have no trouble, going to another studio. But promise me that before you make a deal, that you think about calling me and saying you want to come back."

I promised I would.

Then he said, "Just between us, with what's been going on here, I wish I was leaving with you."

That was the last time I saw the old warhorse.

What about Freed? Was that the last time you saw him?

Yeah, but one more thing about this shitheel. I once looked at a DVD of **Meet Me in St. Louis**, made about fifteen years ago. On the DVD there was some added documentary footage, where the narrator, Roddy McDowell says something about how, "Freed convinced Judy Garland to do this picture."

I was never so fucking annoyed.

Groucho Goes Fishing

Irv, didn't Groucho Marx once say, "Reverence and irreverence are really the same thing"?

Not to me he didn't.

Oh.

I don't even know what that means.

Perhaps he meant that at their level best, they're both holy?

If he said it, it's not one of his most famous quotations.

Okay. Will you tell me about the time you went camping with Groucho in Wyoming?

That wasn't famous either...

Fine. First though, I have to ask you something else.

Go ahead, kid.

Why did L.B. Mayer tell you that he wanted to leave too, when you left MGM? Why would he? Mayer's the boss.

Up to a point. He said it because he'd just been knifed. By Dore Schary. Schary, the former writer and producer, went behind Mayer's back, reporting the activities of the studio to the chairman of the company, Nicholas Schenck back in New York. Schenck and Mayer hated each other. It was a contest for power and Schenck had the upper hand because that hand held the majority of the stock in Loew's Incorporated, the parent company.

How did it feel, leaving in 1947 after ten years?

Good. I wanted to make more movies. But if I could, I wanted it to be at some other studio. Mainly what I wanted was a rest. For three years, from when I put "The Life of Riley" on the air, I had a real load, writing movies during the day and thinking out problems at night. Working with my radio writers on the weekend, and then working usually from about midnight to four a.m. or so, rewriting the radio script for that week.

When did you sleep?

When you're thirty-two, you manage to survive. Especially I had food and a roof and a wife who watched over me and made me take care of myself. And when I came home and told Eve that I had left Metro and twenty-five hundred a week, I expected her to be surprised. But instead, she said, "Great. Now there's only one thing for you to do: go fishing."

The timing of that idea was perfect. The Riley radio show was about to do its last segment of the season, which meant I had thirteen weeks of free time before we started again in October. And I was a nut for fishing. But not just any old fishing. I didn't like ocean fishing because being on a boat in all that water was too confining and the view is monotonous. Unlike river or lake fishing, the only scenery on the ocean is more water and occasionally one of the other guys on the boat throwing up. (And cursing me for talking him into the trip.)

So I had to round up some friends who would be game enough to do what I'd always wanted to do: go fishing in a lake that was ten thousand feet above sea level in a remote part of Yellowstone National Park. Very rugged country. L.K. Sidney, my friend at MGM, had fished up there. It was called Hart Lake and he told me of hotel to book which would also get us a guide to take us up to the lake.

He laughed when he said it. "You'll find Moran, Wyoming, is kind of Wild West. Not exactly Beverly Hills."

I knew two guys who jumped at the idea. One was Frank Ferrin, the Chicago ad exec who put "Riley" on the air after discovering it in the bottom of that pile of audio platters, for which I loved him. And Manny Rosenberg, who had managed the Little Carnegie Playhouse when I worked there as a kid, and was now co-producer of the popular "Sam Spade" radio series.

The plan was for Manny, who was in New York, and Frank in Chicago, to meet me in Salt Lake City. And as I was about to call Moran to book some hotel rooms, I suddenly thought of my friend Groucho. I knew he was very depressed because he was out of work. I knew his main sport was watching baseball games, going to theater and symphonies—he loved classical music—or sitting in his big armchair at home, reading some good book and listening almost constantly to Gilbert and Sullivan albums on his Capehart, an expensive phonograph system that would automatically play a record and then turn it over. Groucho was a Gilbert and Sullivan freak—he would ruin his own dinner parties by forcing his guests to listen to "The Pirates of Penzance" and all the other hazzerei.

I was a little apprehensive about asking him to join us in what could be rough country, but I felt maybe it would help shake him up a little. His ego was bleeding. So I took a shot.

I dialed his number, it rang, and he picked up.

"I'm not buying anything," the voice rang out.

"Groucho," I said, "how are you?"

"Who wants to know?"

"Listen," I said. "Couple of guys I know and I are gonna do a ten day trip."

"Don't forget to pack. You may need a change of clothing."

I gave him a courtesy laugh.

"I thought you might enjoy coming along."

"Where are you going?"

I told him, adding, "And they've got some great fishing."

"Are you kidding?" he said. "I'm sitting here smoking a Havana, enjoying Gilbert and Sullivan on the Capehart with my beautiful wife Kay, and you want me to leave this woman who is twenty years my junior and who I think is a nymphomaniac? It's out of the question. Brech, your mind has been shattered from writing Marx Brothers movies. There isn't enough money in the world to cause me to desert this lap of luxury and force my lovesick bride to endure ten days of sleeping alone. Good night!"

And he hung up. I was sorry I'd bothered him.

A few minutes later my phone rang.

"Hello, Brech?" said Groucho. "My bride is packing my suitcase."

"You're going?"

"That's what *she* says."

"Great!"

"Well, they say the best way for a couple to stay together is to be apart. When do we leave?"

I flew to Salt Lake and Groucho, who hated flying, got there the next day by train. Already he seemed unhappy about the whole thing. Manny and Frank, both fishermen, were enthusiastic about it, and in awe of being with the famous funnyman. I was having second thoughts because I had traveled with Groucho before, with painful results. There were also many times he was funny. Particularly when things got rough.

When the four of us in our rented 1947 red Cadillac, stopped for gas on the highway leading to Yellowstone, Groucho went into the station and came back out holding a brown paper bag. He got into the front passenger seat next to me.

"Whaddya got there, Groucho?"

"Because it's obvious that this car will break down in this blistering desert wilderness, I have something that will save our lives. There are four tomatoes here, and I think there are four of us. Each of us will get a tomato, the remarkable juice of which will barely keep us alive. Until some angel of mercy driving an eight-wheeler stops and uses his radio to call an ambulance, which will also probably break down."

I said, "May I have a tomato now?"

"No. How can you live with yourself," he said. "Doing this to three men, loving husbands, devoted fathers and lifelong Democrats?"

About eight hours later, we rode into Moran on a narrow street where we instantly entered the Wild West. On both sides of the street were little shops like a barber, a drugstore, an undertaker. But they were outnumbered by the saloons and dinky hotels. And worse, the many cowboys standing around all seemed to be wearing guns, in holsters held up by broad belts with cartridges. And the majority of them had bow legs.

Groucho said, "If you lined up some of these guys in the right position, you could play croquet."

I said, "Grouch, I think it would be wise if we don't try and get cute with anybody here. Because if you get shot, not even a tomato will save you."

"Who's trying to be cute?" he said. I heard Frank and Manny giggling in the back seat.

While my two friends from the East unpacked the baggage, I went with my usual apprehension—Groucho was following me—into the Hotel Moran. The first thing we saw was a big circular bar with a few cowboys on stools and a couple of bar girls wearing the shortest of skirts and the slimmest of bras, and the most pleasing of cleavage.

"Egad, we're at the Folies Bergère," said Groucho.

I can still see it in my mind's eye: the saloon, the dames, the Grand Tetons and the great bare legs.

The front desk clerk was a dehydrated man who looked at us with zero reaction, waiting patiently for us to speak. But fate was ugly. The poor guy was made to order for Groucho because he had a tic that made his upper lip jump up and move around to reveal some semi-white false teeth that kept clicking.

"We have reservations," I said. "The name is Brecher. For two rooms."

Out of the corner of my eye I saw Groucho leaning against a slot machine, arms folded, mimicking the clerk's tic. (Except Groucho had real teeth.) I almost choked to keep from laughing and gasped out that we needed a guide. The poor guy was polite enough, I guess because he didn't see what Groucho was doing. To me, it was cruel.

Manny and Frank came in and Groucho joined them in the bar. I signed us in, was given keys to two adjoining rooms, paid the twenty dollars for the one night stand, and wound up sharing a room with Groucho because we were the only non-snorers.

I was tired and suggested we take a nap and then go out to dinner.

Which we did. I mean, nap.

When I woke up, I heard Groucho on the phone, asking for room service.

"Oh no? Well then can you have them send me something from the bar?"

He turned to me. "Want a drink?"

"No."

"Please send me one Old-Fashioned... yeah... thank you."

I felt a slight shiver.

"Groucho, did you see those bar girls?"

"No, what about them?"

"They looked like hookers."

"Really? How much? Not that I would consider adultery..."

"Listen to me," I said. "These broads probably belong to some of these guys with the guns."

"Those fellas? Probably extras. They're shooting a movie."

"Didn't you see all those guns?"

"Props. Why are you so nervous?"

"Only time I'm nervous is when I'm with you, Groucho."

"Trust me, comrade. Fear not. Since you had the gall to invite me on this dreadful journey, I won't let you pay for any breach of decorum."

"Thank you."

And I meant it. Groucho was right. I'm a nervous Jew, worried about knocks on the door.

A moment later there was a knock on the door.

"Come in!" sang out Groucho.

The door opened, and in she came, the sexiest twenty-dollar-a-night bimbo, holding a tray on which there was a cocktail and half-a-breast with a bare nipple looking like an unusual hors d'oeuvre.

"Good evening," she said.

"Evenin'!" Groucho said cheerily.

"I have your Old Fashioned."

"Thank YOU!" he beamed. "You don't look old-fashioned. Would it interest you if we tried something modern? Such as a hop in the hay?"

She dropped the tray on the bed and ran out.

I locked the door and saw myself on a stretcher in an ambulance. Surely she would send her bowlegged boyfriend in to top off Groucho's one-liner.

"If she tells one of those guys who's fucking her what you said," I told him, "he's liable to kill us!"

"I hadn't thought of that," said Groucho. "I was in such heat."

"You must wanna get hurt!"

"No, just laid. Stop worrying. She knew I was kidding."

"You're kidding yourself. I'm getting out of here."

"Well, I hope you're wrong, but why don't we play it safe and leave by the window?"

So that's what we did. I grabbed my suitcase and went first, slipping out and down into the alley. Luckily, we were on the ground floor. A minute later, a more penitent Groucho climbed out with his bag and we shuffled down the alley to the rear door of another hotel, where I telephoned Manny and Frank and told them what happened. They checked out and came to meet us.

Groucho played insistent. "I was not trying to insult the woman," he told our companions. "I was genuinely in love with her. I wish I knew her name."

The next morning we were introduced to our guide, Bob Robards, a tall, good looking young man bubbling with promises of the great time that lay ahead. I instinctively distrusted him. As he drove from Moran for many miles and got deeper into the mountains, he regaled us with stories of his close relationship with his cousin, Jason Robards. We were familiar with the character actor. I even recalled the name of one of his movies, *Broadway Bill*. And this motormouth guide insisted on telling us the entire scenario of the movie to prove he was a cousin. Finally, Groucho, bored stiff—he had generously not interrupted the story of Broadway Bill—said: "You don't happen to have a cousin who was in *Gone with the Wind* do you, because if you do, I'm getting out of the car."

Robards clammed up. But he would get his revenge.

"Here we are!" he announced.

"I don't see any lake," I said.

"Patience, sir. It's up there." Robards pointed to the top of one of the Grand Tetons. We stared at an incline miles wide and thousands of feet high.

"Just ten thousand feet up to the lake," he said, where, he assured us, a real comfy camp awaited, "you betcha!" He then gave us a look that combined pity and contempt, because anyone looking at the four of us knew we had no more business being in this wilderness than Vladimir Horowitz.

We switched from the Cadillac to a five-passenger jeep, which Robards proudly said he'd won in a poker game with a drunken cattle rustler.

Groucho eyed the vehicle warily. "We really gotta ride in that thing?"

"It's safe and sound," said the guide. "And when we get to the top, we'll all take a nice ride on the pack mules."

"Pack mules?" Groucho turned to me. "You son-of-a-bitch, dragging me out of civilization to die on a pack mule?"

But we had no choice. Four intrepid idiots piled into the jeep and Robards started the climb. Four decadent, middle-aged men used to easy chairs, saunas, massages and soothing martinis, now suffered the most violent experience of our lives. For an hour we banged around, back and forth, as the jeep crawled, lurched, bumped, and shot forward. Manny caught Groucho's arm as he almost fell out of the jeep. I had two close calls myself.

Finally, the agony ended, we were on top, and there was the lake. At least three or four miles away. Now we were led by a committee of five despondent-looking pack mules. I had never seen one in the flesh and wished I hadn't been seeing one now. As Groucho cursed me and life in general, we each managed to climb aboard, and with Jason Robards's cousin leading the way, started a terrible trek toward the lake. I say terrible because we had two enemies beside the guide to deal with. One was deerflies. Small Boeing bombers who acted like they'd been waiting months for a meal, able to drill holes in our leather jackets and extract blood. We kept slapping ourselves to ward them off. The mules lurched from side to side to avoid steaming holes in the ground that covered hot springs, some of which would spurt and spray a jet of red-hot water onto the legs of our poor burros.

There may never have been four more miserable, out-of-their-element, putzes. The beating that we took prompted groans, moans and Groucho's epithets, mostly directed at me for seducing him into what he was now sure was a deathtrip. I was now worried this might be the end of our friendship, as well as the end of me.

Several exhausting hours later, we came to the edge of this gorgeous lake and Groucho fell out of the jeep, glad to be on safe ground. We were in totally wild country. Not a boat, no dwellings of any kind, except for the comfy camp we had been promised. It consisted of a tent large enough to sleep two men. One side of the tent had a long rip and looking through it into the tent, you could see two sleeping bags.

Robards was bragging again.

"Did I tell you Robert Taylor was here last week with a party? He got a lotta good fish. And can you believe it, he never gave me a tip."

I said, "I can believe it. He's a Republican. And a Red-baiter. So what happened to the tent?"

"Oh that? A bear did that. There are a lot of bears around here. Looking for food, probably."

"Probably a movie fan," Groucho said icily. "After Taylor's autograph."

On this cheery note, the four of us sank to the ground and waited for dinner, which the guide was obligated to provide as part of our package deal. Travel, lodging and meals, the typical American plan. But what had been disappointment in Robards' promise of a great time ahead, turned into deep, heartfelt hatred when he confessed that all the grub he'd brought in a small ice chest was cans of Spam, white bread, and some bars of chocolate.

"It's my fault," said our great provider. "I left another box in the jeep."

Frank sighed. "That's great. If we ever get back there, we can have a feast."

We started to nosh a little Spam and bread—a terrible experience—but Groucho refused, and slid off into the tent. Frank and Manny jointly decided that since I was closest to Groucho, I should sleep with him. They were worried that Groucho, our senior citizen at 57, might be getting ill.

I felt perfectly well when I climbed into the tent. I tried to sleep, but everything reeked of citronella. Our saboteur guide had doused the entire inside of the tent with it to repel mosquitoes. Overwhelmed, I crawled out and finally fell asleep on some pine needles.

The next morning, the sunrise was beautiful and Hart Lake was a glorious sight. Frank and Manny sat around a campfire that this third-rate Conrad Hilton had built and we drank some hot, but not particularly good, coffee. Some canned fruit and toasted white bread made us slightly more content.

Finally, Groucho came crawling out of the tent. Frank, Manny and I were thrilled to see he was still alive.

"No thanks to *you*, Brecher," he said. "I'll have my revenge. I'm gonna fix it so you have to write another movie for us."

He meant as *punishment*.

When he was through glowering at the guide who offered him coffee— which he refused—he said, "Since you're the manager of this fucking plush hotel, kindly direct me to the men's room."

Robards, apparently immune to any verbal abuse, laughed.

"That's a good one, Grouchy," he said.

He got a withering look from Groucho, who added, "Young man, in the future if you wish to communicate to me, do so through a third party."

Robards pointed beyond the tent to a clump of heavy overgrowth. To his credit, poor Groucho still retained some sense of trying to entertain. So in his familiar crouch, he went perhaps thirty yards and disappeared in the tall greenery. In the meantime, I was taking 16-millimeter movies with my Bell & Howell camera. I took a few shots of the lake, the mountains, and a bald eagle in flight. Then as I sat down, I heard Frank say, "What's the matter?"

I looked and there was Groucho, still in his familiar crouch, but with his pants down, holding his belt and stumbling through a clearing.

"Don't look now," he said, "but is a bear following me?"

Fully visible at the edge of the overgrowth was a brown bear on his hind legs, looking at us curiously. It started to do a dance, which I shot with the camera and I still have on film, the bear dropping down at the end of his performance and finally disappearing.

Groucho was breathing hard and said, "I should have locked the door before I sat down."

We were in hysterics.

After we propped him up and gave him water, Groucho told us, "I was squatting. Hoping that nature would do its duty, and wishing I had a copy of my morning paper. When I happened to look up and notice maybe ten feet away, some bushes moving. And there was no wind. I thought, this is a scientific phenomenon! Then I noticed a black lump with five large claws kindly waving at me. And I asked myself, who in our party has five claws again? And when I couldn't think of anybody who fit that description, I decided to leave. Suddenly the bear stood up. And so did I, barely escaping with my life."

We continued laughing.

"If we're gonna go to the toilet," he concluded, "from now on we go as a group."

We spent the rest of the morning laughing and fishing. Groucho reluctantly agreed to fish, something he had never done. We were out on the lake in a row boat with me handling the oars. I fixed a rod and baited a hook with a worm that the guide had dug up on the shore. Groucho gamely took the rod and let the hook and sinker unreel a great distance down. Robards said the lake was over a thousand feet deep. So Groucho sat there with a fishing line in his hands, amiably. Groucho Marx was generally more amiable when he was exhausted and didn't have the strength to lash out at persecutors like our guide.

Suddenly he got a strike. He fumbled with his rod as I ordered him to reel in. The rod bent back as the fish fought but then finally broke the surface: a huge lake trout. By now the trout had no fight, it had gotten the bends, the same thing that happens to humans if they surface from too far down in quick fashion—their lungs collapse.

Groucho, for the first time on the trip, seemed happy. He had never caught a fish before and this was a real big one, and back on shore we had a delicious lunch of fried lake trout a la Groucho.

We made it back down the mountain via the mules, the jeep, and happily, the Cadillac. Back in Moran, we paid Meriwether Lewis, who by now Groucho called, "Dr. Mengele." We even tipped him generously; we had agreed in advance that beyond his rate of two hundred bucks a day, for the sake of our fellow Americans, we gave him an extra four hundred with the suggestion that he retire as a guide.

Heading for home, we stopped in Las Vegas, which then was little more than sand, a gas station, a general store, and a hotel and gambling casino called "El Rancho." And a new hotel that had just opened a week before at the south end of the sand dune called, "The Flamingo." It had

Groucho and new-found friend.

all the amenities of a modern hotel. It even had beautiful young employees dressed to raise the spirit and anything else that could be raised, for men away from home. The highlight, or lowlight, was meeting Bugsy Siegel, owner of the Flamingo. He was a charmer, couldn't do enough for Groucho and his friends, and wouldn't hear of us paying for our huge meal. We were practically the only ones there, but he wasn't worried.

Bugsy said, "People love to gamble. They'll be coming up from LA and Chi, and maybe New York, too. Soon as we get an airline to stop here, and that's in the works."

As a memento of our adventures, I have movie footage of Groucho walking along the side of the Flamingo Hotel swimming pool ogling some shapely women in bathing suits. And guess what he's holding: a brown paper bag with four rotten tomatoes. Who's to say if tomatoes these days are any less rotten? They sure don't taste as good.

It was on the last leg of the trip that Groucho finally received whatever reward he was entitled to. We stopped to gas up the car, and Groucho called his home, possibly to find out if his young bride was still there.

When he got back in the car, he said to Frank Ferrin: "You know a guy named John Guedel?"

Frank said he knew that Guedel had produced some good radio shows.

"My wife says he called, " Groucho sneered. "Wants to talk to me about doing one of those quiz shows where they give away prize money."

"No kidding?"

Groucho scoffed. "I've been insulted by experts. Whoever this guy is, he's out of his fucking mind."

Guedel wanted it to be a new kind of game show where Groucho talked to everyone.

"Why don't you talk to him?" said Frank. Frank, Manny and I all felt it was a fine idea if the money was right, and it might even be intellectually rewarding.

"No way," Groucho said. "I'm not that desperate. Quiz shows are for morons."

Later that day, we made it home. And about a week later on the front page of one of the trade papers was a story saying Groucho Marx had been signed to do a new show called, "You Bet Your Life." Which he did for fifteen years, starting in 1947, on radio and then TV. It was the one thing that supported him the rest of his life.

In 1947 at the Flamingo in Las Vegas, a town known for hot tomatoes, Groucho has his in a bag.

Irving Brecher

Part IV

Television Writing & Directing

The Undertaker Saved My Life

"Chester A. Riley never says die.
Until he's dead six months."
- William Bendix in "The Life of Riley"

The New York Times *publishes a "For the Record" column in the front section of their newspaper every day. They recently ran a correction having to do with a famous comedy line invented by Brecher. The sportswriter Murray Chass had wrongly attributed it to Jimmy Durante. So setting their readers straight, "For the Record" reported the line was: "Chester A. Riley's catchphrase in 'The Life of Riley,' a sitcom in the 1950s, not Jimmy Durante's."*

I shot off an email informing the corrections department that, "The Life of Riley" had actually first appeared on radio, in 1944, followed by a feature film in 1949, adding for good measure that, "Riley" was a creation of Irving Brecher, "who also came up with the aforementioned catchphrase-in-question, at least seven years before you'd reported."

(For the record, the Times *did not run this correction.)*

How was Brecher able to transition from MGM movies to NBC television? Through radio, the magical medium where he wrote for Milton Berle...

In 1943, you were writing movies at Metro-Goldwyn-Mayer. How did you create a radio show at the same time and then end up in television?

A radio show I didn't want to do and that didn't sell. Start with that!

In the summer of '43, I was in my office, working on the script of **Meet Me in St. Louis**. I had left a sign on the outside of the door: "Please Do Not Disturb." I heard a knock on the door as it was being opened and my friend Groucho walked in.

"Some wise guy must've put a sign on your door in an effort to keep us apart."

I laughed, until he added, "So that you wouldn't write a new radio show on which we'll both get rich."

I said, "I'm what?"

"You're gonna put me back on the radio."

Groucho's radio show had recently been canceled by, I think it was, Old Gold cigarettes. You could see how quietly angry and frustrated the poor guy was. He was miserable, and eating himself. And that bothered me. But I had to tell him the facts of life.

"Groucho, nothing would make me happier, but I'm under contract to the studio and prohibited from doing any other writing than what they assign me."

He was adamant.

"Studios come and go, but you and I go on forever."

"I wish I could, Groucho."

"If you're my friend you'll do it for me. Don't worry, you keep your name off it so the studio never knows."

I shook my head. I was really troubled. I knew it was risky. But I couldn't turn down Groucho.

"You'll come up with something," he smiled. "I know you will."

I was not enthusiastic.

"Well, the only thing I can think of," I told him, "is a couple of pages I wrote when I was still in New York."

A couple pages of nothing really, just concepts. The one I told Groucho about had to do with a father of a family—the Flotsam family—the father was a floater, dreaming about making it big, scheming, and always getting fucked up.

"Sounds like a part for me!" said Groucho.

"Groucho," I said. "The radio listeners will not believe you playing that character. He's basically an average family man."

Audiences saw Groucho in their mind as a guy with a painted mustache and eyebrows wiggling, running around bent over to jump on any broad he came in contact with.

But he was firm.

"They'll believe me. I can act, I can read the lines. Just write it."

And then, what was unusual for Groucho Marx, not the flippant words, but an actual pleading.

"Please," he said.

I knew I had lost, so for several nights I worked on an audition script for a thirty-minute, hopefully funny, family disaster. Groucho meanwhile, had gotten his manager to make a deal with a Madison Avenue ad agency to pay for an audition platter—a 33 RPM record—which we'd record with a live audience at CBS in Hollywood.

The audience laughed at all of his jokes, and when it was over, the agency people and Groucho thought they had a hit. I thought it was funny in the studio, but who knew how it would play on radio? Who would believe Groucho as a flesh-and-blood father? Well, it died because nobody believed. The William Morris Agency played the platter for a number of potential sponsors (after the original agent who'd paid for it had turned it down), and none of their clients wanted it. And finally, Groucho stopped calling me to share his disgust over the lack of intelligence on the part of the people who bought radio shows…

There is a letter in one of his books, where Groucho writes to you and says: "I have a hunch there is deep-seated aversion to accepting me in any role other than the one I have always played."

Yeah. Sometimes it's not fun to be right. Which I was, unfortunately.

Like Groucho, I forgot about the program, until a few months later when I was sitting with my wife in the Fox Village Theater in Westwood. As a prelude to the main feature, they showed a Hal Roach five-reeler called "The McGuerins of Brooklyn." The leading character was a likeable meathead that I'd seen in some dramatic films but only learned his name from the end credits: William Bendix. His comedy timing was very, very good, and on the way home, I said to my wife, "Do you remember that audition we did with Groucho? I think this guy Bendix might be good doing the Groucho part."

She agreed, adding, "You mean as a Brooklyn character?"

"Yeah. Everybody laughs at Brooklyn. I'm surprised anybody lives there."

The next day I contacted the agent who handled Bendix. His name was Stewart Stewart. His real name was Muckenfuss. He should've kept it. Anyway, I told him I wanted to know if Bendix was available for a radio series. Yes. So I supplied the script, after rewriting the main character, somewhat Brooklynish, but not really with the type of English for which Brooklyn is famous. And I decided to change the Flotsam name, first to Riley and then to Chester A. Riley. And "The Flotsam Family" became "The Life of Riley." I knew the phrase had been around for years. I had even seen it in print. It was a perfect title, meaning a life of pleasure, comfort, plenty of money—everything the exact opposite of what the show would be about. After Bendix read it, Muckenfuss called and said, "Bill loves it. Let's make a deal." Even before I met him, I made out a contract covering Bendix's first year with an option for four additional.

Soon after, we were in the same CBS studio with a different cast and the audition went better than Groucho's. The laughs were all there but you had a sense of caring a little about the serious moments, because Riley was not a cardboard character. He was a living father, harassed husband, with a low IQ. The rewrite gave Bendix what Groucho did not have: believability.

I felt pretty optimistic.

But six months later, I was not that optimistic because no buyer had shown any interest. My own agents had obviously given up because they stopped calling. I was back finishing up *St. Louis* when one night I got a call at home.

The long distance operator said: "Chicago calling."

A strange voice on the other end said he was Frank Ferrin from the Leo Burnett Agency.

"Are you connected with a radio record called 'The Life of Riley?'"

I said I was and he went on to tell me what a strange business I was in.

"I represent the American Meat Institute," he said. "I know there's no meat to sell these days, but they are looking for a radio show that will keep the public eager to get meat when it becomes available. The war's gotta end some day."

"Put me down for a pound of lamb chops."

I asked Ferrin how he found me.

"Your name was on the platter. And guess where I found it? For a couple of weeks I've been wading through hundreds of audition records, wanting to find something I liked enough to recommend to my client. Something I think would be a hit, because in this business as you know, your ass is always on the line. I tracked you down by calling the Writers Guild in Hollywood. I wanna buy the show. Will you put me in touch with your representatives?"

"So-called representatives," I told him. "You found the show on the bottom of a pile and they'll wind up getting ten percent of every buck the show earns from now until perpetuity. Or maybe less."

I thanked Frank. And that's how "The Life of Riley" was born. Sixty years ago. And that show has been on the air or sold in audio cassettes and CDs off the internet ever since, from a company called Radio Spirits.

Do you get royalties from those tapes?
Who do you think paid for your lunch?
Sixty years ago…
Yeah. January 16, 1944. It probably had six listeners. The show went

on the NBC Red Network (they had two, the Red and the Blue networks. ABC was the Red) at noon, three o'clock in New York. On Sunday. Nobody much was listening to the radio at that hour and naturally I squawked about the terrible time slot. But the Meat Institute wouldn't pay for a night time spot, and having signed for twenty-six weeks, we doggedly went forward. The acting was good, the studio audience laughed, and the ratings were ridiculous.

Ridiculously low.

But that didn't seem to annoy the sponsor. They picked up the option for fifty-two more weeks. That means for seventy-eight weeks, I worked my ass off. And on around our twentieth broadcast, something near a miracle changed the whole story. Changed my life.

I had rehearsed the cast in an office in the studio in Hollywood. But after I cut it, the script came up a minute-and-a-half short. I needed to fill the time. I looked at what we had for our story: Chester Riley, Stevenson Aircraft factory riveter, instead of coming home after work, has disappeared. He's been missing for a while and his wife Peg is frantic, fearing he's fallen prey to some serious mishap. Various characters drop in to help her which, by design, turns out to be more comical than comforting. Suddenly I thought: what visitor dropping by would really bring her down, would depress her the most?

An undertaker. That would shatter her.

And I found it quite easy to make him funny. What's funnier than death? He had to have a dark, sepulchral type of voice and delivery. "O'Dell." That would make a nice Irish friend of Riley's. "Digby" O'Dell created nice alliteration. Then a light struck. "Digger" would be his nickname.

Everyone on the set hurried me along and suddenly the show began and the story unfolded and there was Digby O'Dell, rapping on the door of a worried Mrs. Riley. She opens it, and the actor John Brown says in the most mournful tone: "It is I, Digger O'Dell, the friendly undertaker."

The audience laughed in surprise.

Then he delivers the cliche that the bereaved always say to an open casket:

"You're looking fine. Very natural."

The audience screamed. And they never stopped laughing through the whole ninety-second Digger routine. Especially on his exit line: "Well, I'd better be shoveling off."

When he left the microphone and sat down, for the first time, a scene ended with applause.

The next morning I got a phone call from Chicago.

Frank Ferrin said, "That undertaker bit you had was hilarious."

"Yeah, I got lucky."

"Now comes the good news," he said. "The sponsor's right hand idiot just called me. They were furious that you'd have an undertaker on the show."

"What? What about the laughs they heard?"

"They hate it. It's too morbid."

What were they upset about? They said they couldn't afford to offend undertakers. Some American Meat Institute members were companies that sold animal fat to morticians. Morticians used animal fat in embalming. Making fun of undertakers would create problems.

"They ordered me to tell you not to use that character again," Ferrin was saying. "Or they'll cancel you."

I was upset. Nobody, be it Milton Berle the first day I met him, or me years later, wants to give up laughs. It's the blood that keeps us alive.

"Well Frank," I sighed. "I guess I'm stuck."

Then I heard him say something I never expected from a man in his position in a field where nobody dares disagree with the guy above.

"SCREW 'EM!" he said. "Put him on next week. I'll take my chances with this dumb bastard."

"Are you sure?"

"Sure I'm sure."

Reluctantly, I wrote in another Digby O'Dell scene. The audience reaction was the same—tremendous. Ferrin called. The sponsor was even more livid. Ferrin stood by me. After the third week, I figured the sponsor was exploring how to break the contract, when I got another phone call from Chicago.

"Wait'll you hear this," he said. "ABC has been getting phone calls from listeners. And telegrams. Applauding Digger O'Dell!"

Letters came to the network and the network delivered them to my office. Letters from all over the country, all about Digger O'Dell. Thanking us for making death humorous. Old people giving their ages. Young people writing to say it was refreshing and candid material about a fearful subject. One prick from the sponsor called me to say it was a great idea to put the undertaker on, "Keep it up."

Which I did.

And there was more fallout. The Meat Institute sent me slabs of bacon. At a time when you had to be a V.I.P. to get a black market pound of meat, where beef and butter were rationed, big hams started showing up at the house. Institutions can be as hypocritical as any politician.

After the seventy-eighth week, the Meat people and I parted. The war was over. They could sell meat; they didn't need me. And my agents, who had never done anything to make "Riley" happen, were now very much involved. They quickly got me an offer from Proctor & Gamble for a plum night spot after "The Ralph Edwards Show" at night on the NBC network. Our sponsor in 1945 was a new shampoo called "Prell." Each month I got a shipment of Prell and my hair grew thinner and thinner.

The ratings grew higher and higher. Frank Ferrin became a good friend. He went on to own his own radio programs ("The Buster Brown Gang") and I produced "The Life of Riley" for nine seasons, beginning-to-end.

How strange. To think of the world in such a dither, and if not for Digger O'Dell, I wouldn't be here today. How do you like that—an undertaker saving a life?

John Brown, who also played the voice of Riley's pal Gillis, was asked to give speeches as Digger. The National Association of Undertakers invited him to their convention. When he came back, he reported that partly embalmed by bourbon and scotch, this merry breed of groundhogs made for a very good audience.

"They were great laughers," Brown told me. "Particularly, one line they quoted to me after. Where Riley says how he wishes he had an easy job, like being the foreman where he works. And I say to him, 'Do not become an envious man. As we undertakers say: the grass is always greener on the other fellow.'"

A Life of Riley rehearsal around the NBC microphone, circa 1944. After this came the movie and TV versions. On my left, Tommy Cook who played Junior and Paula Winslow who played Peg Riley. On my right, William Bendix and orchestra conductor Lou Kosloff. We had eight musicians. On TV we had a live theme song because I couldn't afford to pay for an orchestra. I hired a woman to whistle it for $150.

Bendix with one of the many awards he received just for doing what he was paid to do.

A Rather Revolting Development

Radio Spirits is a company that distributes CDs and audiocassettes of old-time radio programs (1925-1955) through the web. On their site it reports: "'What a revoltin' development this is' was the catch phrase sweeping the country in the summer of 1943." Who knew?

"It was 1944!" *growls Brecher.* "The show had just been created!"

Radio Spirits runs ads in journals like Radiogram. Radiogram *comes via SPERDVAC, the "Society to Preserve and Encourage Radio Drama Variety and Comedy." In the summer of 2001, going through the mail, Brecher found his semi-regular issue of* Radiogram. *But this one had a surprise inside, a big, black headline across the top of Page 3: "Comedy writer Irving Brecher dies. Made 'revoltin' development" a national phrase for frustration."*

Irv looked at Norma.

"I don't know if I should finish this breakfast or not, because I'm dead."

"Really?" *said Norma, used to the shtick.*

Brecher showed her the magazine. "And I'm an honorary member of Sperdvac!" *he told her.* "I went to one of their meetings… but that doesn't mean I'm not dead. I can't believe this fucking thing!"

I offered to shoot an e-mail off for him. "Yes," *he said.* "Will you please tell them that I am still alive? Because otherwise, they'll stop sending the magazine."

Irv finally spoke with the editor, after the e-mail came back.

The way he tells it: "The editor said, 'I guess we should have checked.' I said: 'Might've been a good idea.' I was careful not to go crazy. What I finally said at the end of the conversation was, 'I can't wait to read your obituary.'"

I never heard back from Radiogram.

Comedy writer Irving Brecher dies

Made 'revoltin' development' a national phrase for frustration

Also wrote Marx Brothers comedies and MGM musicals

Comedy writer and producer Irving Brecher, whose radio series *The Life of Riley* brought working class situations to the sitcom, died recently in Los Angeles. He was 87.

Brecher, an honorary member of SPERDVAC, began writing at the age of 19

Jackie Gleason's Favorite Jew

"She'll just start in Burlesque and then sink
lower and lower until one day . . . Television!"
– Chester A. Riley

You said Groucho's "You Bet Your Life" went on TV after it began on radio. The same thing happened with your radio show "The Life of Riley."

When "You Bet Your Life" began, there was no TV. The next year, suddenly, there was. Hundreds of TV sets around the country. It was a thrill for TV owners to dabble with the new medium, even though what was on the tiny screen was mainly test patterns, or occasionally something less interesting. Milton Berle changed all that. He became a phenomenon. And '48 brought me another experience where something I didn't want to do, but was forced into it, became a big break.

Like doing Riley originally as Flotsam for Groucho and it becoming a hit with Digger.

Yeah.

Like being reluctant to do this book. A pattern perhaps?

You say.

So what was it that you were resisting this time? I mean, that time...

Hold it. First, in '48, my agents brought me an offer. A brand new company called Universal International was interested in making a motion picture based on my radio show. This pleased me, but surprised me, because several movies based on popular radio shows had all bombed. "Amos & Andy" and "Edgar Bergen & Charlie McCarthy" are two I recall.

But of course I was all for making movies and the studio's offer was generous: I would own half the picture and be paid decent fees to write, produce and direct. So in January 1949, I began shooting *The Life of Riley*. As the date approached, I began to do what I was very good at—worrying I might screw up. The night before the first day's shooting I didn't sleep. I left my home in Bel Air and drove over Coldwater Canyon to Universal at about six. The only living creature was the man at the studio gate. As I headed to my bungalow, a pair of deer ran by. The studio was surrounded by woods and wild game would often invade, animals undoubtedly hoping to become movie stars.

In my office I tried deep breathing to calm myself, and then used a technique I used often in times of crisis: talking to myself in the bathroom mirror. Scolding myself, calling myself names, ridiculing my fear of failure. Of disaster. *"What are you worried about, schmuck? Let the other guys worry!"* And other sage advice. It had worked for me in the past. This time it seemed to work—until I threw up.

Strolling onto the set, I waved good morning to the crew and greeted warmly, numbly climbed into a chair with my name printed on the canvas back. So far, I was a director. My cameraman was William Daniels, the man who shot Greta Garbo's movies. Bill Bendix came in greeting everybody and said to me: "Ready when you are, I.B."

For the first scene, we'd be shooting the end of a piece of action featuring Riley and his friend Gillis, played by James Gleason. They stood across the street from Riley's small, rented house. His landlady was on her porch next door. She was waiting to trap him because he owed three month's rent. Borrowing a nickel from his pal, Riley phones the landlady. She hears the ring and goes inside, allowing Riley time to race across the street—narrowly missing getting run over—and through his front door, just as the landlady came back out, missing her victim, ending with him flopping in relief on his couch. Which then collapses.

As soon as I yelled "Cut!" and "Print it!" I was no longer nervous about directing. It was no big mystery—nothing more than making sure the actors spoke their lines properly, with the right inflection, and moved—even though some directors made it seem like it was tougher than splitting the atom. Which of course, led to big money for them. The great ones—William Wyler, Ernst Lubitsch, Billy Wilder, there were a number—really brought the script to real life. Anyway, the next morning as I was shooting in Riley's dumpy living room, it was a real shot in the arm to have the head of the studio, William Goetz, come in all smiles.

"I was running yesterday's dailies," he said. "You done good."

And then he added what means the most to studios (money): "The best part is, you shot two days work in one."

Naturally, I was all thanks. I was almost tempted to forgive him. Two days before shooting, Goetz called my agent to say he wanted me to give up directing because he was worried about my inexperience. He wanted to put some veteran hack in my spot who never had his name on anything watchable. I was very disturbed and told my agent I refused to be dumped. And since my deal had terms where I could only be replaced if I fell behind schedule, Goetz had no choice but to let me at least start the film. From then on I experienced the most pleasant thirty days of my life. The picture was sneak previewed in downtown Los Angeles and was an out-and-out hit with the audience. The executives enthused.

What did *Riley* cost to make?

Six hundred thousand dollars.

Do you remember the premiere? Where was it held?

Cincinnati. Proctor & Gamble, my radio sponsor, were based there and the premiere was a fundraiser for a local charity. After that weekend, the film "went wide" as they say, in dozens of theaters. And at forty cents a ticket, it grossed over two-and-a-half million dollars in its first year. That's nothing today, but those were real dollars. They had value.

Now as I said before, about big breaks? Here's what happened.

P & G canceled the show on radio. I'd been on the air with them five years and I honestly felt I was part of a love affair with Howard Morgens, the lead man, and his other execs, Gail Smith, Gil Ralston and Al Halverstadt.

I don't know how you remember names from the 1940s...

I want to. They were wonderful to me. Two of them flew out from Cincinnati to my home. They said they wanted to discuss the situation. They were close to tears. "Even though we love Riley," Morgens said, "we have to cancel." The brand that's paying for the radio was being switched to TV. Their board insisted they make the move. I think they moved their money to the "Red Skelton Show." But their genuine unhappiness about parting moved me. I still have a warm feeling. Canceled, I fell into what I first thought was a pit, but later it became a gold mine.

You bought P & G stock in 1949?

Overnight, I got a new sponsor for the '49 season. Pabst Blue Ribbon Beer. The show took off and resumed its popularity—meanwhile the movie had run, and one probably helped the other. And when we started the Pabst contract, I was approached by the head of Warwick and Legler, their ad agency. By approached I mean attacked. Paul Warwick was a small, tough bulldog. He was not the least bit long-winded and acted like a mob boss.

He said, "Nice layout, kiddo."

We were sitting on my patio in Stone Canyon.

"Thanks, Paul."

"We're putting you into TV."

"What?"

"Tuesday nights on NBC in October."

I couldn't believe it. This was July.

"Who says?" I said. "Not now. Maybe later. Who's got sets? There's no audience yet."

"I got a sweet deal for you," Warwick said. "So you can keep paying the mortgage on this hut."

That sounded good.

"How about a drink," I asked, trying to be the host. "Pabst Blue Ribbon?"

"Never drink that piss. We got a good time slot, so when the sets are there, Riley'll be there, peddling Pabst. Now let's talk money. We don't need your agent, they only fuck up deals."

I started to act out my idea of tough.

"Look Paul. No way. Even if Bendix is available, which I doubt because he's owned by Hal Roach who wants to use him for movies where the money is big."

Warwick calmly flicked his cigar ash on my Chinese rug. Eve had a flair for decorating.

"We don't care who you use," he said. "Bendix. Al Capone. Your uncle, your cousin, your rabbi. Hey, a rabbi could make a good Riley."

"No rabbi would work for Pabst," I told him. "It's not kosher."

Then I added, "Forget about it. I got enough to do with the radio. I don't need TV."

"Yeah we'll forget about it, after the contract is signed."

Before I could say no again, Warwick laid his sentences out like a judge about to send me away. "Let me straighten you out," he said. "I give you credit for having some brains—that is, for a Hollywood writer. You're making a couple of grand per broadcast and you might make a couple dollars from the movie. From what I hear, it's not doing too well."

"You hear wrong."

"Here's the point. We want you to do the TV or we dump the radio."

"I'll get a new sponsor."

"Don't bet your ass. By the end of this season, a lot of shows are being canceled because the ad money is all going to TV. TV is taking over. And that's where you'll be."

And that's where I wound up.

A few days later I had a lousy contract ($8200 per show) and an obligation to pull a TV half-hour out of the air. I didn't understand why it didn't matter who would star as Riley. I should have suspected something.

But Warwick was good. He slapped me on the back and said, "You'll find someone. There are lots of hungry actors."

I had no choice but to go east and start casting.

At that time, a nationally-shown TV series emanated from New York, live, and was broadcast simultaneously in cities in the eastern and central parts of the U.S. There was no transcontinental cable, no carrier from New York to California. So the show would be kinescoped—photographed on film right off the TV screen (there was no videotape yet)—and the kinescope would be shipped to Los Angeles and San Francisco where it was shown with a kind of fuzzy quality in cities west of the Rocky Mountains. A second-class version of the original show. It wasn't until coaxial cable was laid across America that the kinescope was no longer needed.

In August, the William Morris Agency supplied me with an office on 7th Avenue and helped me find actors. I looked at dozens of men who wanted the job as Chester A. Riley. Bendix was so good, I knew I'd never match him. Even Lon Chaney, Jr., auditioned; none of them came close. After forty actors, nothing. October was coming. Then I suddenly remembered seeing a young comic a couple of years before in a nightclub in L.A. called Slapsy Maxie's, owned by the boxer, "Slapsy" Maxie Rosenbloom. I didn't remember the name of the stand-up, so I asked George Gruskin, my agent who covered nightclubs. He rattled off a few names. And then I hit the jackpot.

"Jackie Gleason?"

"That's it! Can you bring him in?"

"Don't touch him," said Gruskin. "He's playing lousy little clubs, and yeah, he's funny, but the guy is totally irresponsible. He gets drunk, he owes everybody money, he'll give you nothing but headaches. Lay off him."

I was at the end of my trail. Pabst didn't care who I cast, but I did. A wrong actor could destroy my property.

I insisted and I got my way.

The next day he came in with his agent from MCA. I can see Jackie now: Handsome, about 175 pounds, big gap between his two front teeth. Coal black hair and a big grin. The kind of personality you immediately like. You knew there was fun inside.

We talked. He knew the radio show. Could he feel comfortable doing TV? He went right into character, improvising dialogue and falling over a chair. Physically, verbally, facially—instant funny. I told my agent to sign him if we could afford him. Jackie happily accepted five hundred bucks per show for twenty-six shows, with an option for thirteen more. (Compare that with the insipid performers today who slave for five-hundred thousand per episode.)

Having Gleason was a relief. But worry had grown into anguish, because starting in October, I would have to be in New York doing a TV show, which would take several days a week of rehearsal, plus a script that had to be written. Once that episode played live, I'd have to take an airplane for eight hours to Los Angeles to get my "Riley" radio show on the air. I knew what would happen; on one of those flights the plane would crash in the Middle West. Either that or I would have a heart attack from the pressure. The absolute necessity of being on time to the very second is the worst kind of pressure. So I went to see the president of NBC, Niles Trammel. He had treated me kindly in the past. I came with Abe Lastfogel, the head of William Morris and at that time the most powerful agent in the field.

Niles Trammel was a gracious Southerner and he greeted us warmly. With him was his second in command, the brilliant Sylvester "Pat" Weaver. With his creative touch, he had made NBC radio number one and he was on his way to pushing NBC television to the top.

I laid it out quickly after the usual schmooze: the impossibility of being able to do two jobs, one live radio and one live TV per week from opposite coasts. I wanted to do the Gleason TV show on film, in a sense as a short movie which I could produce in Hollywood. (No flying back and forth, no heart attack.)

"Beside," I told them. "If it's on film, they'll get the same clear picture on both coasts instead of what they're looking look at now, that blurry, grainy kinescope."

Niles nodded as if I were making sense. But Weaver cut in.

"You know what, Irv?" he said. "I love your show and I sure like you. But we would be cutting our own throat if you were put on film."

"Why, Pat?" Trammel asked.

"We're a network," Pat explained. "We feed all those cities from here in New York, all the way to the Rockies. They pay us to allow them to carry our programs. If Irv's show is on film, he doesn't need us. He just ships the show on a reel to any city. They could play it whenever they want. They don't need NBC."

"You're running old movies now which were on film," I argued.

But he waved it away.

"Niles," he said. "We'd be out of business."

Now Trammel got the point. He shook his head and patted Weaver's arm.

Listen, Pat Weaver was a true pioneer. And Sigourney Weaver's father, too. I liked Pat; I love Sigourney. Pat created "The Today Show" starring the very amusing Dave Garroway, which was a show never equaled in terms of originality and entertainment. And before there was such a thing as cable TV? Weaver formed a company that linked homes by showing motion pictures currently in theaters, at home on the TV. Each residence got a coin box where homeowners deposited a certain amount to see whatever was being offered that night. Oddly enough, I had a home in Palm Springs and was among the first to install the system; I think it was called, "Subscription TV." When I paid the fee into the box—a dollar or two in quarters—I got the local movie. But soon came the court battles. Theater owners conspired with some phony facts to make the operation illegal. One of their arguments was a single fee dropped into the box meant any number of viewers could watch. Exhibitors preferred each moviegoer buying a ticket.

Weaver lost the fight. That was show business.

But I prevailed!

"Alright, son," Niles Trammel said to me with kindly eyes. "We'll try it your way. For one season. But we reserve the right to go back to live if we so desire."

The way he pressed down on Weaver's arm, I thought he was asking his forgiveness.

"I doubt it would be a problem," is how Trammel put it to Pat. "Although doing it on film," he put it to me, "would cost quite a bit more than your budget, wouldn't it?"

I nodded. Pabst had agreed upon $8200 for each episode. A line producer had budgeted a half-hour film and told me it would cost two thousand more per show.

"Suppose Pabst won't pay the increase?" asked Trammel.

"Then I will." I was desperate. I had no choice.

Pabst had a choice.

They said, "Let Brecher pay it."

I went back to Hollywood and we started shooting with one camera, a whole show in one day. We shipped the show four weeks in advance, it got good reviews and respectable ratings. Jackie Gleason was absolutely wonderful, actually broader and funnier than Bendix.

But around the nineteenth week, Paul Warwick from Pabst was at my throat again.

"Seven weeks to go," he said. "With an option for thirteen more."

I said, "Yeah, and it's only costing me two thousand a week out of pocket."

"Stop," he said. "You're making me cry. So instead of thirteen and losing another twenty-six thousand, we'll just pick it up for six. Happy now?"

I said, "Paul, that way I only end up with thirty-two. I can't sell a series of thirty-two episodes to anybody. They deal in thirty-nine. Per season. So we'll do thirteen or we'll do zilch."

"You'll do six," Warwick said.

I said, "Goodbye."

And that was it.

So I wound up with twenty-six half-hours.

Then I found out that they'd screwed me. Warwick had planned all along to start putting on the prizefights from Madison Square Garden. Boxing, brought to you by Pabst beer. Riley was just holding the time slot for them. If I'd known that, I'd never have done the show.

But we won the Emmy for "Best Filmed Comedy Series." The genre called "Situation Comedy" developed later. I didn't know what to call "The Life of Riley." But looking back, it was the first televised comedy story, as opposed to people coming out and telling jokes. A short film rather than a fifteen-minute sketch show. When "I Love Lucy" had its 50th anniversary, CBS exploited it as being the first sitcom. Lucille Ball was a terrific broad, but in point of fact, we beat her to TV.

Anyway, you know, with those points sticking out of it? An Emmy makes a good backscratcher.

And whatever happened with William Bendix as Riley?

Wait. TV had become red hot. Milton Berle was a sensation for Texaco. They couldn't make sets fast enough and companies were rushing to buy airtime on the new networks to plug their garbage. So I guess that's why I got dragged in. Seduced is a better word. By filthy lucre.

By the late '40s, Bendix was so well known on radio that people were shouting "Hey Riley!" at him on the street, at the ballpark, and in the grocery store. And he hated it. He sent his agent to see me. Ol' Muckenfuss. Stewart Stewart. He said Bendix wouldn't sign for any more shows unless I changed the name of it to, "The William Bendix Show."

I looked at Fuckenmuss and decided to play with him.

"Makes a lotta sense," I said. "In fact I like it. Great idea. We change the show and Bill is happy and millions of people listen every week. "The Bill Bendix Show" is in the top ten. And then one day, Bill makes a mistake and dies."

Mucky got an odd sort of look on his face.

"But that doesn't stop the show," I went on. "We get another Bill Bendix to play Riley. Makes sense. Let me think that over for the next few years."

That ended that idiocy. It was funny in '49 when Bendix told me TV was just a fad. It shows you that as a forecaster, Bendix was no Nostradamus.

In '50, Gleason and I parted friends. And then it happened for him. The Dumont Network took him to do a variety show. No surprise. Anybody who'd seen him on the little screen doing his shtick as Chester A. Riley could sense he had more than enough talent to assure his future. Dumont was a struggling network and Jackie quickly became its number one attraction. Couple of years later he was at CBS and became a multimillionaire, thanks to a contract with the CBS boss Bill Paley that paid Gleason sixteen million bucks.

I like to remember how during that first autumn we worked together, he was amazing. On time, too. With Christmas coming, knowing Gleason was an ardent Catholic, I called his personal manager, "Bullets" Durgom. Bullets was a cute little Lebanese guy with a hairless head that looked like a 45-caliber bullet from the side.

I said, "What should I give Jackie?"

"Give him a coffin," said Bullets. "A cheap one, but solid. The son of a bitch owes me so much money, I'd like to bury the bastard."

"Sounds like you love your client."

"He's a pain in the ass. Now he's bugging me to lend him money to have his teeth capped."

Made sense. Because of the separation of two upper teeth, Gleason was whistling on the soundtrack recording. Often we had to stop and have him do his lines again.

All of a sudden, I felt overly benign.

"Tell Jackie I'll pay half the dental bill as a Christmas present."

Bullets said, "Are you kidding?"

"A couple hundred bucks won't break me."

When I hung up, my secretary, who had been listening in on the second phone, made a circle with her finger around her temple.

I said to her, "You think I'm crazy?"

And I laughed it off.

Bullets called back saying Gleason nearly cried when he told him what I'd said. He'd never heard such a reaction.

"Nearly cried?" I asked.

"Yeah. Sweet, huh?"

"Yeah. By the way, how much will it cost to cap the teeth?"

A pause.

Bullets said, "Jackie says it's three thousand."

I almost dropped the phone. Fifteen hundred? I felt like an idiot.

"Well, okay."

And when I came into rehearsal the next day, Gleason lifted me off my feet. He picked me up and hugged me and said: "You're the nicest Jew I ever met."

I laughed.

What did you do after the show was cancelled? You were out of TV, so what trouble did you get into now?

Well, I played gin rummy in the afternoons. I played tennis. I took it easy. And my wife and I took our two young children to Palm Springs some weekends. We had bought a vacant lot and were working with an architect, so we stayed in a little motel nearby. One Sunday morning I came out to the pool. There was a pleasant-faced, middle-aged man sitting there and he introduced himself.

"My name is Feder."

"Brecher. Glad to know you."

"Brecher," he said. "Where have I seen that name? On television! With Jackie Gleason! Am I right?"

"Yeah. Think he was funny?"

"Funny, shit. I'm a dentist. I capped his teeth. And he never paid me."

"Well, he just signed a contract for sixteen million bucks," I said. "That should cover the bill. How much does he owe you?"

"Two thousand dollars."

"He told me three thousand! He lied in his teeth."

"You mean *mine*!"

"He's a fucking embezzler. I gave him fifteen hundred instead of a thousand."

But I told Dr. Feder that I thought I knew how to get even.

I had read that Gleason—living like an emperor, weighing 300 pounds—was coming out from New York, on a private railroad car with his entourage, the band, the cast, the hookers, to celebrate his fat CBS contract. The meatball was holding a press conference at the Bel Air Hotel to kickoff the new season.

So when I got back to town, I called my friend Bullets Durgom. I told him about the dentist.

He laughed, but without humor.

"Typical," said Bullets.

"I'm gonna be at the press conference," I said. "With all the newspaper and radio reporters to salute the king. I'll tell them my Christmas story."

"Great," said Bullets. "I love it."

The next morning, by special delivery, I received a check signed by Jackie Gleason for five hundred dollars. At the bottom of the check it said: "Reimbursement for dental work."

I still have a photo of the check.

I keep it framed, hanging in my bar.

Apparently, Jackie was not embarrassed by anything. A few years later, I think it was '55 or '56, I'm at McCadden Studios in Hollywood, shooting an episode of another TV show I had thought up, called "Peoples Choice." This series starred an actor named Jackie Cooper and a dog named Cleo. My secretary's name was Lois, and she stuck her head in my office.

"There's a long distance call. From Scottsdale, Arizona."

"Who's it from?"

"He wouldn't say."

"Put him on."

The voice was familiar. Millions heard it every week. "Reginald Van Gleason," a character of Jackie's.

"Helloooooo dear pal. I'm smiling at you, with your teeth!"

I had to laugh.

"How are you, Jackie?"

"Very rich."

I knew that was true. We chatted warmly.

"So why are you calling me?" I asked finally. "You need another cap?"

Gleason got serious.

"I bought a script for my next movie. It's a comedy and I want you to direct it. The character is sort of a Chester Riley. His name is Gigot, a Frenchman. It's funny."

I told him I appreciated the offer.

"Let me read it, and if I think I can do a good job, I'd be happy to do it."

"Great, pal. Away we go!"

He said he'd mail me the script right away.

I never heard from him again.

Jackie Gleason pays for dental work and waits for his cue during a break shooting "The Life of Riley." Sid Tomack, in the middle, played Riley's pal Gillis, the chum with the turned-up hat who drives you crazy. Gleason copied him when he created The Honeymooners' Art Carney character, Ed Norton, who wore the identical hat.

Somebody Loves Me
(and I think it's George Burns)

> Hank: I watched a documentary about the actor
> John Garfield [ne'e Garfinkel] on Turner Classic
> Movie channel last night, and it said he died
> at 39 when the House Un-American Activities
> Committee hounded him because his wife was a
> Communist and he refused to name names.
>
> Irv: Fuck Turner. Garfield was on top of a
> hooker.

Can we discuss some of your later movies at MGM now?
Go ahead, kid.
Somebody Loves Me **came out in 1952 and—**
That wasn't MGM. I wrote and directed it at Paramount.
Whoops. Sorry.
George Burns talked me into it. Jack Benny was very cute in it.
Burns and Benny, sounds like a hit!
Wait. Burns said he could get Paramount to produce it. It was set during the vaudeville era. Blossom Seeley was an old-time blowsy singer— once married to a baseball pitcher named Rube Marquard—now married to her fellow ex-vaudeville star, Benny Fields. George Burns wanted to help them out financially; they were old friends of his from way back in the early days of vaudeville. So he sold an idea about Seeley and Fields to a producing team named Perlberg and Seaton. George Seaton was a friend of mine and he asked me to write and direct a movie, reflecting primarily how Blossom and Benny Fields fall in love and the consequences to their careers.
Hence the title, they *loved* somebody?
No. The title *Somebody Loves Me* was also a popular song, also from way back, by DeSilva, Brown and Henderson. Do you know it?
Skitch **Henderson?**
No. No. Way Back. [*Brecher sings*] "Somebody loves me/I wonder who? /I wonder who it can be? /Somebody loves me/I wish I knew/Just who

it can be, worries me…"

Nice.

Good song. Big, big standard. There were other great numbers in it too, like "Way Down Yonder in New Orleans."

Tell me about the two vaudevillians.

Blossom was a small, blond, now elderly woman, who still loved show business despite a long period of being passed up. Her husband was a big shlub, still dapper with a perfectly-combed toupee and healthy tan. Their eagerness to fill me in with what they thought would be funny movie material, actually filled me with sadness.

Why?

Because clearly time had passed them by and they had the illusion that this movie would re-ignite their careers. I'm afraid I knew better, that this was the beginning of television taking over. Being in your seventies was no help in becoming successful TV entertainers in 1952.

And the woman who played Blossom, Betty Hutton. A real looker?

And a pretty big star. She made some wonderful movies at Paramount like *The Greatest Show on Earth* and *The Perils of Pauline*. She sang the song "Somebody Loves Me" in the movie.

Do you want to sing it again?

No. But she sang it very well. Now I'd heard Betty Hutton could be a tough customer for a director to deal with. You know how Mel Torme is called "the velvet fog?" Well, she was known as "the velvet swamp."

So I was somewhat apprehensive when we first met, but she was quite upbeat and enthusiastic about the script. And as we got chummy, she confided that after the movie got shot, she would be marrying Norman Krasna, my friend. So obviously she was very happy—wearing a pretty big diamond engagement ring—and raving about how wonderful he was compared to her string of ex-husbands.

We rehearsed the musical numbers, and it was just a day before actual photography was to begin when my assistant director, Arthur Jacobson, belted me with the bad news: Betty Hutton was "hysterical" in her dressing room. Krasna had called off their engagement and we were told to call off shooting indefinitely. The producer, William Perlberg, grabbed me and said he'd tried talking to her, but she told him she just could not work. Delaying shooting would cost thousands, he told me, adding: "See if you can calm her down."

I knocked on her dressing room door and a voice said to come in, and inside was a very unhappy young woman sitting on a cot drying her eyes.

I was sympathetic, which was easy because I liked Betty; she had a little girl quality that I found appealing. We talked. She grew a bit calmer. And then the trouper in her—she really had a deserved reputation as one who simply lived for performing—gave her a second infusion of resolve, protected as she was by a natural talent for playing the romantic victim. In a sense, she was defiant about this turn of fate. She vowed to be on the set the next morning, and she was.

Did you ever find out why your friend Norman Krasna…?

Why Krasna dumped her I never discussed with him. Go read her book.

Did she do a book?

I don't know. Are *we* doing a book?

Hang in there! Just keep remembering. We'll get this done.

There's a good chance I'll be done before the book is.

Oy vey. Irv the Nerve… so how did things work out with Hutton and *Somebody Loves Me*?

She performed heroically and I finished shooting ahead of schedule and under budget. But the thing I remember with the most pleasure about that job, was when I stopped action to let everyone watch Bobby Thomson, the New York Giant outfielder, beat the Brooklyn Dodgers and win the World Series with that immortal home run. We all saw it on a little TV set on the stage.

You were a Giants fan.

I was thrilled.

But not so much with the movie.

The movie never had a chance to be a hit because the producers made a fatal mistake. To play Benny Fields, we needed a young, attractive actor who would be a credible song-and-dance man and could handle the comic dialogue with a flair. Instead, Perlberg signed a dramatic Broadway actor named Ralph Meeker. Totally miscast. He had a naturally sullen look and probably did a good job when he was a heavy.

I protested, but I made the mistake of finally accepting Meeker in the role when I should have walked. I should have walked, but at the time there weren't many young Fred Astaires around. (Well, there was one—Tony Martin, a handsome, very popular singer.) So while Hutton was great and there were a lot of laughs along the way, if there was any chemistry in those romantic scenes, it was Alka-Seltzer.

Ha! What do you mean, you should've "walked?"

I didn't need the money, but I knew if I quit, I would make a number of enemies. So I gave up, wrote the screenplay too, and was generously paid. I didn't want to say, "Shove this up your ass." I knew I did a good job so I let it go.

And how did Meeker turn out in the role?

Meeker was a flat-assed shit. I mean, a reasonable dramatic actor, but in demeanor he was just not a light, sexy, musical comedy type who could render the way Fields really had been. Hutton, several times, whispered to me how she wished that she had anybody but Meeker. And you couldn't believe him as a singer, even though he was dubbed by a professional.

How did he dance?

He fucking clogged. Like an elephant.

So the picture suffered.

Yeah, but it stopped suffering and died.

Was George Burns unhappy with how _Somebody Loves Me_ turned out?

He didn't give a shit.

Did it help his friends, Blossom Seeley and Benny Fields?

Well they got a paycheck! And Burns and I became fairly close. That led to two major events in what I like to think is my life. Although at times I wish it were somebody else's...

One event was in '55, a few years after _Somebody Loves Me_. I did a new TV show in which Burns was a financial partner. That was a result of chicanery. I'll tell you about that. But the best thing that happened was for another piece of my life which I loved: doing standup comedy. A most rewarding one, at a roast celebrating his 95th birthday.

Burns lived to be 101. How old were you when he turned 95?

It was three days after my 77th birthday. January 20, 1991. There were more than 300 Hillcrest club-members there. Of course it was a sellout. Men only. And it was the biggest ego-enhancing monologue I ever did. The loudest laughing audience I ever worked on.

Well, I'd sure love to hear it.

I'm glad.

Have you got it on tape?

Yes. I hope it's still good.

[We continued as I went to fetch it for his VCR.]

Who else roasted George?

There was Milton Berle, Red Buttons, Danny Thomas, Tony Martin,

Jack Lemmon...

Wow.

Sammy Kahn, Larry Gelbart, Hal Kanter, Jan Murray, Yakov Smirnoff... the comic who gave Russia a bad name.

Not as good as the others?

Stunk.

We'll fast forward.

During dinner, sitting there with all these heavyweights had me nearly catatonic. I didn't even have my usual martini because I needed to be as clear as possible.

[On the tape: From the piano we hear "There's No Business Like Show Business" and see it playing George Burns into the room. The huge Hillcrest dining room. Large round tables, ten or twelve men at each, standing and applauding as Burns strolls in slowly, taking it all in. Jack Lemmon jumps onto the piano bench and plays the next number, "That's Entertainment." Burns steps up on the elevated stage and sits in the middle of the dais. Hanging high behind the men seated alongside Burns (the men Brecher just named, a collection of giants Larry Gelbart has hailed as, "Mount Rushmore with cigars"), we notice a framed picture. It's a lively Al Hirschfeld depiction of natty Nat Birnbaum in song-and-dance mode sporting tux, straw hat and cigar.

At the podium in the middle of all this is the short, good-looking and ever-affable Hillcrest emcee, Barry Merkin, last seen on tape hosting another club panel Irv killed on: "Movies Don't Just Happen."

"These fellas up here have made it," says Merkin. "They've all made it big. They don't need a great talent, a famous emcee to introduce them. As a matter of fact, any schmuck can do it. So I'll do it! Irving Brecher!"

Brecher cuts a tall, hearty figure, approaching the lectern with admirable command—in stunning contrast to the frail one now hunched over and staring, unable to see the screen but smiling at the sound of himself nearly 15 years later—a sharp performer in a smooth blue suit, deftly pulling out a pair of reading glasses with his left hand while waving a sheaf of note cards with his right. "These are my adlibs," he announces.]

```
(Turning to Merkin)
Thank you, schmuck.
(Laughter)
For that long-winded introduction.
At least you mentioned my name.
```

And thanks for putting me on first, ahead of these great, great comedians.

At least *you* I can follow.

(Laughter. Brecher looks at Burns seated just right of the podium. Burns is quietly smoking his cigar, staring straight ahead pokerfaced, possibly after many martinis.)

What is so unusual about our guest of honor is that in a profession so frenetically competitive, where the pressure to make it big is so intense that often friends turn on one another, George Burns has not one single enemy.

They all died.

(Extended tremendous laughter followed by applause. One more seat down the dais is Danny Thomas. He turns to Burns, holding his long cigar to the side. Leaning directly into the ear of the tiny luminary, Thomas shouts: "Great line!" This causes Burns to lower his cigar and join the applause.)

I'm proud that George and I have been friends, for most of my life… about thirty percent of his. (Laughter)

I've loved George for his impish humor, his zest for entertaining, his modest way of handling great success. And loving him, I've worried about his destructive habits.

Like twenty cigars a day. I begged him: "Cut down… cut down." He said, "It can't hurt. I don't inhale."

And four, five martinis. I pleaded, "George, alcohol is poison." He said: "I don't inhale." (Laughter)

Worst of all was the salt. I've watched him for years. He puts salt on everything. Even on pickled herring.

I told him years ago: "George, you're taking years off your life."

Ninety-five. Big deal. If he'd listened to me, today he'd be at least a hundred.

(Laughter. Irv looks down at George next to lectern, who stares straight ahead, cigar in mouth.)

George, Methuselah didn't smoke or drink. And Methuselah lived to be 900 years old. Of course he was lucky. At that time, there were no doctors.

(Mirthful banging of tables and the clattering of silverware. Burns almost smiles.)

Tonight we also are celebrating, the anniversary of another venerable institution, Hillcrest's 70th. Hillcrest, among country clubs, is also something of a celebrity. It's always had notable members: Judges... lawyers... medical men ...un-indicted bankers. (Laughter)

But it's only fair to credit much of Hillcrest's fame to the matchless entertainers that were here. Most of them, sadly, are gone: The Marx Brothers, Jack Benny, Jessel, Jolson, Danny Kaye, The Ritzes, Holtz. They're all legends. Happily we still have other legends: Milton, Danny, Tony, Red, George.

And we have some legends-to-be in Jan Murray and... Rickles...

They're not old enough yet!

And Jack Lemmon, dear Burt Lancaster, Sidney Poitier...

We also have many men who lent color to this club. Men who you newer members don't know about. They joined during the Depression of the 30's. The club was hungry for more dues-paying members.

It was actually desperate for money. It was so broke that the board passed a rule: You hadda have two sponsors to *resign*. (Laughter)

One choice candidate who applied for membership was a little lad named Ben Siegel. Handsome, charming, a classy dresser.

Suits by Brooks Brothers, vest by U.S. Steel. (Laughter)

The committee asked Bugsy, "What business are you in?"

He said, "I give out contracts in cement." (Laughter)

"We're very selective," the chairman said. "But we do need new blood."

Bugsy said, "Fine. Whose?" (Laughter)

Bugsy quit, he went east to become CEO of Murder Incorporated.

And then there was Manny Lowenfeld. He owned a pawnshop.

You think he was tough? I'll tell you how tough he was. Over the pawnshop door, he hung three balls.

Real ones. (Laughter)

But my favorite departed member was Al Hart, the Hungarian banker. Al, to many was a loyal friend. Al was also very charitable.

Especially to nymphomaniacs. [Laughter]

Al was truly a horny Hungarian. We thought of him as a cockamamie Casanova. At one point, Al's doctor warned him not to drink. But one day we smelled the booze and I was alarmed for him.

I said, "My god Al, you've been drinking. You've got liquor on your breath."

Al smiled dreamily.

"I didn't have a drink. This new girl I got. She douches with scotch!"

I really do miss Al Hart. He may have been tough to others but to me he was like a warm, tender father. I called him "Dad" and he called me "a dirty cocksucker." (Laughter)

Lastly, there's that member that would steal your heart—and sell it to a lab. C.K. The

club kleptomaniac. He has retired. This man
has stolen anything he can carry: bottles
of ketchup, hair tonic, bathmats, telephones,
Kleenex… some of it unused. (Laughter)
    I personally witnessed this packrat's greatest
single exploit. His career high.
    One day I went into the men's room, he was
unscrewing a urinal from the wall.
    While George Burns was using it. (Laughter)
    It was quite a sight watching this guy carry
the urinal out to the parking lot, with George
following.
    You see George likes to finish whatever he
starts, and so do I!
    (Extended, rousing applause as Brecher returns
to his seat on the dais among the other giants.)

That's great standup, Irv. Thank you for letting me see that.

Norma said she got a call at home that night from Milton Berle at the club.

Really? Why?

He told her I ruined the event. I remember when it ended and the crowd thinned out, we went over to the roundtable and Danny Thomas said, "Kid you were beautiful," and put his arm around me. And Berle said, "You ingrate. Made us all look like bums. What's yer phone number at home?"

I said, "Why? I'm not home," you know.

He goes right to the phone and I heard him say: "Norma? Your husband ruined the night. We couldn't follow him."

I have run a number of tapes where Irv made appearances. But yeah, I have to go with Berle on this one. (Except for maybe Danny Thomas; that guy was one helluva storyteller.)

Cleo the Derisive Basset Hound

"He was sitting there when I arrived, feet up
on his desk, smoking his cigar, not wearing his
toupée. That's how close we were, he didn't wear
his toupée—but I kept my hair on."
- Brecher on Burns

Now what about this TV show where you and George Burns got involved?

Do you want to know how things happen in Hollywood?

You bet!

How for instance, a TV series can come into being because a rich man wants to please the younger woman he married by giving her a career?

Nat Birnbaum?

No! This genial chap was young Harry Karl of Hillcrest, who inherited a huge chain of low-priced shoe stores. Essentially a playboy, Harry was hooked on marrying beautiful young women; Debbie Reynolds was one of them. He was a big spender and a good sport and I liked him, even though he never gave me a pair of shoes. In fact, I'll tell you the kind of shoes they were. During the Watts riots, the police could tell who looted Karl's Shoes: the people who were limping badly.

My involvement with Harry was triggered by one of his marriages, this one to a voluptuous beauty named Marie MacDonald. One day he approached me at the club and said: "I'd like to get a TV series for Marie."

I was not particularly interested in this goal, but one of my agents, George Gruskin was. And he leaned on me.

"It's time you went back to work," he said. "There's a half-hour slot still open on NBC for the fall season. Think up a show."

I reluctantly mentioned a half-hour mystery I'd written years before on radio back in New York. I remembered vaguely it was about a young couple and the girl was the daughter of the mayor. I said I'd try and write a pilot.

Gruskin said, "I know how we can sell it. Have Marie MacDonald work naked."

The humor of my agent.

But ten days later, when I finished writing, Harry Karl had already told Gruskin that his sexy bride had changed her mind. The "future Lucille Ball" had backed out. She was worried that if the pilot became a series she'd have to get up too early in the morning, and so she preferred starring in features, because they only take four or five weeks of getting up early...

But I really owe Harry Karl something. Gruskin thought the idea was perfect for another one of his clients, Jackie Cooper, the former child star who made the world cry in *The Champ*, a classic MGM movie starring Wallace Beery. That was in 1931, and by '55, Jackie Cooper was popular on the Broadway stage, playing grown-ups. So George Gruskin and I flew to New York and met with Jackie and his manager (an attorney named Mort Rosenthal, who also managed one of my comedic idols, Victor Borge).

Cooper liked the script so I came back to the coast and had a budget made. And this is where George Burns comes in.

George Burns had his own style. A style I liked. He was impish and had this attitude about life: he didn't take it seriously. When I was a kid, I saw Burns and his wife Gracie Allen perform at Keith's Fordham Theater in my native Bronx. Vaudeville. With George Burns, everything related to show business. Once after he rebounded from a serious case of pneumonia, I asked if he had ever during his hospital stay thought he might not make it this time. He blew smoke in my face and said: "I knew I wouldn't die, because I'm booked to play the Palladium in October."

George Burns also told outrageous lies and told you they were lies.

Now he and Gracie had a hit TV series and his company was partners in other half-hour shows like, "The Bob Cummings Show" and "Mr. Ed."

And another one of my agents at William Morris, Sam Weisbord told me: "I can get you a deal with George Burns. No sweat. George Burns loves you. And if he likes the idea, he'll finance the pilot."

I said, "I had a producer look at the script and the pilot would cost less than thirty thousand. I don't need financing. I've got the money."

Weisbord said, "We'll talk about about that later."

Soon we were in George's office. While I tried to breathe, Burns smoked one of his twenty-cent cigars. His brother Willie was there. Willie handled the money and contracts.

"George," I said. "I've got an idea that could make a fresh kind of show."

"Okay," he said. "Shoot." He leaned back and closed his eyes. I cleared my throat and began.

"George, this first program opens with a young guy, Jackie Cooper, as Socrates 'Sock' Miller. Sock works for the U.S. Bureau of Wildlife and he lives in a trailer. With him in the trailer is his amusing aunt, Augusta. 'Gus' for short. She's a one-line shooter and she's there whenever we need her. Sock studies the lives of endangered species, which we see some of throughout the series. At this particular moment, as we fade in, he is walking through the woods followed by a dog. You may know the type; it's a basset hound."

"I don't know any dogs," said Burns. "I know some people, but I have no business with dogs. If it will help the show, I'll have my cat introduce me to some."

"Anyway," I continued, "Sock Miller reaches a tall tree, followed by this basset hound. Sock takes out his hunting knife, and looking around to make sure no one is watching, he carves a heart in the trunk of the tree. He caves 'S Loves M' in the heart. And then the dog says—"

Burns interrupted. "The *dog* says?"

"Yes. The dog says: 'I don't know what he sees in her.'"

Burns said: "The *dog* says?"

"Well, her lips don't move. We hear what she says in her *mind*. She throws the lines like Groucho."

Burns turned to his brother and said: "Willie, give Irv the money."

So we became partners.

Cleo chewed up the cover of TV Guide twice, this one in 1957

Weisbord pulled me out of there and started explaining it to me. "You can't afford to put up the money. Before you get on the air, they'll want you to pay for four or five completed half-hours. Let Burns take the risk. Say somebody gets sick, you don't lose all that money."

"And what does he get for putting up the money?"

"Fifty percent."

I paused. The nice thing about owning "The Life of Riley on radio and TV was not that I got one-hundred percent of ownership, but that I had no partners to argue with. So I told Weisbord: "I like George, but I really don't want any partners. This way, no grief. I'll finance it myself. But I'll do one thing for Burns. I'll shoot it here at his studio so he can make the money on the physical production."

But Weisbord was adamant and I finally gave in.

Televisions were in high demand and sponsors were hungry to get on during the "prime time." Gruskin showed the finished pilot to Shaeffer Pens. They laughed. And passed. Then it was snapped up by Borden's, the national dairy company. (Our company was called "Norden Productions," after my wife's hometown in Norfolk, Virginia, and Burns's McCadden Productions.)

"Peoples Choice" starred Jackie Cooper and Patricia Breslin, as Amanda Peoples. They were perfect, but it was their co-star that was responsible for the show's popularity.

I lucked into her in terms of casting. Among the trainers who brought me dogs to look at was Frank Inn, who came in from Sun Valley with five or six basset hounds on leashes. I said, "Thank you Mr. Inn. They're sad, sweet-looking animals. But I need a beagle. These hounds are too lethargic."

Frank didn't have a beagle, but he urged me to give him a chance. And while they were milling around, one puppy slipped the leash and came running across my office, jumping right up into my lap. I was smitten.

"Frank," I said. "Do you think you can train him?"

"It's a her. And I can train anything."

I looked at this beautiful, forlorn puppy with the long floppy ears.

"Cleo," I said. "You're gonna be a star!"

With Frank Inn's patience and skill, the dog became a smash. Cleo did her shtick on cue, but her one-liners made her unique. All movie and TV animals at the time were made to move their lips via mechanical or chemical devices. These were cruel. Mr. Ed? Fucking electric wires that made him twitch!

Instead I tried something different.

Whenever Cleo saw or heard something to ridicule, we'd cut to a close-up of her, eyes into the camera, and you heard her thought. It came in a female voice with a Groucho Marx type of delivery and was usually some kind of stinging criticism, put-downs and off the wall commentary directed at Cooper and his girlfriend Mandy Peoples. This "thinking aloud for comic results" device was copied years later in **Look Who's Talking** using a baby and John Travolta. I prefer my dog. Writing her "strange interludes" was second nature to me after writing movies for Groucho. Cleo was a real thinking man's dog. And I struck gold with Mary Jane Croft for her voice. Mary had often played on my "Life of Riley" radio show.

The zingers never failed to get a laugh. Cleo made the cover of TV Guide twice, and people began breeding basset hounds. You started seeing quite a few of them around. She received fan mail from around the country, proposals for marriage signed by "Rover" or "Prince." I showed some of these to Frank Inn. He sniffed them and quipped, "If you want my opinion Irv, these were not written by animals."

Inn had begun his own business in 1954, after working for Rudd Weatherwax, the owner-trainer of Lassie, who was good looking, but dumb and never said a funny word, unlike Cleo. Frank was a wizard. He brought her every day in his pickup to our studio on Las Palmas. He never once got angry at the animal. For one scene, he trained her to walk right up to a fishbowl and stick her face into it without harming the fish. Despite the runaway popularity of Cleo, Frank never demanded we increase his fees. I liked that; I suggested he train the actors.

Our show ran until 1958. Jackie Cooper when on to star in "Hennessey," playing a Navy medical officer. I went back to writing movies. And Frank Inn went on to make famous other four-legged performers like Arnold the Pig and Benji.

Now did I tell you where my agent screwed me? After "Peoples Choice" finished its run, we sold a hundred-and-four of them to ABC for syndication. They paid a million dollars for the shows. So for putting up the 27 thousand for the cost of the first half-hour, my partner George Burns got half-a-million. And one day at the club, he innocently mentioned why he thought my agent at William Morris had originally brought me to his office.

"They were trying to get me back as a client," he said, seeming quite pleased with himself. Burns had been a client of William Morris ever since his vaudeville days when he was a starving tap-dancer. He married Gracie and when they started to make it as a team, William Morris handled him in radio and movies. Then a rival agency, MCA lured them away.

"So when they brought you to me," Burns said, "they were kind of making love to me, trying to get me to switch back by making me this barrel of money."

This was news. Not the kind I enjoyed hearing. That's show biz, "a lotta cat-fat." That's what Cleo called a bunch of bullshit. I started the series calling it "hogwash" but Borden's Dairy objected, so I came up with cat-fat.

So now I saw why George Burns was *kvelling* about the show. What was a good business move for him, going with MCA, William Morris saw at outrageous disloyalty. Nobody walked out on Abe Lastfogel, an icon of the profession! It was like insulting the Pope. My friend Fred Allen put it best: "You can stuff all the sincerity in Hollywood inside a flea's navel and still have room for eight caraway seeds and an agent's heart."

Cleo starred in her own Golden Book for children.

Anyway, despite delivering me to Burns, William Morris was never able to lure George back. And shortly thereafter, I left them, too. But George Burns and I remained friends until he reached 101.

And let's not forget how "Peoples Choice" launched one of Hollywood's great, albeit unknown, romances.

Yes. As I look back on my experiences working with beautiful actresses like Carole Lombard, Lucille Ball, Judy Garland, Betty Hutton, Myrna Loy, Ann-Margret—all were wonderful and very appreciative of my efforts. But Cleo was the only actress who ever licked my hand.

John Wayne Got Me Blacklisted

Hank: Irv, why are so many movie stars so short?
Irv: Maybe part of them was cut off by the agent.

On Brecher's ninety-third birthday, he raises a martini glass to a group of celebrants gathered around a table at the Water Grill in downtown Los Angeles. "I'm very happy to have been granted ninety-three big ones," he toasts. "But I would like to stick around to see America come alive again."

Brecher is convinced mankind is going crazy.

On my next visit he tells me about the last time he saw America go crazy.

In 1952, you had finished the movie *Somebody Loves Me*, right?

Yeah, and one day the co-producer of the picture, William Perlberg, showed me a book. Called *Red Channels*.

This was the book of names—

An anti-Communist smear. My named appeared in it. And my hatred 54 years later is still fresh as the poison ivy that I wished they had wrapped all those red-baiters with before they buried them. Which they should've done earlier. Much earlier. The fucking blacklist!

Who published *Red Channels*?

That shit state senator of California, Jack Tenney. He published hundreds of names, in his successful attempt to cause perfectly decent Americans to lose jobs, some their careers, some their families. Some even committed suicide. All a result of the House Un-American Activities Committee hearings, held by Tenney and the other son-of-a-bitch witch-hunters all over the country. But the worst was here in Hollywood. The book also mentioned Perlberg, his co-producer George Seaton and Gregory Peck among others. It seemed like anyone with a name in the industry who was even moderately active in liberal causes was in Tenney's witch-hunt.

And guess who was up front, fingering actors, writers, and directors? The brave, patriotic hero of Hollywood who went and fought three war films for his country. John Wayne, super-patriot who received several hundred thousand dollars per war—talk about your "combat pay." A hundred-and-thirty-eight percent America, saluted with a medal: the

Distinguished Double Cross. Wayne and Robert Taylor, Gary Cooper, Ward Bond. They were all part of testifying, smearing fellow performers with a brush handed to them by the paranoid Senator McCarthy, Richard Nixon, and God knows how many other ruthless and reckless self-appointed saviors taking bows with a flag stuck in their ass.

And you were blacklisted for being a communist?

Yes, but mine was an odd case. I came out lucky. What happened was, I was sitting with a really sweet man, Jo Swerling, who wrote the original script for "Guys and Dolls," which was partially rewritten by the talented Abe Burrows and became a smash hit on Broadway.

Jo and I were at his house in Beverly Hills, working on a play together called, "The Pink Beach." I got a call there from my agent Abe Lastfogel. He'd been looking for me to tell me that Bill Goetz, the man I'd worked with on the **Riley** movie, was buying the film rights to "Guys and Dolls." That is, Columbia Studios was buying it, and Goetz wanted me to write and direct it. That was strange to hear; I'm talking on the phone, I'm looking at my friend Swerling. I told my agent I'd love to do it, but I had to clear something up first. I hung up the phone and told Swerling. Only a doll like Jo would react to being snubbed—bypassed regarding his own creation—by being genuinely happy for me.

"Are you really sure that it wouldn't bother you?" I asked. It bothered me. Swerling, who had also once worked with the Marx Brothers, was that kind of gentle soul and friend who understood what the studio wanted: Never trust the playwright to translate his own words to the screen.

"I insist you take it," Jo said. "At least I know if you're doing the screenplay, you'll save a lot of my lines."

I was relieved. So Lastfogel took me to see the head of Columbia, Harry Cohn. He was a savvy picture-maker with the personality of a piranha and had made movies like **From Here to Eternity** and Frank Capra movies like **Mr. Smith Goes to Washington, Mr. Deeds Goes to Town**...

When we got to his office, Bill Goetz was there, quite excited about making **Guys and Dolls**.

"Don't I know you from someplace?" said Cohn after Lastfogel introduced me.

I said, "I was here several years ago when you asked me to write another **Jolson Story**. I said I was flattered, but told you I didn't think I could do anything to top the original film."

"Yeah," said Cohn. "But something else..." He turned to my agent. "Go downstairs and see Ben Kahane. Ask him what we heard about—what's your name—Brecher?"

Lastfogel, Goetz and I were puzzled. But we went down to see Kahane. He was head of business affairs and I knew him socially; we'd been in each other's homes.

"Harry said something about Brecher," my agent told him. "What's it all about?"

Kahane winced. A drawer was opened and shut. A dossier appeared. A single sheet of paper was pulled out and he handed it across the desk. On the paper appeared my name and under it, "List of Affiliations: Member of the Writer's Guild, member of the Hollywood Democratic Committee, contributor to Russian Relief." And below the list, in big red letters, I saw the words: "Loyalty Questionable."

I hit the ceiling. "Where did this come from?"

Kahane said John Wayne and Roy Brewer, who I knew to be the head of one of Hollywood's craft unions.

"Those vicious bastards! Slinging shit all over people who are better Americans than they are and their fucking smear group. I can't believe that anybody would think I was a commie!"

Lastfogel dragged me out of the office and tried to cool me down.

"Go home. Have a couple drinks. I'm gonna make some calls."

A few hours later, I heard from him.

"Listen, kid," Abe said. "I talked to one of the assholes in that gang. He said you can probably clear it all up by writing a letter. To Wayne, explaining why you were in those groups that they think are full of Reds. Make it plain that you're a loyal American."

"They can drop dead," I said.

"Easy, easy..."

"I won't do it."

"Don't cut your own throat," Abe said. "Unless you straighten it out you could wind up like a lotta others."

It was hard for me to write such a letter. The idea revolted me even more than finding out I existed on their hate list that the studio executives consulted to find out who not to hire.

I had nothing to hide from these hollow-headed menaces, unlike some writers. Actually, a few months earlier, one of the best writers I had on the "Riley" staff, Reuben Shipp, was dragged out of the studio by men from the FBI. Next I heard, he was deported to Canada for being a communist. His career was ruined. In the five or six years that Shipp wrote for my radio show, I never heard the man express anything that smacked of subversive ideas. If he had any, he was a better actor than the ones on the show.

But as long as this epidemic of idiocy continued in the country, I realized that if I ever wanted to do movies again, I'd have to knuckle under and write the letter.

"To the great patriotic Warner Brothers war hero Marion 'I'm braver than Errol Flynn' Morrison," I began.

"Cut it out," said Lastfogel. "You don't wanna inflame Wayne."

"No, but I'd like to set fire to him."

I swallowed my disgust and rewrote the letter, saying that my membership in these suspect groups was simply as a registered Democrat.

"I would also like to bring to your attention," I wrote, "that I was a contributor to 'Bundles for Russia,' a relief program supported by another person you may know: Eleanor Roosevelt. You may even recall her husband. He used to work in Washington."

The letter went out and two days later I got a call from Abe Lastfogel. One of Wayne's bootlickers had advised him that my "Loyalty Questionable" had been canceled. I was off the list.

They're not off mine.

Weeks later at the club, I ran into a producer named Sol Lesser. His name had been on the bottom of my "Loyalty Questionable" file at Columbia. "Information requested by Sol Lesser," it said. Lesser owned the *Tarzan* movies. The only business contact I had with him was when he asked me to write a script for a 3-D feature . This was a hot style, a form of film coming back into popularity. All it meant was you could see more of a lousy actor than before, and Lana Turner's tits took on a whole new dimension. I said to Lesser that I'd think about it. I could only assume that because he contemplated hiring me, he checked up on my Americanism. What really burned my ass is that neither Kahane or Lesser had the decency to tip me off about the list. That's what friends are for.

"Listen, you prick," I stopped him outside the Hillcrest men's room.

He seemed shocked. "What did you call me?"

"Sorry," I said. "*Mr.* Prick. You put me on Wayne's shit list!"

"I didn't mean anything," said Lesser. "I just wanted to be sure it was safe to hire you."

"Then why didn't you tell me I could be in danger?"

"I should have, but I was afraid you'd be mad at me."

"Why should I be mad? It could only put me out of business, that's all. But if you ever speak to me again, you better have a bodyguard."

I can be very tough when the other guy is smaller than I am. He simpered a bit and ran into the bathroom.

Meanwhile, the witch hunters kept hard at it, but all of these snakes like Tenney were eventually stepped on by their own chicanery. It was a joy to read one day that the head of the HUAC, Jay Parnell Thomas, went to jail for tax evasion. Even though he loved America! Cheating the America he had so valiantly been protecting.

And the Red Scare of that era finally ended in the late '50s.

Eventually. But not before the HUAC sent "The Hollywood Ten" to prison.

Well, that came earlier, in '48.

Yeah. And some of them had screen credits on the most fervent patriotic movies of the time like, *Pride of the Marines, Pride of the Navy* and other pictures hailing America's greatness. These were tremendous box office hits that brought huge profits to the studios. If this was how the secret communists planned to destroy capitalism, the CEOs of our corporations should hire more secret commies.

And whatever happened to the movie version of *Guys and Dolls?*

After all this, Columbia failed to acquire the rights to do it. They were outbid by Samuel Goldwyn and ***Guys and Dolls*** was written and directed by Joe Mankiewicz. In 1955.

The year I was born.

Mazel tov. Let's get a sandwich.

Jack Lemmon came by the set of *Sail a Crooked Ship* because he heard we were having so much fun.

Irving Brecher

Cry for Happy (1960)

> We see a Japanese cowboy on his horse,
> galloping along the dusty trail. He's chasing a
> bad guy and when they reach town, the villain
> quickly dismounts and ducks into a saloon. Our
> hero jumps off his horse and starts for those
> swinging doors. But halfway through them... he
> comes back outside and removes his cowboy boots.
>
> A scene in *Cry For Happy* (1960)

First of all, what does that mean?

What?

"Cry for happy." It seems really profound.

That comes from a Japanese expression for a feeling. A feeling of being overjoyed.

Overcome with emotion.

Sort of, yeah.

And the movie came from...

I adapted a paperback novel of the same title, written by George Campbell. He was a retired U.S. Navy Captain, writing about his time spent in Japan after World War Two with some fellow soldiers and a geisha. Glenn Ford and Donald O'Connor starred. Produced by Bill Goetz and directed by George Marshall. He had done a lot of comedies, for Laurel and Hardy, and W.C. Fields, and movies like **Never a Dull Moment** and **The Perils of Pauline**. He started in silent pictures. And Goetz was a friend of mine, as you know.

Son-in-law of Louis B. Mayer.

Ran the studio at Universal where I directed **The Life of Riley** motion picture.

Ran the studio?

And made a lot of flops.

And now he's at Columbia.

Studio heads move around a lot. He had his own production company. Anyway, Goetz called me in and said he bought the paperback.

Did Donald O'Connor dance? You had already worked with Fred

Astaire and Gene Kelly and—

No, but in one scene Donald O'Connor is on the make, gently trying to get someplace with Myoshi Umeki, the geisha who broke your heart as Red Buttons' wife in **Sayonara**. As O'Connor gets fairly amorous, his pretty target slips out of his embrace and through the curtain—the tatami—and into the safety of her night chamber. O'Connor is crushed, so he turns to the camera and says: "We won the war and lost the peace." The audience got it, naturally.

What do you mean?

A piece of hump! And the Sherlock office came after me.

You mean—

The industry censor. If they'd had their way the line wouldn't have been in the movie.

I said to him: "What's the matter with you? Since when is peace a dirty word. It's right there in the script: p-e-a-c-e. You have a dirty mind!"

What could they do? It was the biggest laugh in the movie.

The Gagman, going for the jocular!

Huh? It was shot for Cinemascope width, so when they compressed it into VHS, it cut off the sides so you get sometimes half a person.

But I went there. To Japan! For a month of good times in Tokyo and Kyoto.

For research on geisha.

It was the only movie I ever enjoyed doing research on. It was a lot better than sleeping overnight with the Marx Brothers.

We had a charming, Japanese Princeton grad as our consultant. The same fellow Goetz had worked with when he produced **Sayonara**. So we got special treatment. White men are rarely permitted to stay in "first-class" geisha houses, which catered to very select clientele. As opposed to the other type of house which keeps horny men happy.

So how was it?

We were there a couple nights.

No, I mean how was it being catered to by a "first-class" geisha?

First-class.

Come on.

They were really sweet and somewhat naïve. They asked a lot of questions, simple ones, about America.

Nice girls.

And very anxious to please. They did, several times.

Uh-huh.

Bathing, massage, etcetera. A lot of etcetera.

And then what happened?

The etcetera was the best part.... Then? I recall just before coming back, I bought a very new item they had—a transistor radio.

One of the little ones?

They were a sensation then.

That's it? Anything else you can tell readers about, you know?

Sayonara!

The Eternal Comedyship of Ernie Kovacs

"If there is any similarity between the
characters in this film and people who are now
living... they'd be better off dead."
- On screen as *Sail a Crooked Ship* FADES IN

Brecher is laughing because he just got two residual checks in the mail. One is $4.10, from German TV, for **Ziegfeld Follies** *of 1943. The other is for four cents from the Director's Guild of America. This is payment for a voiceover he did, the introduction to* **Sail a Crooked Ship**, *which Brecher directed at Columbia Studios in 1961. This picture starred Robert Wagner and Ernie Kovacs. Kovacs I knew as the pioneering genius of TV comedy in the 1950s, a quirky man with an incredible mind who had influence on Carson and Letterman and anyone who tries to push the medium creatively. I was very excited to ask Irv about the movie...*

You directed the brilliant Ernie Kovacs?

Yes, and he was predictably brilliant in *Sail a Crooked Ship*. Sadly, it was the last movie he ever made.

Why was that?

A week before the picture was to open, he was driving home from a New Year's Eve party at Billy Wilder's house... and he hit a telephone poll. In Century City. Where the Hilton Hotel is.

Yes yes, I'd read he was driving on Santa Monica Boulevard, leaning over to light a cigar or—

Nobody knows how it happened. He was alone, except for all the alcohol he had in his veins.

Oh my god. I loved him on TV. Percy Dovetonsils... all those outrageous characters.

Ernie Kovacs was one of our freshest, most novel comedians in early television. Wonderful and off the wall.

So when did this happen?

New Year's, 1962. The next week, the movie opened, but most of the potential audience shied away. Nobody wanted to go see a dead man in a comedy. Understandably. Ticket buyers who liked Kovacs didn't want to see him on screen while conscious that he was gone.

Wait. You were friends with Billy Wilder; were you at his house for that party?

No.

Where were you?

Oddly enough, I was in Chicago. And not because I hated the forced gaiety at New Year's Eve parties and was usually in bed a couple hours before the ball fell down in Times Square. But that night I was alone, at the Schubert Theater in Chicago. A Columbia producer, Fred Kohlmar, had asked me to write a shootable script of a Broadway play called "Bye Bye Birdie." I hadn't seen the show and it was on the road and closing its run on New Year's Eve in Chicago. So Kohlmar sent me to see it; I'll tell you about that later; you were asking about *Sail a Crooked Ship*.

Yes. Okay. I'd love to hear what your relationship was like with Kovacs.

First I'll tell you how the script happened. Ruth Brooks Flippen, the wife of comedian Jay C. Flippen—-

Jay C. Flippen from "McHale's Navy" and other TV shows.

I don't care about that. Please don't interrupt and I'll tell you about Ernie Kovacs. Ruth Brooks Flippen wrote and rewrote the script, with me in my office at Columbia in between set-ups on the set. When I think of it now, I get exhausted. But when it was happening, it was exciting and stimulating; obviously when you're young, you have the desire to do anything. Ruth did an excellent job. The movie has no gaps. Everything's moving all the time. No lulls, and in comedy, that's something you hope you can get. Ernie Kovacs plays Bugsy Fogelmeyer, a bird-brained bank robber in Boston. Only he plans his getaway, you see, by sea.

On a crooked ship of some kind.

It was a small picture. We made it up day to day as funny as we could. Robert Wagner was particularly great. Frankie Avalon, the singer, was in it. Frank Gorshin...

Frank Gorshin! He does a one-man show about George Burns now.

I don't care about that. There was lots of comic business from Harvey Lembeck and Sid Tomack and Jesse White. I know, you want to tell me about Jesse White now...

Hilarious actor. Never mind the Maytag repairman ads.

I wrote a vaudeville act at one time for Sid Tomack. It was called "Reese Tomack and Reese." They were all comedians and the two Reeses made Tomack the patsy.

Do you remember the act?

It was so fucking long ago! In vaudeville the acts were only four minutes, nine minutes at the most. It was no big bulk to write, so I don't remember them.

Okay, so let's get back to Kovacs.

You know how some people, especially babies, have security blankets? Ernie Kovacs had one. He carried it with him every time I saw him when he wasn't in front of a camera. It was a big box of Cuban cigars, which were illegal contraband. But that didn't phase him. Ernie was obviously an addicted law-breaker.

I eventually became very fond of him. But it wasn't easy. Kovacs, I was told by one of my spies, was very unhappy when told that I was directing. He didn't know me. He had no reason to believe a stranger could direct him as well as one of his friends like Richard Quine could. Quine directed him in **Operation Mad Ball**, with Jack Lemmon and Mickey Rooney. I mean, Kovacs was a TV guy doing more films now and he was popular. Columbia wanted David Miller to direct, but he wanted a hundred-and-twenty-five thousand dollars because he'd had a couple successes. They couldn't handle it. Since I was anxious to direct, I took twenty-five thousand. I didn't really need the money; George Burns and I had just sold "Peoples Choice" for a million dollars.

Anyway, the resistance I felt from Kovacs came the very first day of shooting. He stopped short of being rude but his manner made me feel uncomfortable and unwanted.

Bob Wagner, the star, was the opposite. Here was a pleasant, light-hearted young man who I thought had reason to be: he was married to the darling Natalie Wood.

But with Kovacs acting very distant, I tried to win him over. Early on we were rehearsing a scene in the wheelroom of an old Liberty ship. This was all on a set at Columbia. Bugsy Fogelmeyer has a floozy girlfriend played by Carolyn Jones [Morticia in "The Addams Family"]. They're on this hijacked ship together and Bugsy is in charge of a gang of bankrobbers. Carolyn Jones comes into the wheelhouse where Kovacs is barking out orders to his navigator. Beautiful Carolyn Jones, she's wearing the slinkiest of black gowns, looking very seductive. Bugsy hugs her. And we see that her gown is cut in the back, revealing a lot of naked skin all the way down to her... what do you call it? Her coccyx. Bugsy gets his hands moving all over her bare back. And happily, I thought of a line to give him that wasn't in the script: "Baby, aint you got this dress on backwards?"

After I threw him the line, Ernie flashed his big smile.

"Perfect. I wish I'd said that."

"You will," I said. "When you see the movie."

The minute I gave him that line, things changed. From then on, he was a real pleasure. We started playing gin rummy in my dressing room in between set-ups. And as good as he was as a comedian, the reverse was true of his gin rummy. He was one of the few people I could consistently beat at the game. He was that bad. I insisted on keeping the stakes low because, avaricious as I am, playing Kovacs was like stealing.

"Keep my tab, we'll clear it up as soon as I get even," he said cheerfully. That never happened. But knowing Ernie and his outlook on life and people, it was worth tearing up the tab. And more. He was fun to know.

For Christmas he sent me a basket of premium whiskey and a book, "How to Play Gin Rummy."

Sail a Crooked Ship has a funny conclusion I'll tell you about. You never expect tits to solve their problem. What do I mean by that? Bob Wagner is a captive on board as the ship tries to escape to sea. He is locked in a cabin with his girlfriend, played by Dolores Hart. A Coast Guard cutter comes along and demands through a bullhorn that Bugsy identify his ship. Which Kovacs ignores of course. So Wagner attempts to alert the Coast Guard. In desperation, he tries to knock out their searchlight by throwing steel ball bearings through his porthole. He's pitching these ball bearings (the ship is lousy with them because Captain Kovacs thinks he's Commander Queeg in **The Caine Mutiny**), but it doesn't work, so he asks his girlfriend for help. She takes off her bra. And while she holds the elastic ends of the bra on either side of the porthole window, Wagner uses it as a slingshot. He fires off several steel balls that miss. Finally he hits the Coast Guard searchlight. The Coast Guard comes aboard. End of Bugy's criminal career.

Kovacs was a big talent. A big loss. He was a big, extremely likeable and refreshingly different funnyman.

*There is a photograph hanging in Brecher's study of Irv standing with Robert Wagner. On the back of the picture frame, Wagner wrote: "One of the highlights of my career was making **Sail a Crooked Ship** with you, Irv. And of course, more importantly, our friendship. I love you always."*

What a lovely thing.

Yes, he's such a lovely person. Totally unusual, in my experience. I just watched the movie again when Bob brought me a video of it. He was perfect in his leading role and to see it took me back to pleasant days. I enjoyed seeing what I was involved in. Working with Wagner was one of the better experiences I had as a director. And we've kept in touch ever since he took advantage of Dolores Hart's tits. As for the beautiful Dolores? Shortly after the release of the movie, she became a nun. I hope the convent has cable TV so the other nuns can see her take off her bra.

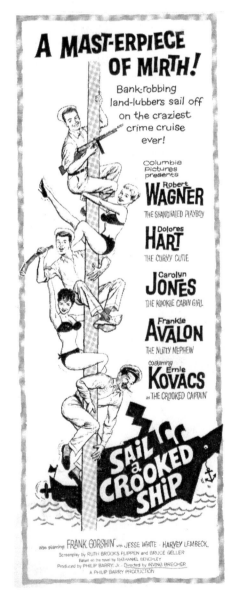

Irving Brecher

PHOTO OF ROBERT WAGNER WITH IRV ON THE SET:

In *Sail a Crooked Ship*, Robert Wagner tried his first role as a comedian. He was great—he made me look good as a director. Here the director is telling his leading man he'll never become a California governor because he doesn't grope the actresses on the set. (Photo by Bill Crespinel)

Bye Bye Brecher?

> Maureen Stapleton: Don't try to pay me back,
> son. I forgive you. So what if you're an
> ingrate? So long as you're happy.
> Dick Van Dyke: I don't wanna be happy! I wanna
> be married.
> - *Bye Bye Birdie*

Late one night, I catch the tail end of Bye Bye Birdie *on an old 9-inch black and white TV. Happily transported back to 1963, I think of my sisters who were teenyboppers in the '60s going ga-ga at this Conrad Birdie guy in his oozed-on, gold-lame greaser suit shaking that Elvis pelvis to woo Ann-Margret. She played fifteen year-old "Kim MacAfee" of Sweet Apple, Ohio. And oh how my sisters flipped for that famous chorus-as-partyline telephone tune scene—Jill and Nancy with their own "Princess" line always singing, "What's the story, morning glory?/What's the word, hummingbird?" and "He's in love with Kim/Kim's in love with him!/Goin' steady, goin's steady/Goin' steady" like the kids onscreen. Then came "One Last Kiss" before Conrad's conscription ("It never felt like this/ Oh! Oh! Oh!"), broadcast on national TV of course ("Ed Sullivan! We're gonna be on Ed Sullivan!"), and giggling at Paul Lynde in his nutsy-cuckoo youth as Kim's daddy MacAfee, shrieking, "What's the matter with kids today?" as everything is flipping off and out of control around him.*

Anyhoo, by this time, Brecher's old studio system had flipped out too. Like a lot of the culture, studio films looked like a real drag compared to what was starting to happen in the counterculture. This was Brecher's last musical, a satire on rock-and-roll, protest marches, media madness, and better living through chemistry, all kicked into high gear by Dick Van Dyke's pre-Rob Petrie, pre-Mr. Fantastic, elastic physical shtick. Did I mention Ann-Margret? Oh! Oh! Oh!

I can still see her onstage in Las Vegas...

Irv, in *Bye Bye Birdie* Ann-Margret is dancing a music video over the credits. It's like twenty years ahead of its time.

I got a kick out of doing that picture. Ann-Margret is the thing that made it bigger than it might have been. I recommended her to Fred Kohlmar, the producer.

You discovered Ann-Margret.

We were very very lucky in casting her. I had seen her in Las Vegas when my wife and I went up there in 1962 to see George Burns perform, I think it was at the Sands or the Sahara.

Wait. Was this the same time in 1962, you'd just seen the play in Chicago, the night Ernie Kovacs died?

No, no. Let me explain it to you. When I came back from that trip to see "Bye Bye Birdie" in Chicago, I agreed to make the movie. Fred Kohlmar promised that he would make a deal for me to direct it. Kohlmar had run *Sail a Crooked Ship* and was impressed with it.

But the "Birdie" you saw didn't have Ann-Margret.

No, but several movie scripts had been written, one by Mike Stewart, the original playwright. But Kohlmar told me none of them were considered good enough to shoot. Columbia had been sitting on a very expensive property and was very anxious to get a profitable film made.

I read the play had five writers before Mike Stewart.

Well, when I saw the play, it was easy to understand why it had been such a big hit. Excellent songs and choreography, and some nice comic performances by a new face, Dick Van Dyke, and a talented Chita Rivera. But the last part was flat and predictable. It was devoid of any big laugh comedy. I knew it needed something radical. So on the flight back, I went into a type of self-hypnosis that helped me come up with the changes.

Like you went into at MGM, a trance to conjure scenes for the Marx Brothers?

No, different. Anyway, when I came back and said I'd do it, Fred Kohlmar offered me a hundred-thousand dollars and that verbal promise to direct. When I was about two-thirds through with the script, he came to me with a very troubled look and with great embarrassment. He told me he couldn't sign me to direct because the higher-ups insisted that George Sidney do it. Sidney was an experienced director who had been paid big numbers for a different picture that had been abandoned. So they wanted Sidney to shoot *Birdie* for no money to wipe out what they already paid him! I was mad—not at Sidney, he was a friend—and momentarily I was tempted to walk. I was even thinking of suing them, demanding an injunction against their using the part of the script I had completed, full of all sorts of wild notions.

But you didn't walk.

I could have stopped everything, but they had my idea about how to end the picture by now. So in the end, and because Kohlmar and I had been friends for quite a while, I gave up and finished the script.

And now comes Ann-Margret? Sex kitten of me youth, on the telephone with her legs in the air?

Whoa, darling. She came onstage in Vegas before George Burns performed. This kid, a real beauty and a damned good singer. And we were casting and coming up empty in the key role of the ingenue who has a boyfriend but falls for Birdie, the Elvis character. I told Fred that I'd seen the perfect girl and if she could act a little, she was a real possibility. He arranged to have the girl flown down and brought to the studio. She came in nervous and excited and adorable and Kolhmar told her a little about the script and suggested she read a scene or two with me doing the other characters.

Just like you read with Judy Garland for *Meet Me in St. Louis*.

Well, Judy didn't want the part. Ann-Margret sure did. There was nothing to this. Almost instantly you knew this kid was good. The movie proved it; she became a star overnight. She went on to do great dramatic roles in movies like **Carnal Knowledge** with Jack Nicholson.

And she was great in *Tommy*...

And *The Cincinnati Kid*...sexy.

To this day! *Grumpy Old Men*...*Grumpier Old Men*...

Like who could ask for anything more?

How did you like George Sidney directing?

George Sidney did not like the script, but he got the hots for Ann-Margret.

She was twenty-one at the time she played Kim.

The rumor was, it caused his marriage to break up.

I read Paul Lynde's autobiography and he says that he and Maureen Stapleton—who played Dick Van Dyke's mother and kept sticking her head in an oven to make him feel guilty—were the only ones on the set who didn't try to fuck her. Ann-Margret, I mean.

I didn't.

Well, there ya go.

So much for *his* memoir.

Ha! And how did you get Ed Sullivan in the movie, playing himself?

Ed wasn't in the play but I knew him from my days in New York. His newspaper column used to run some of my jokes, in the '30s. Whenever he came out west, Groucho would entertain him. Anyway, he was out here with his TV show and I added that part for the film.

I can't believe George Sidney didn't like the script.

I heard he was not crazy about it. But he was crazy about Ann-Margret.

So he took a shot at both.

Ha!

The smash hit that *Bye Bye Birdie* became revived George's sagging career. That was okay with me because I liked him. The movie got some very favorable reviews. Not only raves for Ann-Margret, but for Paul Lynde, one of my favorite funnymen. He came from the Broadway production and it was his first picture. He got a hundred-percent out of every line I wrote for him. I liked where lovesick Dick Van Dyke, heading to a bar, asks Lynde to come along and Lynde says, "I'd like to go with you, but I'm a happily married man. I'm not allowed to enjoy myself."

Lynde was so great. He died much too young. He was a gay actor who was so entertaining that I think even homophobes would've loved him.

Irv, I read where the composer Charles Strouse called *Bye Bye Birdie*, the first rock and roll musical. You have a line in there where Janet Leigh says: "The world is changing." Did you see it signaling that kind of cultural shift?

Well, Conrad Birdie is going into the army, the women are marching on Washington and the mayor of Sweet Apple can't keep his wife's legs from spreading when she hears that music.

I guess music, youth, politics. Do you think it was in touch with a late '50s, early '60s *zeitgeist*?

I added Russian ballet.

That wasn't in the Broadway version?

No. But the Charles Strouse-Lee Adams songs were. Numbers like "Put on a Happy Face" were sublime. Did I tell you Carl Reiner said he first saw an unknown Dick Van Dyke in his first part as Albert in *Bye Bye Birdie* and hired him for television.

The Dick Van Dyke Show!

Yeah.

Wow. And how about Albert's gal? The scene where she's in that short, tassled skirt coming on to those Shriners...

Janet Leigh. I thought she was a nice girl, but it was bad casting. Her body was sensational at one time. By the time she got to play Rosie, she had lost it.

Aw, come on, Irv. "Put on a Happy Face" and [Sings] "Me and little Rosie..."

[Sings] "We will be so cozy..." Yeah.

Yeah!

No. She was over the hill physically. But you see, those bastards at

Columbia, they didn't want to use Chita Rivera from the stage show. Rivera was a fabulous broad. I wanted her, but I was not in charge. They wouldn't use a Latin woman. It might upset the racists.

Well, her name was Rose Alvarez. So much for what we said about cultural shift...

Yeah.

But Dick Van Dyke. Albert Peterson, he's the hero who saves the day.

Yeah.

And this is where you say you saved the picture?

Well, it's probably the best example of my adapting a movie because I took a script that was not shootable and saved them a bundle. I told them it had to have a bang-bang ending. It needed to conclude on a humorous note.

You changed the ending.

First I changed Dick Van Dyke from an English teacher to a chemistry professor. Now he could invent something called a "Speed Up" pill. In one scene he demonstrates it on a pet turtle belonging to Paul Lynde's kid.

Randolph MacAfee.

His turtle. Van Dyke feeds him the pill and the turtle races around the house. That made it possible for Albert and his girlfriend to feed the same drug to the conductor of the Russian ballet. And knowing where I was going, I enjoyed writing the script.

The whole thing ends up on national television.

The Ed Sullivan show sequence. Part of his lineup that night was the Moscow Ballet Company, doing a scene from "Swan Lake." With just a few minutes left on the Sullivan show, Albert needed to do something to make sure there was enough time for the big farewell kiss planned between Conrad Birdie and Kim MacAfee, the fifteen year-old from Sweet Apple. So Rosie drops some of the drug into a glass of milk she gives to the Soviet conductor. When he takes the podium we see one of his eyes do a crazy wiggle. Suddenly he starts increasing the tempo with his baton, which causes the symphony to speed up, which forces the ballet performers to pick up the pace. The studio audience gets hysterical, too, and it turns into a riot.

Yes! The anarchic comedy again..!

Kim kisses Conrad Birdie, and Bobby Rydell punches him in the nose—and pandemonium. Finally, we wrap up the love stories and other loose ends. You know, George Sidney was the one who told the Turner Archives Project about me.

No. Really?

Which was nice of him.

Here I am hating this guy for taking your director job on *Birdie*, when in fact if not for Sidney, I'd never have met you in that hotel suite in Century City.

Not only that, but his father was the guy at the Capitol Theatre in New York who threw out the jokes that I wrote for Milton Berle.

He kept appearing in your life. And then you worked with his son. I like how that comes full circle.

By '62, his son was forty-nine and I was forty-eight.

You say it revived his career. How about your own?

That was it for me. My life turned into a day-to-day struggle.

That was it for the movies?

A few years later, I was supposed to write and direct the film of Neil Simon's play, "Star-Spangled Girl." But the producer Howard Koch said the head of Paramount, Robert Evans, thought I was too old. I got so disgusted.

I don't know if you know this Irv, but *Variety* ran a story about a proposed remake of *Bye Bye Birdie*.

On television.

No, this is for the big screen.

Any mention in *Variety* that it was already a popular movie?

Nope. No mention. Just how they had some director fresh out of USC who was going to make a hip-hop version of the original musical, aimed at younger moviegoers.

You make sure to tell Variety that the original screenwriter is available!

Hey, Irv.

What, kid?

[Sings] "Grey skies are gonna clear up..."

[Sings] "Put on a happy face."

[Sings] "Brush off the clouds and cheer up..."

Yeah. Put on a happy face.

Yeah.

Oh that picture was a smash...

Newspaper advertisement, 1963

Part V
Irv Brecher in the 21st Century

l-r: Nancy Bennett (my niece), Norma, me, Hank, outside WGA Auditorium.

Jan Murray Takes a Bash

> Hank: Do you remember the first time you did
> stand-up?
> Irv: It was for a stag at Hillcrest. In '43. For
> an MGM lawyer named Isadore Prinzmettle. I
> remember Yip Harburg singing a parody of a song
> in a new musical called Oklahoma: 'Ev'rything's
> Up To Date in Vulva City.'

The first time I saw Irv Brecher do live stand-up was at the 85th birthday of his pal Jan Murray, held at the Improv on Melrose Avenue in Hollywood. A dozen stand-ups fought for stagetime to shout out salutes to the great Murray Janovsky, a tummler who went from the top of the Catskills to the top hotels on the Vegas strip. Jan had a brilliant nightclub act and was also the first comedian to ever host a game show on daytime TV. (He did about six of those, from "Dollar a Second" to "Treasure Hunt.") I met him at Morey Amsterdam's funeral, caught up with him again at Buddy Hackett's funeral, and used to watch him emcee the L.A. Chabad Telethon, which he did it for eighteen years. Irv said Jan and Toni Murray hosted the best Passover seder in town—"It was a hot ticket! Sid Caesar would get up and do the Four Questions, each in a different style of gibberish." I did a Q & A with Murray for a funny new magazine called Heeb, *and he was not happy about that name. Neither was Irv.*

But Murray's bash turned out to be a big night for Brecher.

"It's so crowded," said his delightful wife Norma. "The walls are bulging!" She sat in the Improv's main room, crunched at a table with Friar's Club and Hollywood friends of Jan's—Sid Caesar, Shecky Green, Louis Nye, Red Buttons. Younger comics like Jimmy Brogan and Max Alexander got up and then of course, their elders went on... and on, but I ate it up, right, because Irv invited me. Finally, maybe two hours into the show, Budd Friedman, founder of the Improv, introduced him:

"Our next comedian who's gonna come up here... just had an eye operation. He's written countless films over the last fifty years. Ladies and gentlemen, Mr. Irv Beckman!"

Buttons helped steer Brecher to the stage. 87, blind in his right eye and post-surgery that tried to save the sight in his left, Irv reached the microphone stand. He tucked his cane under one arm and fumbled with some 3-by-5 cards before dropping them all over the stage. The two hundred people in the house didn't know whether to laugh—were they taking pity?—but the man was ready to take them on:

I made some notes but I can't read them.
[First laugh.]

I'm very happy to be here with Jan and Toni and their beautiful extended family.

Of all the great comedians I've known... and worked with... Jan is perhaps the softest, gentlest, and kindest of them all. And the laughter I heard tonight... I thought it was the greatest two days of laughs I've ever had. [He's out of the gate.]

Yes, I did just have eye surgery. I knew I needed it when the other morning, I woke up and my vision was so bad, I couldn't find my hearing aid. [And gone!]

Anyway, I think it was a good idea to have this close to Cedars-Sinai Hospital.

Jan, congratulations on your birthday.

I was 85, three operations ago.

And I think it's a great tribute that the comedians who live here... all of them wanted to come out. You know, comedians come to big roasts because they want to be seen. But to come to a small, second-rate show like this... it means that Jan Murray is paying for their dinner.

Jan, I remember on your 80th birthday, you invited a lot of us to Palm Springs to the Sheraton. And Toni told us you're planning to take her down there to recover from tonight's forgettable experience...

Let me caution you. Palm Springs has changed since you were last there. And not for the better. It used to be a sleepy, lazy town, but now it's become very commercial. A big city.

Except for one thing: it still attracts people who are looking for eternal youth.

For example, my wife and I were strolling down Palm Drive one afternoon.

We're approached by a woman who might be in her sixties.

The way she's dressed... we can see she's evidently a hooker.

And she's using a walker.

She says, "Hello, big boy."

I said, "Excuse me, may we pass?"

She says, "What's your hurry? How about a little party?"

I said, "You got your nerve. Can't you see I'm with my wife?"

She says, "We can make it for three. It's only fifty dollars."

I said, "There's no way... my wife won't give me that money!"

And we shove past her.

The next day I was alone. And she never showed up.

I needed to cool off so I dropped into a coffee shop and ordered a cold drink.

I was sitting at the counter... when out of nowhere, a slick-looking young man comes over to me. He says, "Sir, you don't know me and I don't know you. But you look like an intelligent businessman. And I have a business proposition you can't afford to miss."

That was annoying.

I said, "I'm not interested in any proposition. I just wanna finish my drink."

But he was stubborn.

"I can see the way you're dressed, I'm sure you're affluent. And I'm sure you're smart enough to recognize a bargain."

I was getting mad. "What bargain?"

He says, "A cemetery crypt. At Palm Springs Memorial Gardens."

"A crypt?" I practically screamed at him. "Are you crazy? I don't even live in Palm Springs. I only come down here two weeks a year."

"Perfect," he says. "This is a time-share. You spend a couple weeks in the winter in the crypt in Palm Springs. And say you have relatives in New York who miss you. We ship you there. Or any other place you choose. Next year, we're planning a cruise..."

I said, "Listen you son-of-a-bitch, you must be out of your mind."

He said, "And it's a steal. Only three thousand dollars."

I said, "I know I'm old. But just being old doesn't mean I'm an idiot. You're insulting my intelligence."

I got it for two thousand.

From the laughter and applause greeting the punchline, it was clear Irv had annihilated them. A couple friends of mine who do comedy for a living came over to tell him they enjoyed his act.

"Irv," said one. "I liked your story about the crypt. I thought you were going to say it was a 'tomb-share' instead of a time-share."

"No," he said.

"You might wanna use that," she told him. "Tomb-share."

"Never make a joke on a joke," he snapped. "Time-share is what they understand. If you start them thinking, you blow it."

Later, Irv was telling us how Jan was one of the finest "anecdotal comedians" ever, and, "a match for his great friend, another brilliant storyteller, Danny Thomas. For your information those two were the best in the long form. The hunks. Stories."

Meanwhile, Norma gushed. "All these young ones kept running over to him," she told me with an affectionate pride. "Like the last one, what was his name, the young comedian?"

"Vinnie," said Irv.

"Vinnie," she nodded. "He was at Irv's feet. And he was funny. He was a funny comedian."

"Oh, he got screams," said Irv.

"But I thought the most interesting," she continued, "was Saul Turteltaub."

Turteltaub, a TV and film producer, remarked, "This is a giant in our industry and how come I don't know about him?"

"That's very nice," said Irv.

Brecher said he didn't care too much for the venue, however. "It's oppressive. It's dark and dingy."

Norma says Irv is grumpy by impulse. But really, he's jello.

"Well," she nudged her husband. "The owner said, if you ever want a gig you're always welcome here."

"That's all I need," said Brecher.

But in a flash, after sighting Improv owner Friedman a table away, he fired away: "Budd! I may take you up on that. But if you ever introduce me again, please use MY name."

Friedman looked puzzled.

"And fuck Beckman!"

The following week, Army Archerd's column in Variety ran this item:

"The giants of comedy were on hand for Jan Murray's birthday to give their all and tell all. Buddy, Shecky, Sid, Red Buttons even dropped his pants for laughs. The guests of Toni Murray included the funnyman Tom Poston, his bride Suzanne Pleshette, Carl Reiner, Cyd Charisse, Tony Martin, Monty Hall and Nanette Fabray. Veteran writer Irving Brecher noted that it was a good idea to hold the event at the Hollywood Improv, close to Cedars-Sinai. Brecher announced that he too was 85, "three operations ago."

Brecher Plays Cedars

"To Sunday dinner on the old plantation: Chicken
okra, cohn pone, sho'tnin' bread, pickled
wootamelon and a stomach pump!"
— Groucho as as S. Quentin Quale in *Go West*

In the years I've been following Brecher to various performances, spasmodically taping or scribbling the retortage of my mercurial-minded friend, I've observed him in different habitats: his club and his home, of course. But also at the Directors Guild, the Writers Guild, the Hollywood Arclight Cinema, the Los Angeles County Museum of Art, the Jules Stine Eye Institute at UCLA, the Westside Pavilion, Hillside cemetery, Langer's Deli, the Shanghai Grill. But after dozens of recordings of Irv's act, this was the first time I ever watched him do stand-up in hospital.

I guess I should consider myself lucky that the first time I step foot in Cedars-Sinai Hospital is to see a comedy routine. In October 2006, Brecher was invited by Fred Kahn, his former doctor (now retired) to be guest lecturer at the monthly luncheon of the "Doctors Emeritus Society." These were retired physicians who had spent their careers at Cedars, the famous medical center in Beverly Hills, just off George Burns Boulevard. When I quoted the famous S.J. Perelman line: "I don't know anything about medicine, but I know what I like," Irv fired back: "As much as I don't like hospitals, I'll take the job."

"When do we get started?" he asks.

"After everybody stops going up for more," Dr. Kahn tells him.

We're seated around a table of eight Society members plus Norma and Fred, in the Harvey Morse Room, a conference hall at Cedars. There are ten other tables just like ours, half-full of elder practitioners partaking of fish sticks and oatmeal cookies from a cold lettuce buffet. Fred says the men usually hear talks on subjects like pain or urology, or sometimes a marine biologist will relate new stories about Darwin. I'm wondering what they'll make of a guy who tells stories about Harpo Marx playing golf with no pants on.

"Is somebody gonna take away the dishes while I'm talking?" asks Irv. "Because if he walks around like that, I'm going home."

"Stay right here, Irv," says Fred. "No one's going to do anything. Besides, it's a buffet."

The coordinator of the Emeritus group, Sylvia Stern, comes over to tell Irv this is the biggest crowd they've ever had and mentions "the famous urologist" attending the event. While she kibitzes, I take in the room. Harvey Morse is vast, like a high school gymnasium, and marked by a mural running the length of an entire wall called, "Jewish Contributions to Medicine." It starts with a giant Moses at one end in beautiful and respectful tones of sweeping greens and browns, and progresses through a history of Jews who won the Nobel Prize or were inventors of miraculous drugs. I write down the names of colossal and colossally-accomplished women I wish I'd learned about in school: Rosalyn Yalow, Rita Levi-Mantalcini, Gertrude Elion, Gerty Coro.

Then I turn to Irv.

"What would you say have been your contributions to medicine as a Jew?"

"The money I spent in drugstores."

That's enough of a warm-up for Irv the Nerve. Every time I've seen him, he's had a great record when it came to public speaking—making audiences laugh while remaining deadpan, never laughing at his own jokes. But since losing so much of his vision, he's appeared even more anxious.

"Irv! Irv!"

He looks around for the sound. "Who's that... is that Jan?"

Jan Murray has arrived, with his friend and doctor, Jack Matloff.

"How are you Jan?" asks Irv.

"I'm all right. I passed away three days ago."

Jan tells me he gets a kick watching his pal perform; he's seen Irv, "in action thirty, forty years already."

But he doesn't do his polished nightclub act anymore. Crippling asthma knocked him out of the spotlight, he says. "For about ten minutes I'm all right. And then I'm gasping. You can't ask the public to spend money to see an old Jew gasping. It's not nice."

When I tell him I think Irv is nervous, Jan says then for fun he will, "do to Irv what Milton Berle used to do to me: sit right up front. First row. When I played New York, I'd come out and see Berle sitting there and I wanted to die from nerves. I was a kid! Here is a guy right in front of me that I know knows every joke. Knows everything! And instead of worrying about the audience, I'm worrying about this yutz here."

As Fred Kahn, at the podium, begins to introduce Brecher, Jan waves a hand at me, whispering loudly: "What is Irv worried? He'll kill 'em for crissake."

"...was his friend Groucho Marx who called him, 'the wicked wit of the West.' And as you saw on the brochure we mailed to your homes, he has performed for the Friar's Club, at Hillcrest, and at big fundraisers... so it is with great pleasure that I ask Irv Brecher to come up..."

Norma and I help him up, first untangling his sports jacket from his chair, and using his four-wheeled walker—Norma calls it, "the Rolls"—he manages to push himself thirty feet to the lectern. In my mind this takes forever—the applause has died down by now—but like a horse at the starting gate at Santa Anita, Brecher settles in. Leaning to rest on the dais, he pulls out some 5 by 7 inch cards with notes scrawled on them in black magic-marker. Clearing his throat twice...

This is the first time I've gone to a doctor, where the doctor hasn't kept ME waiting.

[No response. Strange. In all the stand-ups I've seen, he always got an opening laugh.]

This is not the first time I've been to this hospital. I'm happy that today I was able to get here using a walker. The last time I was here, I was on a gurney.

[Silence. Perhaps the retired physicians can't hear him? Anyway, if it's a surprise, he doesn't tip it off.]

I have the highest regard for medical men. And particularly, I have gratitude for Dr. Kahn, who took care of me for over fifty years. If it weren't for his skills, I wouldn't be standing here today.
You see I don't drive.
He brought me here.

[One or two titters; one comes from Norma. I'm laughing inside because he is fumbling to see his cards, which throws off his timing.]

But the world has changed. Doctors really
cared about their patients. I remember the
time when you phoned the doctor and he would
come over in a matter of minutes. The new young
breed of doctor is too busy, waiting for the
Triple A mechanic to get his Mercedes started
so he can get to the golf course by tee time.
The only time the doctor will make a house call
is if you're having a dinner party.

[A single loud guffaw splits the air. It's
from Jan Murray. Suddenly, I get a crushing
feeling: this is Brecher's last gig.]

I know you're out there. I hear breathing. But
it's probably mine...

[His face brushes up against the microphone
and the sound booms to distortion.]

Is this the Harvey Morse room or the Harvey
Morgue room!!

[The Emeritus Society stares at him. They seem
to listen politely, those that are still awake.]

I want to thank you for the warm reception
you were thinking of giving me.
    But apparently changed your mind.

[Enjoying his own anger. He's on a roll now.]

But I have a high appreciation, especially
for you who are gathered here.
    I know that you are all retired and I thank
you for that.
    By retiring, you've obviously saved hundreds
of lives.

[Big laughs come from Jan, Norma, Fred and a few ordinary civilians.]

Fred? Fred, I wanna thank you for inviting me. This is the first time I've ever been to a Jewish wake.
By the way, if anybody wants to hear any of the stuff I did, call me.
I'll read it to you over the phone.

[Some laughter and applause. It's all over in ten minutes.]

"That was very good," says Dr. Kahn, after we get Irv safely back down from the dais. "They really did enjoy it."

"No they didn't," says Irv. "They're half-asleep. And half-senile."

Fred tells Irv that the Emeritus Society members won't remember any of this by the next meeting.

"Yeah," Irv says to that. "The nice thing about speaking to a group like this after a week of working on the material, is you can use it again the next time."

Jan Murray comes over with a big smile.

"Jan," Irv says to him. "They're not an audience. They're a jury!"

"No no..." says Jan. "I didn't tell you this before you laid an egg; I didn't want you to be nervous."

"Didn't tell me what?"

"If you had four doctors in a regular audience, they'd shriek at you. But a whole room of doctors? No chance. A whole room of lawyers, or accountants. No chance."

Irv tilts his head at this. "I think you're right, Jan."

"I know I'm right. When they're all the same, they understand nothing."

"You're absolutely right."

"Hey, I have sixty-five years experience doing this, kid."

"Yeah."

"I came off the road where I played mammoth theaters. Killed them night after night, I slaughtered them. But a convention in Palm Springs, every time it was a solid group, I bombed. Didn't get one fuckin' laugh. I think they wanted to be paid for their time. The same as these schmucks that were here today. Irv, I wouldn't worry about them. Just don't play to these kinds of audiences."

"Now you tell me."

On the way out, I ask Jan if he ever played Cedars-Sinai.

He says: "Do you know how many rooms I've played in sixty-five years? Think I remember if I worked this room? I remember the emergency room here, that's what I remember."

"I should never have done Cedars," says Irv, still angry afterwards at Junior's where we've come for soup. "They don't laugh unless they're reimbursed by Medicare."

Wicked.

I say "Gee whizz and here I thought it was a good sign when I got a parking space right outside the hospital on George Burns Boulevard."

"Well, it's okay," Brecher blows ahead of me as usual. "People like George Burns knew, we're fucking dying and we might as well make some fun of it."

Jack Benny of the Mounties

Irv, you seemed kind of nervous before the Cedars gig.
Totally nervous, going in. But after doing a standup, I feel elated. And relieved. After, it's a great feeling, and to hear the laughter, too... but right before, terribly nervous. I don't suppose that would ever change. Jack Benny told me he trembled every time he walked on stage. And that was thousands of times.

I loved Jack Benny. My parents loved him. I think my grandparents loved him first.
The sweetest, most unassuming man, and a gigantic star.

We even had him in our games as kids. We'd say: "Wanna penny? Go kiss Jack Benny!"
Yeah?

Where did you meet?
We didn't kiss.

I don't know what that game was even about, now...
I first met Jack on Broadway in New York, when I was hungry. Milton Berle introduced us. It was outside Lindy's restaurant and I was living hand-to-mouth, trying to write for the vaudevillians. Any vaudeville act who had ten dollars. And there were lots of them.

I was in awe when we met because it was my dream to one day write for Jack Benny's "Jell-O Hour." I think I blurted out how much I enjoyed his radio show. He was very gracious. Berle mentioned that I did some writing for him. Jack nodded approvingly and went on his way.

And then you went into Lindy's with Milton and Henny Youngman came in with corned beef hidden in his pants.
No, but I made it a point, when I could, to be seen with Berle, because that gave me some small stature with the vaudeville actors that hung around Lindy's. Just being there gave THEM, they hoped, membership in the big time.

1935?
1934, '35.

'36?
'34. Because it was four years later that I met Jack Benny again, in Los Angeles. I had just been brought over to MGM by Mervyn Leroy and after doing some work on *The Wizard of Oz*, I think I told you, MGM

had a radio show...

"MGM Good News." At Metro. 1938.

The producer L.K. Sidney wanted me to write a weekly guest spot and I got a kick when he said Jack Benny would be on the upcoming program. And I wrote a ten-minute piece where Jack would talk about music with Meredith Willson, the show's orchestra leader and a very good straight man. It got a lotta laughs, particularly about Benny's fake braggadocio regarding his skill as a violinist. Ridiculing the lack of talent of virtuosos like Yehudi Menuin, Jascha Heifetz—

Irv, why do you think so many of the greatest violinists were Jewish?

Nobody knows. Jewish parents in Europe may have been hungry and victims of pogroms but they all believed that their children should be educated. And for some, their first love was to become a musician.

Anyway, when the show was over, Benny came over and put a friendly hand on my shoulder and with his genuine humility, thanked me, and I was thrilled because in my book he was the best and certainly the biggest in the business.

A few days later I got a package from Dunhill's and in it was a card and a Huckster cigarette lighter. A solid gold cigarette lighter. Engraved on the flip top was: "To Irv From Jack." I was so thrilled that I took up smoking. I guess he sent it because it seemed in those days everyone smoked cigarettes. But before I could develop lung cancer, Groucho talked me into switching to cigars. His theory was cigarettes can kill you. Smoke cigars. Nobody ever died from halitosis. The worst that can happen is you have no friends.

Ha! Why did they call it a Huckster?

That was just some advertising man on Madison Avenue who flaunted expensive lighters. I think they sold for $160 in those days.

Can you tell me more about Jack Benny?

Perhaps the best indicator of his character and behavior as the number one radio star back then was the opinion of his staff writers. They loved him.

The famous "kids in the hall" as they were known.

They were not kids. He had men. He always gave credit and he was very generous in a financial sense.

But you didn't get to be a writer on his radio show?

I was already doing movies. In fact, I put him in *Somebody Loves Me*, which I directed in 1952. Jack Benny was in and on everything. He made cameos over and over because it wasn't about the money. He was doing a friend a favor. In *Somebody Loves Me*, he came on and played a little violin and told some jokes, and was very cute in it.

And interesting that that movie was about the vaudeville days. Blossom Seeley...

I didn't care about that.

One night a little later, he called me up:

"Irv, what are you doing for the next ten days?"

"Nothing really, Jack."

"Same for me. Want to take a ride? Will your wife let you go?"

"I think so. She likes me. But she likes you more."

He said he wanted to drive up to the Sierras. So the next morning he picked me up in his long, brown, Cadillac convertible. I remember the top was down and I tossed my valise and golf clubs in the back and he said: "Careful. Don't hurt the cigars," with mock concern. He had a big box of Havana cigars. Which were contraband.

Just like Ernie Kovacs, always with the Havanas, you said, like a security blanket.

The great comedians were all hooked on big, fine cigars. Groucho, Jack, Berle, Kovacs, Burns and Danny Thomas. They probably enjoyed smoking them, but they definitely needed them as if something to hold onto, an imaginary crutch, when they were performing.

So tell me about going on the road with Benny Kubelsky!

Jack loved driving. And he was not a gabby guy. To further convince me that he was the least self-important of all the comedians I knew, he rarely talked about himself, the past, or the future—so we talked about baseball, golf, how hard it was to find a restaurant that made really good coffee. Or how much he admired other people.

When we got to Lake Tahoe, we got a very nice reception because he had performed there. We had a bungalow at Cal-Neva Lodge. Betty Hutton was performing there. I had just finished directing her in *Somebody Loves Me* and we went and saw her show, which gave her a chance to tell the audience that Jack Benny was there.

Jack would always rather have been the audience in public. He never sought attention. Unlike the other comedians at the round table, he had the highest appreciation of other people's talent. Almost a naïvete, a sweet simplicity. I found him to be a sucker for me if I said something that he thought was amusing. And he was a pushover for George Burns, who always knocked him out.

From Tahoe we went to Reno and did a little gambling. Jack was no

Chico Marx. He didn't care much for gambling. Jack was a passionate, not very good, golfer. I was ordinary and really disliked golf. But if the company was to my taste, I pretended to enjoy the nonsensical pastime. We played a little more and it was time to head home. Jack had to get back for the new radio season and I was looking forward to getting back to my wife and kids and no golf.

We drove into a little mountain village with a lake famous for fishing: June Lake. We finally had a chance for some real fun. We went into a cafe and had lunch and suddenly, while sitting there, I heard my name. I turned to see Al Shinberg, an assistant director I knew at MGM. He said Mervyn Leroy was shooting a movie a couple of miles away near Mammoth Lakes. A remake of a musical called **Rose Marie.**

That was all Jack needed.

"Let's drop in on Mervyn," he said. He and Leroy were good friends.

Al said they were just about to shoot a big scene: "We got hundreds of extras painted up as Indians and Jeanette MacDonald and Nelson Eddy are in big trouble."

Jack had Al dress us up, in ill-fitting uniforms, as two Canadian mounties. He found us two tired horses older than the hills and lakes—two swayback horses. Shinberg led us through a lot of foliage out to a huge clearing, from which we could see what looked like a thousand fake Indians with warpaint, brandishing bows and arrows, positioned in a meadow. We went on these old stale horses and hid behind a tree on the rim of the meadow. We saw about a hundred yards away, the small figure whom we knew to be our friend Leroy. Too far to recognize, which means he couldn't tell it was us, either.

He was shouting on a megaphone, giving last minute details.

"Nobody move an inch until I say! When I call action, do exactly as we rehearsed it. Mr. Eddy and Miss MacDonald will come riding toward the camera and you will all begin moving toward them. Now settle down... wait..."

Nobody moved.

Except Benny and I. We starting our horses forward. Some Indians parted—they were not so brave—and the horses continued plodding across the meadow.

"CUT!" shouted Leroy. "What the hell are those horses... get 'em out! Get 'em out!"

All the action was stopped. But we kept coming.

Benny shouted at him: "Moiven! Moiven!"

Suddenly Mervyn recognized us. His outrage turned to hilarity as he fell down onto the grass. I almost fell off my horse—I was never good at keeping a straight face when a "rosey" was going on. We reached the little man and it was a happy reunion. But we had to cut it short because MGM was spending five thousand dollars for this three-minute interlude.

We got out of there on foot.

Now you have to tell the readers what a "rosey" is.

A rosey is a rib, a prank. A hoax.

Great rosey.

Yeah, it was. To give you one example of Jack Benny's childlike quality in the way he appreciated something, which I found so unusual in men I knew: On the drive back, we went down a one-lane dirt road because he saw a sign saying, "GOOD EATS."

"Let's get some," Jack said.

Behind a gas station with one pump there was an old shack, weatherworn and smelling of frying food. Inside was a man in a Texaco cap, turning hamburgers over a griddle and the grease was bubbling as it turned the burgers almost black.

"I'll have a hamburger," said Jack to the chef.

"Yes sir. Hamburger?" he said to me.

"No thanks," I said. "I just had some grouse for lunch."

The nauseating smell—I believe it was Valvoline motor oil—forced me outside and I just sat in the car. A few minutes later, the number one comedian in America came out, biting into a bun and saying like he actually meant it: "This is the best hamburger I have ever had!"

"Jack, " I said. "Why don't you have your New Year's Eve party here?"

Jack was a laugher. He always choked.

I can't recall exactly where this place was, so I am unable to recommend it.

The only time I ever heard Jack complain was about the coffee at Hillcrest. He couldn't understand how they could spend thousands on a new kitchen but couldn't produce a decent cup of coffee. I got a postcard from Toronto once after he had gone to perform up there. "Dear Irv, Finally got a good cup of coffee. Love, Jack."

When he died in 1974, my sense of loss was intense. Then I heard from his daughter Joan. She said she had been going through her father's desk and found a slip of paper on which Jack had made note of something. It had my name on it. All Joan had was something she figured was a punchline. She asked me if I knew the rest of the story.

I told her about a day that Jack and I had been at Hillcrest. And we were outside the club afterwards, waiting for our cars. Jack happened to look up and notice something. Two strange, white streaks, high across the sky.

"Are those jet trails?" he asked.

"I guess so," I said.

"Isn't that amazing," Jack said. "That jet must be thirty thousand feet up. My god, that's high!"

"Yes," I said. "Even birds don't fly that high, and that's their *business.*"

Jack doubled over. Really knocked out.

That's what Joan found among the scraps of paper in her father's desk. Just that one line.

Fake Mounties, 1954. Jack Benny (eyeglasses in hand) and I rescue Mervyn Leroy from the movie he was directing, *Rose Marie*, a musical by Rudolph Friml and Oscar Hammerstein II

Honeymoon with Friends

> Brecher, helping his wife Norma make barley
> bean soup:
> "It needs more spices."
> "Some more thyme?"
> "A couple years maybe."

Just before 5767, the Jewish New Year, Irv calls and tells a joke on my answering machine: "A girl is leaving her fancy eastern college to go back home. Her roommate asks why and she tells her she has to, because, 'It's the high holidays, and we blow the shofar.' And her roommate says: 'You Jews are so nice to the help.'"

And speaking of Jewish jokes, I found a cassette tape in a box in Irv's bedroom closet the other day. A label said: "NORMA-IRV-WEDDING JULY 20 '83." Irv says to pop it in. After listening, I ask permission to transcribe it immediately. Assuming the role of archivist, privy to certain historical materials, I inform Brecher that such a document belongs in The Museum of Comedy. (However, in lieu of such a building-to-be-built-one-hopes-sooner-than-later, audio has been made available online.) The wedding tape is Danny Thomas, Milton Berle, George Burns, and Red Buttons inhaling large amounts of microphone— Brecher, too, tummeling among these giants—to entertain the fifty or so guests by cutting Irv to the quick, trilling Yiddish ditties, and telling two or three of the best dirty jokes ever. (Transcriptions available, at Irv's discretion.)

The more I get to know you, the more jealous I become of your extraordinary friendships.

You wanna know about friends? Here's what friends do for you: When I began dating Norma in 1980, George Burns was already quite an elderly man. I guess about eighty-five. We would often have dinner together. He liked Norma very much and he started to sell Norma on marrying me, which was something I wanted. After many suggestions given around various tables, Norma was still kind of cool about it, so one day George became more insistent.

"Norma, marry this guy," he says. "He's got a great track record as a husband."

"Well, I'm not sure," she said. "I like Irv very much. We have a lot of good times. It's fun and I think he's very funny. But I'm not sure."

Burns turns to me and says with Norma there: "Listen kiddo, you insist that she marry you and make it something important—get your name in the papers—I'll be your best man. I'll stand up for you. But my dicky won't."

In fact, my best man was my best friend Edward Marx. Eddie at the time arranged the financing for huge projects like the Los Angeles Forum for the Lakers and hotels in Palm Springs and Las Vegas, and unfortunately for me, was also the best two-handed gin rummy player I ever got clipped by.

Well, now that I've heard the wedding, what can you tell me about the honeymoon?

We took a trip to New York and stayed at the Lotos Club, where I was a member. It occupies an old mansion just off 5th Avenue on 66th Street. Mark Twain founded it. Now it has a membership primarily of lawyers and educators and politicians. Nixon was one. Anyway, the most memorable part of our honeymoon, that I'm willing to speak about publicly, was the time spent with a wonderful couple that my wife Eve and I had fallen in love with when I first met them at MGM. Frances Goodrich and Albert Hackett. They were one of the top screenwriting teams—***Seven Brides for Seven Brothers, It's a Wonderful Life, Thin Man*** movies—but they earned international fame for their play, "The Diary of Anne Frank."

When I called to say I was in town with Norma, Frances invited us to lunch on the east side at a very stuff place, the Colony Club. (For a hotshot screenwriter, Frances did not look the part; she was a tall, prim woman who wore white gloves and was a descendant of the Goodrich tire family.) I was very nervous because Frances and Eve had been so close and I hoped Frances would like Norma.

After introductions at the table, while Norma was talking to Albert, Frances studied Norma, then nodded to me, and leaned over, whispering: "Darling, Eve would have approved. Now eat your soup."

After lunch, the Hacketts invited us to dinner—"just the four of us"—at their place. A week later, when Norma and I arrived at their apartment house on Central Park West, , the doorman, dressed as an admiral, sent us up in the elevator. Dinner for four turned out to be thirty people surprising us as we walked in. Norma was knocked out.

By the surprise.

I was surprised. And flattered. She was knocked out. Big talent, everywhere you looked. Harold Ross, the crusty owner-editor of the *New Yorker*. Harold Rome, the composer of shows like "I Can Get It For You Wholesale" and "Fanny" and among other hits, "Franklin Delano Jones."

"Franklin Delano Jones?"

Harold Rome wrote songs of social importance in shows by George Kaufman and Moss Hart in the '30s and '40s. Mark Connelly was there; he worked with Kaufman on plays. Paul Osborn was there, who wrote *Sayonara*. And Julius Epstein, one of the writers of **Casablanca**. Al Hirschfeld, the great caricature artist who drew something wonderful for every Sunday *New York Times* arts section and did the Marx Brothers and **Meet Me in St. Louis** movie posters. Norma said he pinched her behind. She didn't mind.

Hackett and Goodrich. They're all gone now.

That party was not only one that sticks in my memory because of all the interesting characters there, but also because Frances Goodrich had the finest collection of Edward Hopper paintings anywhere. Everywhere you looked there was a stunning example of his style. Yellows. The moods created. Parties like that were so different from the other kind of party that too often I've suffered through in the last twenty or thirty years. This party and some others in New York and Hollywood, were alive with wit and serious talk about primarily politics; the others were wasted evenings where all the host and his acolytes talk about is money. Their money. Your money. While the Hackett-Goodrich party featured portraits by Hopper, the last few parties I've been condemned to sit through featured other pictures—of dead presidents.

And I can't wait to see George Bush's picture, on the new half-cent the Treasury is minting to honor his service to the people. I wonder if it will help bail out Wall Street....

Irv on Norma

*Now, about twenty-six years after that party at the Hacketts, Brecher just
came back from another. Norma's 80th birthday, thrown by her three children.
About fifty friends celebrated with her at Hillcrest.*

How did she handle turning eighty?

I think she handled it remarkably well. I see a lot of women lying or
complaining about their numbers. Norma really takes it in stride. To me,
she isn't really eighty. Her looks and mind; she's maybe fifty. So now that
makes me forty-four years older. I feel like I'm robbing the cradle, except
it's an electric bed.

Anything about the party you'd like to tell?

It was all women except for her son Michael and me. Michael is a brilliant kid, the kind of lawyer I personally admire. Most of the lawyers I
know do the easy kind of work. Boiler plate, trusts and buying and selling.
Michael primarily does litigation for people getting screwed by insurance
companies or other big corporations. I like that. If you're gonna have a
stepson, get one that reminds you of Jimmy Stewart in **Mr. Smith Goes
to Washington.**

Who spoke at the party?

Michael spoke, and Norma's daughters Jane and Ellen.

Um, you didn't make any remarks?

I forced myself.

To do some stand-up.

I recalled how I felt the moment I saw her on a blind date that a mutual
friend of ours, Mildred Bressler, arranged. I said, "I know it's a cliche that
it was love at first sight, but the fact is, it was not love. It was lust." I said
I found that if you handled it right, lust turns to love. Which it certainly
did in my case. I said we've had a lot of fun, along with some sad moments,
as illness or death constantly remind you that the clock is ticking. I said
that I've especially enjoyed our travels together. Trips to Israel and Europe.
Cruises through the Panama Canal. Twice. And a particularly fun cruise

to Alaska in '95 to see the icebergs, which I now hear are much smaller, in spite of inflation. Boy was Al Gore smart. Far back he saw what was coming. I often wonder what would have happened if the biased just-asses—huh?—had been honest and put Gore in the White House instead of Bush in the Fright House.

This is part of your stand-up?

Could be. And I said, "I love Norma and because she loves to travel, I still take her on fun vacations. Tomorrow we leave for two weeks in Costco."

Ha! Tell me about that first blind date. It was 1980, yes?

It was at a small dinner party I didn't want to go to.

Why not?

It was only seven weeks after the death of Eve on August 8th. I didn't want to go anywhere. Then I went and met Norma. I remember we talked about fishing. She liked to fish for walleye. I liked the steelhead trout in the Rogue River in Oregon. Later, I heard she told a friend she didn't believe this guy she was talking to at the dinner was a fisherman. My father loved to fish. He used to catch striped bass in the Atlantic with his dad. My father wrote poetry. He wrote calligraphy. He played piano. The only thing he couldn't do was make a living. Luckily, I could, and when I made it, I brought him out to California. He fished out here in Santa Monica and sometimes on a boat out of San Diego. He was a great fisherman.

But Norma was the main thing about that party I'm remembering—how striking was this dark-haired beauty from Davenport, Iowa. With what I find rare in most women, a genuine sense of humor. I mean lots of women on a date do a lot of laughing. At nothing funny. I assume it's nervousness. Not Norma; she only laughed if I said something that deserved it. And as the evening went on, I found myself really wanted to know her better.

Wait. You didn't talk about movies?

Oh sure. She was a big movie buff and we got to talking about some of our favorites. And then neither of us could remember the title of a French classic we both loved. All we could recall was the star, Jean Gabin. At the end of the evening, I made my reluctant exit, determined to see her again, and soon.

I was an amateur at dating. I'd never done it. I'd been married for forty-two years.

I was too shy to call. I needed a good reason to give me the nerve.

I could not get her out of my mind, remembering her sexy eyes, the Middle West accent, and a body that wouldn't quit. The next night: Bingo! I'm in bed, 10 o'clock, and it comes to me. I called the hostess of the party and asked for Norma's phone number, which Mildred happily gave me. I had butterflies when I dialed it. After a couple rings, I heard that voice.

"Hello," it said.

"Le Grande Illusion!"

"You got it!" Norma said, laughing. "I've been trying to think of that movie but you beat me to it."

"You're right! I win. I get to choose the restaurant that I want to take you to."

"Not tonight. I'm in bed."

"I'd rather not hear the details," I said. "I wanna be able to sleep."

I called her the next day. And from there, we're now here. If it hadn't been for Jean Gabin, I might still be a bachelor. Although I doubt it. Norma would have forced me to marry her. I know the type.

Here I am with Norma, my second and, quite possibly, last wife.

Norma on Irv

The first chance I got, I asked Norma if she recalled who threw which lines when they met at Mildred's.

When we first met? I thought, here is this sixty-six year old acting like Harold Teen!

I'm sorry?

Oh, that's a bumbling teen comic strip and movie character from back in time. He didn't know about courting a woman. No anchor, no bearings, no script.

Harold Teen.

Irv! He just chased you 'til he wore you down. But first, yes, Mildred Bressler introduced us. I was very close to Mildred. I knew her husband Jerry. He produced the **Gidget** movies and things like **Casino Royale.** Irv loved Jerry, too, and Jerry would say to me, "Do you know my friend Irving Brecher?" Well, I didn't then. The first time I ever saw Irv was at Jerry's funeral. There was a buzz in the house, "Irv Brecher's here..." He delivered a eulogy that just slew me. He caught everything about Jerry with such love and humor.

After Jerry died—that was in 1977—Mildred and I got together quite a bit. She used to go see films at the Academy. In those days, widows were given a pass. Once she called and invited me; she said she was coming with her friends the Brechers. I remember, it was 1979. *The Rose*. I met Irv's wife Eve and I liked her very much. She wanted to know about me; she was very interested. Unlike Irv. He doesn't remember meeting me that night...

No?

No, but a year later we met again. At that dinner party at Mildred's. And we had a conversation about fishing. He went on and on about going up to Oregon and I bragged how I used to fish with my ex-husband in northern Wisconsin. All the time I'm thinking, that man has never been in a boat. And he's thinking, that woman has never caught a fish. But we both turned out to be real fishermen. And the first time he took me to the Rogue River near Grants Pass, I out-fished him. The Rogue is a very wild river; it cuts through a canyon and there are wild rabbits and beavers running and you could hear the swoop of the wings of a hawk. It was warm and the fish weren't biting. We tried every lure. Nothing. Finally, I took my lipstick and painted the lure bright red and cast it out. First cast brought in a huge, beautiful steelhead. Trout.

Can you tell me about your wedding, with all the comedians?

You know, I've seen comedians' wives roll their eyes at their husbands. Sitting there you know, writhing with the anecdotes. With Irv, no matter how many times I've heard his stories, I think I'm his best audience. I laugh.

You have a great sense of humor. And appreciate his.

All of it. His sense of timing; no question, Irv has it. That Jack Benny technique where he could stop and look at you. The pauses. The cadence. It kills him to hear somebody mangle a good joke. And I kind of understood it when we first met, because my father was a very funny man.

What was his name?

Velvel Schneider. Zev. Which means Wolf. And it became Snyder. He was 90 when he met Irv and we went to dinner at my sister's house and I said: "Dad, I want you to meet Irving Brecher." He said: "Irving Brecher? It's alright with me."

It was the Irving part that sold him.

Irv was just hooked. Irv loved him. At the wedding, I remember my father looked over at me and said: "These are the oldest comedians in the world telling the oldest jokes in the world!" But afterwards, you should have heard him tell about it at the Shalom House.

The residential place on Fairfax Avenue?

Yep! He was bragging, he had the time of his life. Growing up with this father that I adored and was so funny and a very good man—I'm sure it had to do with the attraction I had to Irv. And Irv really respected my dad's humor. That says a lot!

Does Irv's humor have a dark side do you think?

Irv has an edge, but it's not a mean or a cutting one. I'll tell you what attracted me along with the humor: the self-assurance. I don't know anyone who ever knew himself so well. And he never tries to be anything else but himself. I love that. Here. I'll tell you why I married Irv. He was funny. And he was so persistent. Right away he was open about it. He fell for me and he really meant it.

After seven years of watching the Brechers at play, I can see he still means it. One afternoon, I asked if he'd reveal his secret.

You've had two wonderful marriages...
Yup. A lot of interesting action.

Are you talking about sex?
No. Marriage! Look, my formula for my personal good luck or success in terms of marriage is, maybe I'm a romantic. But whatever it is, don't get married to someone unless you feel that you cannot enjoy the rest of your life unless you're married to her. That's my reason for having gotten married twice. The first time certainly, and also the second.

What about chemistry?
No wonder you're not married!

Everything's not up to date in Vulva City, I guess.
Listen, a vagina is not the best thing in the world. One size fits all. The best thing is to like yourself enough, without hurting anyone else. Self-esteem. Be sure you don't destroy yourself. That's a hundred dollars.

Ha! So you wouldn't have been able to enjoy your life?
What.

If you hadn't gotten married.
That's the way I felt at the time. And there have been obviously billions of marriages that were happy.

And being funny helps?
Both my wives have told people over the more than sixty years I've been married, that their reason for signing up with me is—well, I tell everybody it's because I'm possibly the world's greatest stud, second only to Little Richard. And Tiny Tim.

Really.
Wives are too modest to admit the truth. Too puritanical, too prudish. So they say it's because I make them laugh.

It's wonderful if, when you're having an argument and it gets very heated and maybe she breaks into tears, and then you say something that breaks her up. And the tears go away and you both start to laugh. In my first marriage, my wife and I were having an argument and in her opinion, I was grievously out of line. She became so upset that she said, "That's it! I'm leaving you." And I said, "That's okay with me. But if you go, I'm going with you." It worked.

So what do you draw from that?
Everything changes your life. And everybody else's needs have some

affect on you.

What was that argument about?

I've forgotten what it was.

But you remember the line that changed it.

The reason is because she told the story so many times as a way of entertaining other people! I've heard Norma say, the trouble with being married to him is that every time you have an argument and get mad at him, he says something that cracks you up and then you've forgotten why you got mad. I can't take credit for this. This is something you have or you haven't got it, and you gotta be grateful if you have it.

Joanna and John

"My daughter Joanna wanted to throw me a big
party on my 89th birthday. But I told her to
wait a year. People who have a big party at 89
don't think they're going to get to 90."
—Brecher on his birthday in 2003

Joanna Giallelis is a delightfully vivacious woman in her 60's who wears wild clothes and jewelry, just about all of which she designed, and lives in a huge house with her dogs Bulgaria and Bear, and some cats and ducks too, up in Benedict Canyon. We've spent some fun times together—she was immediately friendly, open and hilarious, telling stories about being a toddler sitting on the lap of Irv's agent ("They liked me—Abe Lastfogel and all those old codgers"), and running around at NBC studios on Sunset, where every Sunday her father broadcast "The Life of Riley" radio show. Adopted at birth by Eve and Irv, Joanna grew up going to schools with the children of Doheny and Weissmuller, Astaire, Stewart, Bergen, Ladd and Fonda, saying, "if your family wasn't connected to Hollywood, you went to Catholic School." She said when the Brechers moved to Bel Air, the deed to her father's house read: "NO JEWS OR ETHIOPIANS."

Irv, was that true, when you found a home on Stone Canyon Road?

The land was on Stone Canyon. An acre. Bel Air Country Club was across the street. Anyone allowed to build a house in the neighborhood got a free club membership, except for Jews. Eve and I bought the lot anyway, in 1941 for ten thousand dollars.

Joanna said going to school in Bel-Air was amazing. Sally Ride the astronaut went there. And Candace Bergen. But there were only three Jews. One had a father who invented the Toni home permanent, another had a father who invented the first garbage disposal. And then there was you.

Ha.

She said she wanted to go to an arts college but you wouldn't let her go to Bennington.

Why?

She said you were like, no way, "Groucho's daughter went to Bennington College and she came back a dyke!"

I don't think I protested that way, but I could be wrong. Did Joanna tell you about her business? She was the hottest thing in Los Angeles; she had boutiques on Rodeo Drive and Sunset and in fifteen other cities.

What were they called?

"Laise Adzer." It's a Danish name. In one location she had another designer store right across the street called, "Joan Vass." She was a smash.

You've mentioned that Joanna and Norma have become great friends.

Because they agree on so many things, like what's wrong with me.

Like being a grouch.

Okay, so maybe I don't look at the world through rose-colored implants. In fact I really like the world. It's the putzes in it! And I don't resolve to change. If I've said anything snide, I'm sorry. Unless it gets a laugh.

She said when she was born, a famous Hollywood producer came came over?

Hunt Stromberg. He came to our house the night we brought Joanna home. This was when I was writing *Shadow of the Thin Man* which he directed. He brought an antique table that is still upstairs in the study.

Family on the set of the movie *The Life of Riley*: (l-r) John, Eve, Irv and Joanna

She said at Hillcrest, Georgie Jessel once told her that you and Jack Benny were like, "a tic on a Louisiana dog."

Ha.

Joanna remembers that as a wonderful time. A boy's club. How she loved being with you and Danny Thomas and George Burns.

Yeah.

She said she was just out of high school and you caught her smoking pot and told her that you knew jazz musicians who smoked pot and got very worried.

I knew what that life was about!

That's exactly what she said. And you made her call the pediatrician so he could tell her what she was doing to her health.

I don't remember that.

She also told me a lot about your son John.

My son... my son John, who I loved and unfortunately that did not help, because he was a schizophrenic, which we did not know when we adopted. He was loving and kind and totally irresponsible and starting at the age of thirteen he became an alcoholic. He made an old man of me. My career was stopped.

This came when, just after you made your last movie, *Bye Bye Birdie* in 1963?

I stopped around '65. I was a little over fifty years old. I had made a lot of money. I wanted to do some more work. But I was beset by the problems of this young man. When you write comedy for a living, it is not easy—you have to somehow develop a kind of armor—so at a certain point you can be creative and at your best despite all the horrible stuff that's around in life.

And for forty-two years, he tyrannized his mother—then she died—and me and his sister. But what's the point of this?

To let people know all about you, Irv.

Other people have the same troubles. I sound angry.

Your sadness comes from the same place as your humor.

The only escape from that is to try and be amusing. Know what I mean. This can kill you unless you have some recourse. Some self-therapy. In my case, it's making people laugh. My wife, or a friend, or an audience seated at an event.

Doing something creative was your way.

Maybe that was the easy way out.

I don't think so. Mark Twain called the creative act the only defense

against the ruin of the world.

I'd sit and try to work and then would come the call. Tyranny on the telephone. We had terrible scenes. Once he picked up an electric typewriter and threw it across the room. He threatened to shoot somebody once in a house he had in Malibu. It burned down in '93. John escaped with his life. His dog caught on fire. A big Labrador, his fur was burning. When I think about all that went on, I don't know how much entertainment there is in the world. Not even if you count living.

Joanna said he moved in with her after that.

She was extremely generous to her brother. Nobody could be more supportive than my daughter was. Finally he exploited her and became a problem.

She said she finally got him to go to the Betty Ford Clinic and he lived in Palm Springs.

Where he died from alcohol. Fifty-five years old.

She said you got him jobs time and time again, at production companies...

In fifty-five years he never earned a dollar.

She said once you got him hired at the William Morris Agency and in the elevator he tried to have sex with Abe Lastfogel's secretary who went running and told Abe—

He always got fired. We tried everything. But you see, stay in denial for a while and after you come out, you still feel a tremendous sense of obligation because the child is yours and then he's in his twenties. Then he's in his thirties. Then he's in his forties. Then he's in his fifties. And it's a one-way street.

Is that enough for the book I hope? I don't want this to end up a therapy book. This should go in the "Help Sell" section of the bookstore. Not "Self Help."

Ha. Do you have a story about him you'd like to tell?

More than one! At the house on Stone Canyon, I grew things. The earth was so rich. And the property had trees, some over a hundred years old, that had fed the earth with leaves. So in that soil, I grew up squash and strawberries, corn, cantaloupe. Some zucchini grew to six pounds, which is larger than a watermelon. Not that you'd be impressed with that today. But that soil was wonderful. I told you about the dill and the garlic pickles I made.

Yes! And gave away in jars to friends like Billy Wilder.

Oh, he couldn't get enough of 'em. And Gene Kelly and Fred Astaire.

Everybody loved 'em. I grew them from the late '40s all the way to 1976 when I sold the house. I had one acre.

We drove past it on the way to Joanna's.

Where she used to live. Now she's in Benedict. Anyway, at the bottom of our property in Stone Canyon was a large piece of flat land. Then it went up a hill and then on top was the house and pool. So what was down below could have been a tennis court, but I didn't want that, I wanted the land for the greenery. The flowers may be better back east, but the vegetables are better out here. But deer would come in from the canyon during the night and eat the corn and the string beans. The only way to keep them away was to hang strips of cloth that had been soaked in lion urine. We were able to get it at the nursery. It was so expensive, I considered buying the lion.

Or using my own urine.

We often had parties at the house, some which included the dozens of people involved in my TV series. People would spill out on our front lawn around the pool and in the house—sixty to a hundred people. And Phil Silvers was at a barbecue one night. His first time at the house. That was in the '50s. Phil Silvers was a big noise. Funny man.

I was standing out on the lawn grilling steaks. My son John, six years old, came over to us and started doing somersaults on the lawn and demanding: "Watch me Dad! Watch me!"

John, when he was young, before his illness really took over, was a delightful child who would sing little songs and was a joy to play with.

Phil Silvers was the star of "Bilco" on TV and was only happy when he was "on," so he started in on the little boy: "What's your name kiddo?"

"John." I had named him John Leroy, after Mervyn Leroy.

Silvers said, "Are you this man's son?"

"Yes."

Still somersaulting.

"Well then, how come you're out here fooling around while your poor father is standing her sweating from this fire, working to feed you? You think that's fair?"

Tiny John stood, looked up into Silvers' scalp and said: "Do I know you, Stupid?"

Silvers fell down.

The other story about my boy I like to tell is this one:

When he was seven, we were driving to Palm Springs, and leaving town we passed the Hollywood Forever Cemetery.

John pointed to the graveyard and asked, "Is that the place where they put people?"

"Yes. It's called a cemetery," I said. "It's where people kind of go to sleep, close their eyes."

"You mean die?"

"Yes, John."

"Well what happens after you die?"

I said, "After a while, you turn to dust."

The kid thought about that and said, "Will I turn to dust?"

"I'm afraid so."

He thought a moment and said, "There's a fat kid in my class who always picks on me. I hope I get in his eye."

Ha?

I told that at his memorial.

Father's Day

*"Father's Day is a crock," cracked Brecher. "Mother's Day, too. Only my love
for my beautiful daughter could get me into this hazzerei."*

"Here we go," Norma said, grinning.

*Indeed, daughter Joanna invited us for Father's Day dinner at a family
restaurant where among a mob of Sunday diners, between wincing at the
screaming crying tables around us, Irv joined in, sounding off.*

*"Everybody should know, if they have a brain," he went on, "that these holi-
days were created by the weasels who own stores or factories that began extract-
ing billions of dollars long ago on the false premise that children are obligated to
celebrate parents who in some cases despise them. And vice-versa."*

Norma patted his hand.

"Honey," she said calmly. "You'll feel better after you sing."

"Well, if you insist."

*He looked up in my direction. "My wife and daughter know about the song,
but I'll let you in on it."*

*Thus, I learned that he actually does like Father's Day, but only because it
gives him a chance to sing a song.*

I had a great friend named Harry Ruby. Early on, he'd written lyrics
for a couple of Marx Brothers movies. Songs like "Hooray for Captain
Spaulding." Harry was a delightful guy. Tall with a big head and a hawk-
shaped nose. Groucho said he looked like a dishonest Abe Lincoln. I
think he was right.

I loved Harry. Harry was odd. He never in his life had driven a car
and one of his habits was a daily walk from his home to Nate 'n Al's Deli
in Beverly Hills for lunch. About half-a-mile. But Harry didn't walk on
the sidewalk. He walked in the gutter, close to the curb, looking for lost
coins. Sometimes he would find as much as thirty-five cents. Once he
found a half-dollar. I asked him how well he'd done in all his years of

prospecting.

He said: "Very well. It's all profit and there's no overhead."

I loved his deadpan.

"I'm a great believer in thrift," he'd say. "And I'll give you a tip. If you drop fifty or a hundred dollars into a jar every week, you'll be amazed at how quickly it adds up."

But Harry Ruby's youthful dream had been to be a big league ballplayer. Once in the 1930s, he even had a tryout with the Washington Senators. He trotted out to centerfield and one of the coaches hit a fungo out to him. Harry moved eagerly forward, stuck out his glove, and the ball hit him in the head and knocked him down. He got up and quit baseball.

He became a successful lyricist working with Burt Kalmar on several Broadway musicals. Harry on his own wrote two songs that I love. One was a college number called, "Fight on for Tannenbaum!" And the other he taught me one day at lunch at MGM. This song says so much so quickly, so if you want a free dinner tonight, you have to first listen to this:

[A not-exactly melodic Brecher lets go; imagine Captain Spaulding after falling out of a tree.]

"Today Father, is Father's Day
So we chipped in and bought you a tie
We know it's not much, but it's just that you're such
A heck of a wonderful guy!
You told us not to bother,
You said, 'Don't make a fuss.'
But according to our mother, you're our father,
And that's good enough for us!"

[Applause all around, and some from nearby tables.]

Pastrami on Wry

> Virginia O'Brien: Can't you see I love you and want you for the father of my children?
> Red Skelton: I didn't know you had any!
> — *Du Barry Was a Lady*

*In 2006, I see a movie called **The Holiday**. Fun movie, lousy title. Cameron Diaz switches homes with Kate Winslet. Winslet comes from England to Beverly Hills where she befriends a cranky, nonagenarian screenwriter, played by Eli Wallach, who quips about Louis B. Mayer and MGM where he had all these comedian friends, and then the Writers Guild wants to honor him with a night. I flip out and tell Brecher that Hollywood seems to have stolen his dailies and at least five chapters of his book. But he says to relax. "It's in the air," he says, mentioning the Turner Classic Movie archives and numerous tributes to actors like Kirk Douglas from the eldest generation, adding that he wishes I were Kate Winslet.*

Soon after, we're at Label's Table, splitting a pastrami sandwich with cole slaw and extra mustard. I tell him I want to test his quick retort quotient.

What?

I want to read you a series of questions and see how you respond. They're from a chapbook called "Duplex Planet" by an NPR storyteller, David Greenberger. He gave me permission to ask them.

So you're gonna sell his book now too?

No, no. But they've worked well for him.

Go ahead, kid.

[*Tape recorder is clicked on.*]

What's the worst job you ever had?

Answering this.

Good! See how it works?

But that's no story. Why don't you ask me what is the most *thankless* job I ever had, and I can tell you about the producer at MGM who paid me $500 to write a bar mitzvah speech for his stupid son. Which I did.

What is so thankless about that?

He wouldn't give me credit.

Moving on. Okay, what is the most important invention of the last century?

The mute button on the TV remote.

What's the best thing that ever happened to you?

My bad memory. I keep forgetting to die.

When did you last think about death?

Right now. Every day. All day. Woody Allen's line is the best: "I don't mind dying, I just don't want to be there when it happens."

If you had a robot, what would you want it to do for you?

Go to my proctologist.

Do you enjoy music?

Yes, but even if I didn't, it's very important. If there was no music, thousands of musicians would starve.

Finish this sentence: If I were seventy-five years younger...

I'd move to Israel. And get a whole new set of clothes. I wouldn't be interviewed by you. And I would sell this walker and give away my cane.

What make of walker is that?

A four-wheel walker. With a seat you can flip down. You can fold it up. I intend to use it until *I* fold up.

When did you last drive a car?

2000.

What kind was it?

I had a 5th Avenue Chrysler. Fabulous car. Twelve years old.

What was your first car?

Allan Lipscott and I, while we were writing for *The Mickey Mouse Magazine*, bought a 1927 Essex. For thirty-five dollars, so help me. Not a used car; an abused car. But somehow it managed to run. Especially when we pushed it.

When I was making big bucks writing the Berle radio show, I bought a beautiful 1937 Buick Roadmaster. A long, sleek, six-passenger convertible. It was $1700.

I can't imagine: to be a twenty year-old New York writer for a Sunday night CBS show starring Milton Berle. Wow.

Then I shipped the car to California when Mervyn Leroy signed me. Then I had five Cadillacs in a row. But the one I should not have bought, was for medical reasons. While writing **Cry for Happy** at Columbia Pictures, I developed suddenly a terrible outbreak of acne on my face. After trying steroids, which is why I'll never get into the Hall of Fame, my doctor prescribed sunlight. He said I should drive my car with the top down. I told him I'd better get a hatchet because I drove a sedan. He didn't laugh.

I thought doctors by themselves laugh, it's only in a group—

Never mind. I traded in my sedan for a new Cadillac convertible. Sedan de Ville. Lavender. Almost purple. The leather inside, too. I drove it for two days with the top down trying to cure my acne, but I had serious car trouble. I noticed that whenever I drove along certain streets where there was construction going on, guys with hardhats whistled at me and threw me kisses. That's when I realized lavender and I do not go together.

Irv, why do you think people kiss?

It's more sanitary than shaking hands.

What is—

Wait. There are so many reasons people kiss. A lot of them are sexual...

Yes?

I can't think of any more.

Did you ever sleep with Carole Lombard?

No. But I slept through Mary Astor.

Huh?

Ask your parents. She played the mother in **Meet Me in St. Louis**. She was well-known; she also had an affair with George Kaufman. Oh, here's something I remembered about Lombard that might be good for the book. My wife Eve asked her what she was doing for Christmas and all that, you know. Lombard said: "Stay in bed all day with Clark and make with the lob."

That was an expression. For dick.

The "lob."

Oh, Eve blushed.

Clark being Clark Gable.

Well of course!

What's your favorite food?

Lemme put it to you this way: I have a living will. In it I lay out what I want or don't want if I have a catastrophic illness. In my will, I instruct the doctor not to let me become a vegetable. Unless it's an artichoke. That's my favorite.

Really.

Artichokes.

Why the artichoke?

Because it's got heart.

Want that pickle right there?

Where. No, it's all yours.

Okay. Lightning round.

What?

Lightning round. I think Jan Murray invented it on one of the many game shows he hosted. It means super quick retorts. Your specialty.

Not according to me. According to Groucho and Perelman.

Right. Whom do you prefer: Keaton or Chaplin?

W.C. Fields.

Three Stooges or Abbot & Costello?

The Smothers Brothers.

Richard Pryor said comedy comes from, "a hole in the chest where their heart should be... before it was yanked out."

That's a bit much.

You didn't have a hole to fill?

I had a hole in my wallet.

Your comedy comes from a place very similar to Groucho's, a sort of livewire ire, ridiculing the conventions of society...

That's interesting.

You know how J. Cheever Loophole and S. Quentin Quale step right out of the scenes in their movies and speak directly to the audience? As if you are saying: Listen up! Here's how you tear down the high and mighty!

I think the next table is your audience.

Sorry. Do you have a favorite among your movies?

I would say *Meet Me in St. Louis* was one, and I think with qualifications about the direction, *Go West* might be another. *Bye Bye Birdie* I love. And in a sense because I did the whole thing, writing, directing producing—it was my property—*The Life of Riley*. That feature was based on the radio show, which also sprung the idea for the TV series. All in one year.

That was a busy year.

Not when you're that young. I was 35. Hardly a man is now alive who remembers that famous year. I remember because I *still* don't get residuals from that movie.

1949. Can you tell me what happened to the old studio system?

Once the agents started to get stars ownership, it started to shred. The actors were now telling the studio what to do. People who knew very little about scripts were given directorship and nobody around them wanted to speak up. I prefer the studio system.

Why?

It gave you ulcers but even that was better than having some overpaid star fuck up your script.

Can you describe your writing process? The discipline you needed to—

It all starts with letting your mind focus. I find it hard to talk about this. I don't know how to do it. I can't tell you why I can say funny things anymore than why someone else can sing beautifully and I can't!

What kind of typewriter did you use? Do you remember your first?

The first typewriter I ever had was a Remington where the carriage slipped down. Not like a regular typewriter. After that, when I started to write for the comedians, I bought a Smith-Corona, a little portable I had for years that I loved. I did most of my preliminary work in longhand on a yellow sheet. I either typed it or there was a secretary pool of girls at the studio to type it up. The last one I had was an electronic, called a Citizen. A Japanese typewriter. Good little operator and lightweight. It's not the typewriter, you know. It's the fingers.

You have very long fingers.

I do.

What size are they?

Ha!

What size shoes do you wear?

I used to be 11-and-half. Now I wear 12.

They look like clown shoes. Very long. And what about those socks?

I can't see 'em.

They have little strawberries on them.

They were a gift.

What is your attitude about forgiveness?

You have to forgive yourself for all your bad jokes. But you never have to forgive others, especially if their stuff stinks.

You've had a lot of beefs with people who have screwed you in a deal. Do you forgive them?

Yes, but reluctantly.

That brings me to pet peeves.

Oh good, because I want to talk about that.

People who come up to you because of what you seem to represent and try to tell you jokes. Walking across a room and a guy who is about as funny as septic poisoning will jump out of his chair to say, "I've got a good one for you," and you stand there and listen to it or insult him and ignore it. The other person I can't wait to run into is the woman who the other day came up and said: "Hi. Do you know who I am?" I said to her, "If *you* don't know who you are, how the hell would *I* know?" And I walk away. I'm on the shit list after that, but who cares? What I find almost jokeable is when someone says, "I wanna tell you something interesting." Well, *I* want to be the judge, not them! Once a fellow said to me, "Let me make a long story short…" And I said: "Too late."

I got a long list of things that give me a pain and I think at the top of what I think is a breakdown in our communications, is the rampant amount of computer nuts who spend most of their time screwing around with the Internet, their own blogs or somebody else's. Particularly the young, some of them barely infants who are now playing with computers that Papa and Mama gave them to keep them busy and not annoying *them*.

The language that these computerniks use when I'm around them, is a mystery to me obviously. I don't understand about hard drives and web-sites and bytes and all kinds of stuff. But I think I heard the extreme the other day at Circuit City. My wife needed some ink for her computer and we were in that department. And I'm standing there, I can't see anything, but I'm behaving myself. And I'm hearing people walk by—shoppers, lookers, and then a couple of them, I assume to be salesmen, one of them says to the other, "Hey Joe! I didn't expect you today. Didn't you call in sick yesterday?"

"No, I wasn't sick."

"They said you were in the hospital."

"Yes I was in the hospital. My wife downloaded a baby boy. Seven pounds."

Finally, why do you like Label's deli?

For one thing, it's easy to get in. Second, and most important, their corned beef is certainly better than Nate 'n Al's. Not as good as Langer's. But it's much closer, here in the Pico-Robertson neighborhood. I'm never very hungry, but I hope for an appetite, and know it will happen when I smell the Jews.

[Click! goes the tape recorder as Irv's cell phone rings.]

Whoa, Irv, our machines just went off at the same time.

That's a good marriage. Both go off at the same time.

When asked his opinion in 1979 of super wide-
screen movies, the kind that came into vogue a
few years before, Brecher replied: "Why not keep
the theater screens the same size and simply
reduce the size of the audience?"
- From the book *Popcorn Paradise* by John Robert
Columbo

In the spring of 2006, Norma's went with her daughters to New York and I got to spend four days living with her cranky husband. I say cranky because while Brecher at 92 gets around well enough so that he doesn't need a hired helper, with his rapid loss of sight he tends to bark out instructions when he can't find something he needs: his phone, his remote, or food. Sleeping at Irv's, one assumes the rhythms of the creative nonagenarian/kvetchitarian lifestyle: two tablespoons of flaxseed oil at the top of the morning, followed by cranberry juice and blintzes and lox Norma left for us in the freezer. Plus, lots of thick, black coffee.

I said I took a little cream in my Yuban.

"What?"

"Sometimes those flavored creams."

"You're crazy. The only way to drink coffee is black!"

"Really."

"You're killing it! You don't know anything about coffee. I should teach you."

So, right away I was learning things.

Mornings we passed lounging in his study amid the aural pleasures of books-on-tape. Sent for free by Braille, an institution Brecher has fallen in love with. (Braille also supplies a free playback machine on which to play their special-format cassette tapes). His favorite is the New York Times Book Review. *I thought, no way, but there it was on a single cassette: Read and recorded, a whole section, sometimes 30 pages, from the Sunday paper. Everything but the advertising. (Who does this? I want that job.) Irv said hey, he's never going to read the books, but the review itself is often like listening to a good story.*

In the afternoons, he treated me to Philip Roth novels from cds.

First "Everyman," and then "Exit Ghost." Irv's favorite author is the creator of Zuckerman.

"I'm not egotistical enough," notes Brecher, "to say he's my alter ego too, but I love him for the many things he hates that I hate, and the complaints that he sets down so brilliantly."

Irv calls them "The Gripes of Roth."

Afternoon listening sessions—interrupted by phone calls from his daughter, his broker, his wife, a telemarketer, his daughter, his complaints about his lack of appetite and inability "to fucking see!"—were followed by a nap to prepare us for dinner and "The Jim Lehrer NewsHour." I tried to get him to listen to the "The Daily Show" but he claimed it was "too noisy." So then it was to bed, unless a ballgame came on.

Preceding dinner, he taught me how to mix his six o'clock martini (two ounces of either gin or vodka on ice with a good dash of vermouth and a bit of orange slice) and before we began to slur our words I turned on my tape recorder.

It's interesting.

Huh.

Both those novels we heard by Roth happen to be death elegies.

Yeah, so?

You've dealt with death comedically in your writing. The friendly undertaker. And certain lines for Groucho...

That's right.

This is a good drink, Irv. When did you start drinking martinis?

Bill Powell got me into drinking martinis while I was writing *Shadow of The Thin Man.*

That would be William Powell, who played Nick Charles. 1941 movie. And what was he like?

He was a charming guy, a very well-educated man. It was a joy to talk to him. He pushed a martini at me and I drank it and I think it had a pretty strong effect. I remember getting thick-tongued and he was nice enough to not push anymore on me. Because he had another motive.

That's great. Your first martini was with a man who drank them constantly in *Thin Man* movies. What else do you recall about writing one of those classic, caper pictures?

What I recall is Myrna Loy.

Nora Charles in *The Thin Man.*

The nicest part was getting to know this real beauty. Myrna Loy had everything. She was gorgeous. She was vivacious. She never acted the big star. And she was adorable, beautiful inside and beautiful outside. You just wanted to grab her. She lived across the street from me in Bel Air and Bill Powell lived around the corner on Sunset. And she was cute the way she'd get me to rewrite some of her scenes where she felt her hubby Nick Charles had more good lines. She would say, "Can I vamp you into a few more lines?" And she would flutter her eyelids and purr. She was funny and I was crazy about her. Which did me no good.

What do you mean?

Here's what happened: Powell was a real conniver. He would get me slightly drunk at night at his house, and then bring up slyly the fact that, for the next day's shooting, he really didn't have enough lines. You know, as opposed to Myrna. And did I think it could be adjusted? I'd go in the next morning and clear them, the new lines I'd written, with Hunt Stromberg, the producer. If the lines worked, Stromberg would okay it and Woody Van Dyke would direct them. I told Stromberg what Powell

was up to. And then Myrna would come over because she didn't want to be outwitted in their exchanges!

Gee, that picture got a lotta laughs. Those were the kind of movies you can't see anymore. Pure entertainment. No dirty words, no shock value, no naked, ogling behavior. You don't have to be a prude—and I'm not—to regret the changes in movies.

It was a small idea, a murder at a racetrack. With a bright and funny couple, who would, by brilliant deduction, expose the killer in what better be an exciting climax or you had a dud. Writing for Loy and Powell and a funny police sergeant played by Sam Levine, was one of the more pleasant jobs I ever had. Right after that came Pearl Harbor.

[I accidentally knock my drink onto Irv's pants. Would this sound good on the audiobook I wonder? He squirms, wondering what the hell is going on, but then recovers quickly, bursting out with: "I asked for a dry martini!"]

[Mopping him up with a dish towel.]

Hey, Irv.
What, sweetie?
Did I tell you, I saw a license plate that had "NICNORA" on it the other day.
Yeah?
What did you do during the war?
First of all, I rooted for the United States to win. Then I did what I could. For the USO I wrote monologues for stars from MGM. Some of them were for Eddie Robinson, who traveled wherever the action was, in spite of the danger. He loved making the troops laugh.
Edward G. Robinson.
He came from the Yiddish theatre.
Tough guy. "Nyah... see?" *Key Largo.* I think Bugs Bunny was based somewhat on him.
That's what *you* think. It was a thrill to write material for Eddie. Once he came back from the Aleutian Islands in the Pacific and told me, "I really killed them. Not like I did in *Little Caesar* with blank bullets. This time I did it with your jokes!" Ha.
Who else did you write for?
Spencer Tracy.

Another great actor.

Yes. He usually played the hero. But what he was best at was playing the coward. The USO got a promise from him that they could send him overseas to do a routine on a battleship. I helped him learn a fifteen-minute piece. Between shots of scotch, he'd mutter how he hated to fly. He didn't hate scotch, but I sensed a real lack of enthusiasm about doing the show. So I wasn't surprised when the morning he was supposed to leave for Alaska, the USO was told he had to cancel because he had a high fever. Influenza. It was the kind of flu he caught each time the USO called, until they finally decided they could win the war without Tracy.

I also wrote radio programs geared to keeping up the morale of the nation. These were all-star programs with Groucho, Carole Lombard, Tallulah Bankhead and other big names. Lucille Ball. Judy. I particularly adored Carole Lombard. I had gotten to know her when I first came out here in 1937 and Mervyn Leroy asked me to contribute some dialogue to a movie she was in that he was shooting, *Fools for Scandal*. She was not only sexy, but funny, bright, and great company. Early on, she volunteered to do her bit for the soldiers. But she was killed and this great talent and good person was lost to us. She was on a plane with her mother on her way back from the troops and it went down in Nevada in '42. Carole Lombard... I loved her.

You weren't in the service?

I just missed getting drafted. I was classified 1-A and ordered to report in the spring of '44. Then a new ruling came down in late '43 that exempted any man who was over thirty and had children. I was just over thirty and had a daughter three years old. That saved me from being a war hero: The man who killed Hitler with a funny monologue.

So I was that close to going. And it left me really troubled. Funny isn't it? What you worry about when you're heading for that critical situation; I found myself less worried about getting shot—I was thin and a rather poor target—I was more worried about having to sleep in huge barracks with God knows how many other men, because I was a terribly light sleeper.

I actually had another job during the war. Walking around my neighborhood with a rifle and a hard hat with a red, white and blue insignia on it. We were supposed to watch out for enemy aircraft.

Really? Here in L.A.?

There were many false alarms. Sometimes a shooting star would cause somebody to think it was an airplane. Sure, it happened. My title was

"Air Raid Warden" for the Bel Air district. Everyone in the neighborhood used blackout curtains at night. And fairly soon, the fears dissipated. Bel Air was the elite of the elite. And comical, looking back on it.

How so?

I went through the war there with Jeanette MacDonald. Big movie star. With Nelson Eddy. She could handle a .22 rifle and was very serious about the situation. Once we were at the home she shared with Gene Raymond, talking about an invasion from Japan. We were practicing simulated first-aid and I suddenly laid down on her living room floor. I started to shake and groan in agony. Jeanette reacted quickly:

"My God!," she said. "What's happened to you?"

I said, "I've been run over by a rickshaw!"

That loosened her up. She screamed at that and from then on we had some fun while we guarded Bel Air from the people who fifty years later would own most of Bel Air and the rest of our former country club.

What's your take on the current war, in Iraq?

I'm still angry. Insanely angry.

Norma reads you Frank Rich and Maureen Dowd columns from the *New York Times*. Does that help you keep your sanity?

She's very funny. I'm in love with her. She's sexy, don't you think? Norma said if I ever wanted to cheat, she'd make an exception and permit me to sleep with Maureen Dowd.

I met Dowd that April at the Los Angeles Times *Festival of Books and emailed her a story I'd written about Brecher in* The Forward, *taking the liberty of adding how much of a fan Irv was and what his wife had said. Dowd's return email contained one word: "Fabulous!" I read it to Irv.*

"I know she'll be disappointed," he told me. "But I can't sleep with her. I've got insomnia."

Then he received her new book "Bushworld" in the mail with the following inscription: Irv, you are way too smart and sweet to be trapped in dark and gloomy Bushworld. x Maureen (Cobra!)

"Cobra" is George W. Bush's "code" name for Dowd. Irv made me write her back, telling Cobra to "keep coiling and striking," and adding zingers about "our sneerleader-in-chief."

"I'm proud to be in the Dowd crowd," he said.

Set Up/Punch

*The Writers Guild Foundation honored Irv in the fall of 2007 at their first festival of, "Living Legends: Classic Films and Their Writers." An all-day affair held at the WGA Theatre, the event featured on stage interviews with Fay Kanin (**Teacher's Pet**, 1958), Millard Kaufman (**Bad Day at Black Rock**, (1955), and Brecher (**Meet Me in St. Louis**, 1944). Army Archerd previewed it in his Variety column and I chaperoned Irv and Norma and Irv's niece Nancy Bennett to the theater on Doheny in Beverly Hills.*

We ran into Fay Kanin in the WGA's green room, where she greeted Irv gingerly.

"We've gotta stop meeting like this," Brecher laughed, reaching for her. "How are you, Fay?"

"How are YOU?"

"Schlepping," he told her.

"I'm schlepping too," she said.

"I'm the opening act," said Brecher. "At 11 in the morning. People are still asleep."

"I'm at 3 o'clock."

"I know. You'll have a bigger audience."

"I doubt it," she sighed. "Well, whatever turnout there is, is lovely."

"It's very nice of the Guild to do this."

"Yes it is," said Kanin. "And calling us Living Legends!"

"It's nice to be called Living Legends," said Brecher. "Better than the original title they had for this."

"What was that?"

"'Resuscitated Relics.'"

As laughter from all of us hangers-on enveloped them, Kanin leaned over to Irv.

"I'm insulted," she said. "I won't be a relic for another five years."

Fay Kanin and Millard Kaufman were both 90; Brecher had them by a few. And as Norma and I guided his walker toward the auditorium, I wondered if this would be Irv's last hurrah. He'd been suffering from a lot of problems of late, like heart spasms he felt during "Harpo Night" at Hillcrest the previous week. That had kept him from staying very long among the men gathered in the Grill

Room who all wore boxer shorts in honor of the time Harpo played the club course in a jock strap. I was already nervous, having just read that Al Langer of Langer's Deli had died at 94, and a fellow named Milton Brucker had died, also at 94. And now I was rushing him home because of palpitations and he sat crumpled up in the backseat of the car moaning: "I'm fucking dying"—which he denied ever saying the next day, after the nitroglycerine pills had finally kicked in (miraculous recovery!) and he said he was fine on the phone. "I never said such a thing; I was saying 'let's finish the fucking book!'"

But he had been saying he was "running out of gas" a lot lately, and frightful things like, "I'm heading for the barn"—which made me sad now seeing only half the WGA theatre seats filled. We slowly tugged and then pushed him as he gripped the walker, hesitantly slowing and stopping, down the right aisle to the front of the room where Robert L. Freedman stood waiting. Freedman would be our moderator; each scenarist got his/her own interviewer. Freedman won an Emmy for a mini-series he wrote and directed about Judy Garland that starred Judy Davis. We took way the walker and Freedman helped Irv up two steps to the stage and over to a chair. He was very gracious, letting Irv carry the interview—this bony gentleman in a gray, checkered suit, crossing what had to be the skinniest ankles in Beverly Hills—and dig those crazy blue-and-black polka dot socks. Brecher clutched the microphone against his lips, saying how pleased he was to be honored like this with great writers like Kanin and Kaufman.

"Because of our age," he said to Freedman and turning to face us, "I'm not really sure whether this is a tribute or a memorial."

One laugh and he was off; seventy minutes of Q & A, showing off his unmatched memory unreeling tales not just of the film legends in old Hollywood, but also recalling some of their phone numbers.

The "resuscitated relics" line he'd thought up in the green room got a welcome laugh. When he described **Yolanda and the Thief**'s Lucille Bremer as one of the worst actresses he'd ever seen, but allowing how "Arthur Freed thought she was one of the best lays he ever had," Norma leaned across her seat in the front row and whispered, "He's getting warmed up now."

Rejuvenated by the friendly and sometimes thunderous laughs he could surely hear but barely see as more than a wall of shadows, Irv got so wound up that he finally swiveled around his chair to where he was completely turned and facing the giant backdrop that said "WRITERS GUILD OF AMERICA FOUNDATION."

Freedman gently twirled him back around this way where Brecher, mid-anecdote, hit face front with: "Where's the audience? I thought they left."

Big laugh.

That was hard to top, but he did go on until he got tired, and after it ended Norma and I guided him back up the right aisle. At the halfway point, he was exhausted, and faltering he had to pull the plastic seat out from the walker and sit down on it. And there he sat, resting at a slope on the carpet midway to the lobby. As Norma and I lodged our feet against the wheels to keep him from slipping away, autograph hounds and people taking pictures jostled right through us and jammed the aisle; it was like they had to get to their Hollywood hero and we weren't even there.

Lori Champagne

Fay Kanin and Irv at the Writer's Guild "Resuscitated Relics" tribute.

Homer Simpson and Socialist Dialectic in The Life of Riley

> Riley: Peg, for 5 dollars I can buy Dr Flexo's
> muscle builder! *[Reads]* "Do your muscles sag?
> Are you getting fat and flabby? In 30 days I
> guarantee to make you a Greek god!"
> Peg: You, Riley? In 30 days?
> Riley: Peg, don't you want your husband to have
> a good figger?
> Peg: Not for 5 dollars. I can go see Cary Grant
> for 30 cents this afternoon.
>
> - William Bendix and Paula Winslowe in "Riley
> Getting Old," "The Life of Riley Radio Show"
> April 6, 1951

Listening to old "Riley" radio shows, one thing I've noticed is, you seemed to come up with four jokes about death in half a minute.

Yeah?

So my question is, is that why you created the friendly undertaker character, Digger O'Dell?

Why?

To juxtapose his constant reminder of death and dying with Riley's so-called "life?"

No! I told you how it happened. He was a very popular character.

"It is I, Digby O'Dell, the friendly undertaker!" His accent reminds me of that 7-Up "the Uncola" character. Remember? The Caribbean guy in the TV commercials?

That's what you say.

Yes. A remarkably popular character, because it was this funny undertaker that turned "Riley" into a goldmine, when you sold it to syndication for hundreds of thousands of dollars. I guess you have a secret affection for morticians, then?

I wouldn't say affection. They do what they gotta do. But nobody really wants it done to them.

And what a revoltin' development that sure is!

You know some people still say that when something goes cockeyed.

I saw it as a kid in the "Fantastic Four."

Who are they? Studio heads?

A comic book. A character called The Thing used to say: "Wotta revoltin' development!"

That's nice. Never heard of him.

Well, Stan Lee and Jack Kirby, the creators, must have heard Riley.

I'm flattered.

The Thing was a gruff, working man's superhero.

Riley was a working man.

Irv, did you know there was a seminar at UCLA called, "The Life of Riley as Socialist Dialectic"?

No.

Perhaps because Riley spent ten years at Stevenson Aircraft?

The show started during the war so he was working on war planes.

A working-class riveter. That seminar seems to imply you were really writing about class struggle here.

Huh?

Riley's daughter Babs is a major in Sociology.

Babs was a sophomore at UCLA.

And Riley is always talking about quote, "marrying her off rich to one of those Pasadena socialists."

He said "some Pasadena socialouse!"

Socialouse?

Yes...

He's making fifty bucks a week. He can't keep the electricity on and owes back rent on his little house. And he's from a working-class suburb, El Segundo.

No, El Segundo is where he worked. They lived on Blue View Terrace, a made-up name. I didn't specify. Riley was the funny underdog. To tell you the truth, when I sat down to write the show, I actually couldn't think of someone named Riley. I started to think about families like mine.

Riley was really about a *Jewish* family?

No, I recognized that the problems of the Jewish families I knew were universal in terms of essentially surviving on meager income.

That made me think of "Everybody Loves Raymond" where Phil Rosenthal created an Italian-American family, but he says he mined his Jewish background for many ideas.

Yeah. So?

I'm just saying, who knew? Here's a guy, Riley, living in Los Angeles but still subscribing to the *Brooklyn Daily Eagle* newspaper.

Because he was Riley. He was an odd character. More than that, he and a bunch of fellow losers belonged to their own little club. "The BPLA." The Brooklyn Patriots of Los Angeles. They bowled together and rooted for the Brooklyn Dodgers.

Irv, for a Sunday *New York Times* business section piece called "Class in America," they ran a timeline for the year 1955. It reads: "The Honeymooners makes its debut as TV series. In the working-class sitcom..."

Well, we were on TV five years before "The Honeymooners."

Where does the term, "the life of Riley" come from?

An old Irish saying I liked because it's exactly the opposite of what our hero had.

But you're not saying there was an undercurrent of class conflict in the show?

He suffered all the problems of being poor and tried in spite of that to be proud.

I guess owning a top radio show made you proud and not exactly poor?

"Riley" became the most important project from a financial standpoint of anything I ever did.

What happened after you sold the TV version for six-hundred thousand dollars.

After that license expired in '67, I had it syndicated to independent stations. For example, WOR in New York, ran ten years of the Gleason season of twenty-six episodes. Then, two-hundred episodes, starring Bendix, which NBC returned to me by contract, were also leased to smaller networks—the biggest buyer of those being Pat Robertson for his Christian Broadcasting Network.

Well so much for it being a Jewish show...

It was entertaining! The word church was never mentioned. He never went to church. He was Riley.

I just never knew it was—

The Christian Broadcasting Network shelled out a big number for a five-year run. Which almost converted me.

Ha! And now "Riley" still lives on through the magic of audiotape.

Since the radio show ended its network run in '52, those tapes have been sold by the thousands each year. I never realized there were so many people who enjoyed collecting and playing Old-Time Radio.

So the key here is owning the show.

I was the first owner of a show. Actually, no, there must've been some-one else who owned a show.

And the workers who worked for you as their boss, were they treated well? Make enough to live on?

No, they died. That's no question to ask!

Sorry. In an obituary for Hume Cronyn, it said his sitcom "The Mar-riage" which appeared in 1954 was the, "first network series to be telecast in color." It seems like every show in early TV has a claim to fame.

"Riley" was the first one-camera filmed sitcom. That's all I know. The production crew did a Herculean job. It also helped that Gleason only did one take.

A few years ago, "The Honeymooners" made it to the big screen featur-ing a black cast. Did you ever think of doing that with "Riley"?

Yes! There actually was some discussion about a black version for televi-sion. But it was dropped because they said a black show with a leading character who is a dumbbell would garner resentment from the black audience. And rightly so.

I do see some resemblance to Riley in Homer Simpson. He's yellow.

I don't think so.

Riley always said things like "I'm quoting him verboten" instead of "verbatim." Things like that.

So?

That's how Homer talks.

So does Tony Soprano.

I thought I heard you once on your show.

What?

I heard a "Riley" show on KKGO's "When Radio Was," hosted by Stan Freberg. This character was delivering packages from "Petlak's Depart-ment Store." He sounded like you, is that possible?

I probably did. I did a lot of bits all through the series.

What fun!

I would do it like Groucho in terms of vocal style. Upstart characters who would pop in on Riley for one reason or another.

Stan Freberg said it was a "Life of Riley" from 1948.

Yeah, I remember now. That was a funny show. Everybody got him a coat. Stan Freberg was a funny guy.

Still is. He hasn't "shoveled off" yet, to quote Mr. O'Dell.

Sometimes people still quote Digger O'Dell: "I'd better be shoveling off." It can still get a laugh.

I went and heard the writer Peter Mehlman at the Skirball and he said getting laughter "is the lowest form of comedy."

Ha!

Let me give you one more quote. Gerald Nachman in his book "Raised on Radio," says Riley was a completely original idea in 1944: a blue-collar family show.

And I really created it for Groucho. Very reluctantly. He was wrong for it.

I know.

You know? So stop quoting.

I'm only here for the Groucho. And, of course, stories of your friends in Generation Exit.

What is that?

The generation of dying old Jews who are funny.

Why? What's your interest?

The wisdom. In what there is. In that world that's going away. And what we will become next. You know, about looking forward for my generation, not just you looking back.

Well, it can't be bad for you.

Leaving the wisdom of your generation?

No! Death. Because it's becoming more and more popular; more people are going for it. It seems to be a fad. I'm talking about war. This must be a catharsis. We're going through a fucking war and I'm trying to write about laughter.

Irv, for a guy nearly 95, you seem to have an unusual attitude about "shoveling off." Leaving. About the inevitable.

Well, the main thing, as I've told you: dying interferes with everything. And look what you have to go through, to get to where there'll be peace— you're supposed to believe—to get to the inevitable. Every other day there are visits to several doctors. To get there you have to use a walker and that winds up turning into a wheelchair. The waiter brings you a lamb chop to bite into and you have no teeth. You've watched me eat. Put this in the book: how a blind man eats canned mackerel. That's another thing: There's a show on television you can no longer see because you lost your eyesight. It's very hard to enjoy HBO with two naked people and all you can hear are the groans. When you realize that at a certain stage, even though you're willing to believe that it's inevitable... dying isn't worth all the trouble you have to go through.

Living on Laugh Support

Warner Video Interviewer: Mr. Brecher, if you
could describe the Marx Brothers in one word,
what would it be?
Irv: Jewish.

*Once upon a time, in a Hollywood way back when, Brecher and Marx
are heading west on Sunset Boulevard in Irv's lavender Cadillac convertible
with Berle in the back seat, not happy to be there so he's jostling with Benny
and Burns. And they're all smoking cigars and topping each other with quips,
retorts and anecdotes, winding along the tree-lined boulevard until reaching
Bel Air, where Brech spins a sharp right onto Stone Canyon Road and then one
more immediately into his driveway. As his friends try to keep themselves lit,
he jumps out to grab a jar of pickles made briny fresh from his cucumber garden,
because Gene Kelley is crazy for them, and Billy Wilder, too...*

*But today Irv looks like Harpo, his hair flying out from the sides of his head.
White hair, spread out on a pillow because he's laid out in his bed. He has reached
a point of what he calls, "Diminishment." Thin as Ichabod and beginning to
cough up new things weekly that he's too blind to see as they come out of him.
His only exercise is a stroll in the hallway, pushing the walker down and back.
If he's feeling all right, maybe he'll get up and go to the club for a haircut, or to
Costco with Norma and the help of Eddie and Oscar. But I know his head is
still there when he reveals he's also been having trouble with his balance.*
*"Both bank and physical," he says. His doctor informed him that one of his
legs is an inch shorter than the other. It came from leaning to his left all his life.
His hip bothers him and his teeth depress him and he doesn't feel like talking
because he's not getting any sleep these days. Norma makes us some mackerel out
of a can and we eat it in his bedroom. There's a wrapper of dark chocolate from
Trader Joe's under the bed that he has me break some squares off of for dessert. I
tell him that one thing I'd observed was no matter what, he seemed to try and
make his way through daily life looking for the funny. I suppose, I say, when
you reach this elevated age and find yourself out of the loop...*

You try to find a way to amuse yourself.
Yeah.

You take a shot at it. You grab it

Yeah, "between sips and japes," as Nick and Nora might have.

What?

That's what an *LA Times* reviewer said about the *Thin Man* collection on DVD. That Nick Charles and his wife Nora always unraveled the case "between sips and japes."

Yeah, that's a good one.

Martini sips. But what is a jape?

A jape is a little shtick. Something tricky. A caper.

Can I ask you more about martinis?

Why?

Well, you said your first pop was with Nick Charles.

For Bill [Powell] it was the eight-thousandth.

Did he tell you what he thought made a good martini?

Whatever was available. I showed you what does it for me.

What was that?

It gives me an appetite. Which my doctor says I need.

Outside of the drinking going on in old Hollywood, was there drug use at that time?

We weren't busy at Groucho's parties smoking joints! I went to parties and we dealt from here—our heads. Nat Perrin and the rest, we may have sat around and had brandies, and they did a lot of smoking of cigars... occasionally, Herman Mankiewicz would drink too much, but nobody fell into swimming pools with their clothes on.

Nobody?

We were busy challenging each other with our wit! I wish I had a tape of *that* for you.

So no drugs.

There were people I knew who had to take drugs, like Hunt Stromberg.

The producer of *Shadow of The Thin Man*.

He had an auto accident that left him with a bum hip. Sometimes he would excuse himself and we knew where he was going. To kick the pain, taking a shot of morphine. We assumed that's why he went into the other office. But he was not out of control.

But the writers you knew?

Generally, most writers at MGM knew that they needed a clear head. But the boozers I knew were real boozers.

What did writers make in your day?

I was getting twenty-five hundred a week when I left Metro.

Man. That's what my friends got writing sitcoms out here in the '90s. Did you get depressed when you left MGM in '47?

I was relieved! I went off on a fishing trip with Groucho! I had a radio show, I was 33 years old with a pocket full of money. My son was already showing signs... at age 3. Then he got thrown out of kindergarten.

No.

He threw something at the teacher. So yes, I've been depressed from time to time, sure. For instance, I don't know if I'm gonna wake up and not be here. It's not a good feeling.

How do you deal with that? I go to movies.

I have a method, better than going to the movies and plays and concerts. I lock myself in the bathroom, stare into a mirror, and verbally abuse myself. I tell myself what a schmuck I am and, "What the fuck are you worried about so-and-so, when you can't solve the damn thing?" I act out my anger at myself or whatever it is that I think is dragging me down. It's always helped. It can't hurt to bring it out.

How did you learn that?

Nobody taught me. I just did it one day.

It takes guts to bring all that stuff out. You once told me: "Get past your feelings of being unworthwhile and you get a lot more accomplished."

I did? Lately I'm depressed about the tremendous loss of weight. If I open my shirt you can count the ribs. I saw myself on a tape Jan Murray gave me and I looked like I was fucking dead! Until I started to talk.

Keep talking then.

Okay. What can I tell you?

Did you love movies as a child?

What kind of question is that? Who doesn't? As a kid I loved the silents. Especially comedies with Charlie Chaplin and Buster Keaton. Every Saturday if you had fifteen cents you could see something. I was just thinking: ten years after the first talkie, I was writing for movies.

Amazing.

It's not amazing. Other people obviously were, too. There were hundreds of movies by '37.

What about the first talkie?

I remember the thrill when my father, in 1926, took me to see it! The first talking picture was at the Rivoli Theater on Broadway, starring Sydney Chaplin, Charlie's brother. It was called **The Better 'Ole**. Look this up. It was about war. The 'ole meant the trench. And when the words came off the screen for the first time, it was a sensation! There was only one line of dialogue. Sydney Chaplin spoke the magic words: "The better 'ole." After that, sound movies became the rage. *The Jazz Singer*. I also loved *Fugitive from a Chain Gang*. Little did I know then, that the director of that movie would eventually sign me to come to Warner Brothers and a few weeks later take me with him to MGM.

Mervyn Leroy. Was the experience of seeing a picture in the 1920s much different than today?

When sound came in, it was much more exciting. But there was one problem with it. The noise.

From the sound?

No. On the back of some seats in the theater they had a metal and glass apparatus containing a candy bar. If you dropped in a nickel or a dime, this thing would dispense the sweet. It was hard to hear the movie, because most of the kids were banging so hard on the machine, as the more enterprising boys started coming to the theater with screwdrivers.

You did that?

No, I didn't have a screwdriver.

Backseat candy bars. They just don't make theaters like that anymore.

The bands of young crooks dismantled the machines to get the nickel. Fuck the candy!

Oh.

The contraption didn't last long enough for a kid to develop diabetes.

Ha. Tell me about the kids in your neighborhood.

In the Bronx? Near the Grand Concourse? They used to throw stones at me. A block from Jerome Avenue by the elevated train. I ran to school and ran home because we were one of two Jewish families. There were a couple of Irish kids who enjoyed throwing stones and epithets at me: "Sheeny... Mocky... Yid... Kike."

Mocky? I've never heard that one. What's that mean?

I don't know. Kike is from Yiddish. A kikela, a circle. When the immigrants came to Ellis Island, they couldn't spell their names in English— they made a circle. And the customs guy started calling them kikes. I guess they heard the Jews talking about it. If they said, "Sign your name," the immigrant would shake his head and some of them simply made a circle where the name should be.

I never knew that.

I didn't make that up!

I admire that you made it through that dark and ugly century living by your wit.

That's what kept us alive.

[Pause.]

Anything else, kid?

The author Sandra Cisneros wrote: "People are like walking libraries... Smithsonians, and when they die, all this goes with them unless you document it."

And because dying, wasting away, can be a serious topic.

Yes, so can we end on a lighter note?

Sure.

Do you have a favorite joke today?

Norma's grandson just called and asked if I knew how you circumcise a whale.

How?

Send down four skin divers.

[Pause.]

But I told Norma a line the other day that knocked her out. Henny Youngman—this was repeated to me by Red Buttons—Henny was part of what they called a "tab" show, a variety show, traveling from city to city. And he is screwing one of the beautiful chorus girls, for weeks. One day before the show, they have a terrible fight, their worst ever. And she has to go out with the other girls and dance. Henny's in the wings waiting for her, seething, and when the chorus number ends and she comes off, he says: "You're through. Turn in your cunt."

And so ended a tender romance.

There's something so funny about picturing Henny saying that.

He Who Laughs, Lasts

*Last night I had a dream of Irv doing standup. In Rochester, New York. He does six different bits, characters, monologues, Shakespearean soliloquy. I get there too late and miss the first two routines, but lie to him when he accuses me of missing them; I figure he's blind, how would he know I wasn't there? So I have him do them over again, and the guy is killing and I'm afraid I'm killing the guy by pushing him too hard. But, onward! He does die on stage a few times, but mostly is heroic, comical, dramatical, tragic and mainly, very enthused just about being there. I tape the whole thing - my recorder doesn't work but I borrow one from an old college friend who is there and the sound is a tinny but it works. We're in a black neighborhood and about thirty people have turned out to see him: hipsters, '50s types of madmen like you'd see on an old Oscar Levant TV appearance. Irv finishes his set and his face is shining like Fred Astaire, hair slicked back, really looking good, I'm telling ya! A couple of times I did think he was gonna die on stage - not his act, but for real, like Dick Shawn did; Irv told me the story of Shawn, a standup for years before he appeared in **It's a Mad Mad Mad Mad World** (my favorite movie as a kid—1963, and it had nearly every great comedian of its day in it: Milton Berle, Sid Caesar, Buddy Hackett, Jonathan Winters, even Buster Keaton and the Three Stooges!), and again a standup after he played Hitler in The Producers. Shawn did a lot of off-color material on stage, Irv said, like: "Know why God invented the orgasm? So the [Insert ethnic group] would know when to stop screwing." But when Dick fell down on the stage in _____, people thought he was only kidding, that it was part of his performance. I call 911 to have an ambulance available during the show, telling them, "Don't play the siren, please"—I want them just to be there for Irv at the end. I'm worried, like the time I pulled him too fast up the aisle at the "Living Legends" tribute at the WGA and thought he was gonna keel over right there.*

When I wake up, I can't wait to tell Irv. He says he has strange dreams these days, but he can't remember them when he wakes up.

What do you miss most about being blind?
You miss seeing.
There is a withering pause before he continues.
Mostly I miss the faces of my wife and my friends.

I miss going to the movies with you. It makes me sad.

Of course I miss movies. But I keep running some of my favorites in my head, scenes from so many wonderful pictures. *The Best Years of Our Lives*, the scene where Frederic March returns home from the war and Myrna Loy sees him. What a moment. Scenes from *The Godfather*. So many movies. Maybe hundreds.

Now dear boy, it's getting to be about that time...

You sound like a vaudevillian exiting the stage. Wait, don't go.

I'm headin' for the barn. I feel the clock ticking, baby.

Norma told me she's so worried about your being so thin.

Nature says at a certain point: that's it, g'bye... and awaaaay we go!

Ha ha ha. Jackie Gleason!

Ha.

Do you ever find it remarkable that nearly seventy years after leaving behind this formidable creative output, you have not only the energy to recall the words, but also the skills to still double people over?

Silence.

Irv?

That's a long fucking question.

It's just that I know quite a few guys up in years. So I'm a bit baffled by you.

The truth is I am surprised that I'm still here. But I don't think it's because I quit smoking, or that I take vitamins, or that I do a hundred yards of walking with my walker. What keeps me going is spite. There are people who love to hear that a Democrat died. So I'm living to spite Fox News. I think somebody oughta do a TV series about how a money mad media monster, from Australia, feeds his political propaganda to the dimwits who listen along on his radio and TV stations. The title of the show would be, "Murdoch, He Says."

That's a good one. Would you say all of your work on radio and TV and in film has been essentially comedy?

I thought so. There were times when the audience didn't agree. What do *they* know?

Bert Lahr, whom I know you knew and loved and wrote for in *Oz*, said that comedy is always close to sadness. And Groucho said there's a fine line—that if he didn't know sadness, he wouldn't have spent so much time trying to make people laugh.

Well, I think it's true that being Jewish, with our background of persecution, there's no question that the only escape from that misery was to reach out and do something funny, or say something funny, to change the subject from grief to momentary mirth.

It's "hard-wired?"

That's instinctive. And it has been passed along. Even today with greater acceptance in the world because of the contributions in art and science and music and medicine—Einstein, Jonas Salk—the Jewish comedians instinctively reach for laughter based on the unhappy history of our people.

To this day. What do think of contemporary film humor, what you were able to see of it?

Semen in the girl's hair?

You're talking about the movie, *Something About Mary*.

I don't see any cinematic wit there. I wish there were more movies where the dialogue is as biting as, for instance, ***All About Eve***, or ***Letter To Three Wives***, both by Joe Mankiewicz.

I read an interview with you in a book about comedy writing, "The Laugh Crafters," where you told the author Jordan Young about Carroll O'Connor coming up to you at a party once—

It was at a party at Groucho's. O'Connor was very gracious when I complimented his new show "All In The Family." Which was a smash.

This was the '70s.

He told me that in "All In The Family," they were doing "The Life of Riley." Only with the freedom I didn't have back then. Not only on radio or television, but writing movies up until the middle '50s, we were handicapped by our inability to use certain words or show certain things. I think it was the toughest on comedy. Today it's gone the other way. The use of four, ten, and twelve-letter words, particularly by stand-ups on Comedy Central and HBO, doesn't bother me because it's tasteless. It's boring! More freedom yes, but rarely is the comedy memorable, as opposed to what we got from Jack Benny, Fred Allen, Berle, Bill Cosby, and maybe the greatest comedy of all, the Sid Caesar "Your Show of Shows."

You really wanted to be a stand-up like your friends, right?

I did some. You saw. Some I even got paid for. I never went to do it in a saloon or The Comedy Store. Yes. It made me feel that if I had done it very early, I would've had my own radio show. But I didn't brood about it. We are what we are. But we can modify ourselves somewhat...you know, sometimes I think it's a very big mistake to be alive. That's what happens when you're given life. It's really a temporary thing. In other words, there's a good chance we will not live forever. Don't ask me who told me that. I can't remember. He's probably dead.

When I see you do stand-up, it's like years suddenly come off your face.

I look like Fred Astaire.

Yeah!

That's what *you* say. Until I just said it.

See? You have the timing, the attitude, the rebellious poking holes in the gasbags. All the elements of a great stand-up.

Yeah? I enjoy making people laugh. Wherever an attempt is made to make the audience laugh, I think I've been very good at knowing what would get a result that's desired. Now that doesn't make me a genius, anymore than an egg candler who holds it up against the light.

What?

They call them egg candlers. In the old days before there was a lot of technical production of chickens. A man or a woman would pick up an egg, hold it against the candlelight, and know whether or not it was edible. By seeing through it. I think I had that knack regarding so-called funny lines.

You mean, knowing which came first, the joker or the joke? Where jokes come from?

That's hard to say. I think a lot of the good jokes come from male hairdressers. That sounds weird, but I've been told that often enough to believe it. And some of the funniest stories keep being revised and brought up to date. A lot of them started in the shtetls of Russia and eastern Europe. I know hundreds of stories, but I honestly don't know who originated even *one* of them, with the exception of some of the humor of Sholem Aleichem. He was, as far as I know, *the* most amazingly, creative humorist. One of my favorite laughs that he wrote was about the young Talmudic scholar who raised his hand and said to the "Idiot Rabbi" of Chelm: "Rabbi, why is the sea so salty?" And the rabbi replied: "Because it's full of herring."

Norma told me her father, Wolf Schneider, used to read Sholem Aleichem stories to groups of children and adults. She said she would get all the jokes her father told at home, but her mother wouldn't laugh. She had no sense of humor and thought they were laughing at her. When I reminded Irv of this, he laughed. We both laughed at Norma's mother. Or perhaps I was laughing at his memory of it, of how he remembered Norma telling the story to him. At some level we were both laughing at Sholem Aleichem. Irv was sure right about that guy.

"Why the hell did you strike out? I told you to
hit a home run. Remember, *I'm* the manager."
– Groucho Marx to Joseph Mankiewicz during an
MGM baseball game.

Irv, have you given any thought to having yourself cloned?

Yeah? You know, Bush is against cloning, I don't know why. So many
people have such terrible lives, it makes me think of what I'm about to
give up, and I'm not ready to, either.

What don't you want to give up?

Norma makes me two ounces towards a vodka martini every night and
it feels good. That would be one martini at a decent restaurant where they
don't fuck you on the amount. I'm not a drinker as such. I started it for
medical reasons, for my heart. If you drink a certain amount, it opens
your arteries. If you drink too much it's very bad for your heart.

**Anyway, you can't go, you have a performance coming up at the Aero
for the American Cinematheque—showing *At the Circus*.**

I'll be glad to do what I can, like I did at that Arclight Cinema's screenwriter night with **Meet Me In St. Louis** a couple years ago. Only this time I hope not to have a cold that turned out to be walking pneumonia.
Let's hope not. Break a leg, Brech.
Thank you, dear.

EMCEE: Ladies and gentlemen…"And I guess that takes in most of you" as Groucho said in our special guest's favorite Marx Brothers feature, Night at the Opera… Direct from the Max Palevsky Auditorium! Home of the Aero Theatre, originally constructed by the Donald Douglass Company as a 24-hour movie house for its tireless workers in the World War Two aircraft industry… Recently redone to remain for the new millennium on Santa Monica's tony north of Wilshire Montana Avenue! 'Tis the night before the night before Christmas, where brighter and whiter than the 1939 movie just played on the big screen behind him… a man with size 13 feet and weighing in at 125 pounds, who barely made it out of bed this afternoon but while lying on his side continued to bark out rejoinders and retorts to whomever entered the room… (i.e. behold an irascible, practically-skeletal gentleman and his risible holding-of-the-room routine, etc)… the writer of this picture, Mister Irving Brecher!

[Applause as the scenarist, white hair swept back, wearing a black-and-tan sports jacket, light blue shirt, rust-colored pants, and socks showing some leg, moves, with his friend Oscar's help, from his walker up onto the slightly elevated stage, settling into one of two blue chairs. Soon, freeing himself from the entanglement of a long, twisted microphone cord…]

> Irv [blindly bumps fuzzy end of microphone into his face]: Is this alive?
> AERO AUDIENCE IN UNISON [A couple hundred old and young fanatics and first-timers] Yes!
> Irv: I'm in trouble.
> [Laughter]
> Irv: Can you hear me?
> AERO AUDIENCE: Yes!
> Irv: Then *you're* in trouble.
> [Laughter]

> EMCEE: *The Marx Brothers At the Circus* is nearly seventy years old—

Irv: I apologize. I was only twenty-four when I wrote this movie. I didn't know what I was doing.

[Laughter]

Irv: But before you go on lying about me, I have to say that I'm kind of pleased at seeing the reaction to the movie. I was flattered when I came to the theater and my wife—who sees for me—told me that the marquee said: "Marx Brothers… Irving Brecher… Live."

That would come as a shock to my doctor.

[Big laughter, applause]

There was a moment during the laughter there in the Aero—not repeated, I noticed a few days later when we caught some of the Marx Brothers Marathon that Turner Classic Movies runs over New Year's—a moment beyond those I felt when observing how Irv's imagination in facing the fact of death ended up with everyone in reach in touch with something damn life affirming. This was when this quick-cutting character reverted into a sort-of blithe and fragile friend.

*I remembered the time he had me over to see **Sail a Crooked Ship**. Sitting on the magenta-colored carpet in the study, I was at his feet rollicking back and forth at Ernie Kovacs' burning-it-all-down wild brilliance on the TV screen. Glancing up, I saw Brecher in his high-backed red Barcelona chair with his eyes shut, his chin hidden down into his chest and his arms in a flutter, half-waving out in front. And his skinny legs kept crossing and uncrossing themselves like somebody was tickling him, doubling him over.*

Norma and Irv at the Aero

The Writers Strike of Aught-Seven

When Sholem Aleichem was dying, he made a wish.
He wished that the Jews when they felt bad
would remember him and laugh.
—Ben Hecht in his book, *1001 Afternoons in New
York*

By the end of 2007, Irv's body has almost completely forgotten him. The great gagmaster, our old King Cajole, is a skinny old soul, afraid to weigh himself and nobody else wants to know how low that number is either. He needs eye surgery again, but first he has to go to the doctor to see if he's well enough to undergo the procedure and ensuing complications.

Brecher's mind, however, remains a thing of beauty. Like one of those brains you see in a horror film, carefully preserved under glass. Vibrant, startling. Now, imagine that mind attached to a six-foot shredded meatstick.

I ask him for a state-of-the-tsuris report.

"Fuck, there's no end to this," he says. "They're gonna graft skin from a human heart and put it in my eye. It's a fuck-up, that's what it is. I had this before in the other eye before I got the glaucoma."

"Is that it, then?"

"No. My pacemaker may undergo a recall."

Nice to hear a joke.

And did you hear how Brech is happening? He's in demand all of a sudden, sought after big time. A fellow doing a documentary about the golden age of television wants to come over and film him. Another director called him about a history-of-comedy project. There's an author writing about old Hollywood who wants him. And he just got an advance against royalties from a new website peddling old-time radio shows. The "Riley" tapes. At last they've been transferred from cassette to cd format, just in time to go digital some day, if the radio gods deem it worthy.

In late 2007, a woman called from the Writers Guild inviting Irv over to their western headquarters on Fairfax Avenue for a taping session. The wanted to add him to their WGA Screenwriters Archive.

"This is the last hurrah," Brecher said, rolling in on his trusty Invacare walker, pushing into a tiny square of a room just off a vestibule across from the guild's "Billy Wilder Reading Room."

He sat down okay under some hot lights. But he couldn't see the interviewer. And he couldn't hear her unless she shouted the questions, which she did in a high speed English accent that made it even more difficult for him to understand. He told her about Judy Garland and a bunch of tales about MGM, and about Groucho and Gleason. His hands gripped his thighs as he spoke; it seemed like he could wrap his long fingers almost all the way around his lower body. Afterwards, he said he felt too tired to stop on the way home for a triumphant, celebratory sandwich. Or even half of one. Not even a bowl of soup.

But soon his mood brightened appreciably. In fact, he seemed positively ecstatic each time I came by.

"It's because of Nell," he told me. "You've got to make sure she gets in the book!"

I knew Nell Scovell from New York, back at SPY magazine where we both worked in the late '80s. She was a very funny writer and we lost touch when she left New York to go west and write on TV shows, eventually developing the popular sitcom, "Sabrina the Teenage Witch." We reconnected in Santa Monica after Irv's brilliant 2006 colloquium/live vaudeville act the night he screened **At the Circus** at the Aero Cinematheque. Nell's sons attended a school where I'd applied to assistant teach and I ran into her there. She said she'd taken her boys to see Irv onstage at the Aero and and was blown away. She was a vociferous fan of Irv's work and a dedicated fresser of classic Hollywood movies, so I arranged to bring Irv out to her house one Saturday afternoon. She had myriad questions for him and he had an answer for every one of them. He delighted her boys, Rudy and Dexter, with Marx Brothers anecdotes and then, on the way out, he whispered, "She sounds pretty," as I guided him down their cobblestone path to my car. "What does she look like?"

Out of this came a crush and a friendship he immensely enjoys. He said he got to feel like a mentor for a young writer-director half his age, giving advice to Nell about movies (she was starting to direct), while she entertained him with stories about slaving in the modern TV comedy trenches. They jammed on ideas that she would pitch to producers. With a sweet sort of embarrassment, he thanked me for bringing "another woman" into his life. Norma cracked that if Irv were fifty years younger, "I'd be worried!" He said it had been a long time since he'd been reminded of "schmoozing with Julie Epstein and all the other screenwriters who are now on location."

He meant at the cemetery.

Irv's daughter Joanna passed away in the late summer of '07. It was too painful, he said. "To have a child go before you do." Now both Joanna and John were gone. And it was also amazing to me, how the day after the "Living Legends" fete for him at the WGA Theatre, Brecher was relating stories at a memorial for Joanna in Pacific Palisades. Irv and Norma arrived early at Joanna's friend Miria's house and greeted dozens of her friends. They came up one-by-one: some of them were employees forty years earlier at her designer boutique in Beverly Hills. They crowded around him in the living room while from a sofa, Irv delivered a long monologue of memories. His honesty, his ability to communicate gratitude, made Joanna's friends cry and feel good at the same time.

He wouldn't admit it, but Norma said he was heroic that afternoon.

For months afterwards, it seemed like only Nell could make him smile. "She treats me like some funny grandfather," he said. "Being paid attention to is a gift not every old person gets."

It has been Brecher's fate to always be the youngest in his circle of friends, whether in the Bronx, in Manhattan, or in Hollywood.

"And being the youngest," he explained, "as I moved up in years, everybody I ever cared about has checked out. So now I'm the old one with a couple of young friends." (Don't think for a minute that he revels in being the eldest. He said, "The only thing in my neighborhood older than me, is a sycamore tree.")

When the Writers Guild began their strike against eight movie studios and television networks on November 5, it halted all work coast-to-coast as union members took to the streets and sidewalks. In addition, for the first time they were able to us the worldwide web to air their grievances. To keep the faithful informed and inspired during the long negotiations, writer sites new and old exploded with forums, live rants and audiovisual agit-prop. Irv was riled up. As part of the union struggle for decades, he recalled earlier walkouts.

"I'd like to go join them," he said, "but my walker would just slow down my fellow scribes."

Nell came up with an idea, a way for him to lend support.

Irv reacted gleefully to Nell's pitch: a chance to make a personal appeal, via the internet. "I'll get to take on the sleazy producers," he said, "and encourage the hungry out-of-work writers to hang in there!"

Nell came by with a camera and another union activist and in just a few days, they'd produced a video that appeared on the phenomenally popular website,

YouTube. Here suddenly popping up on your computer was this quaint old crow staring out from the screen, an alter *cocker all arms and legs, firing away in front of a familiar-looking bookshelf in a Westwood living room.*

In a week, two minutes of Irv rung up thousands and thousands of "hits."
"That means," he excitedly told me, "somebody looks at your thing. They click on you!"
This was the first time he'd ever explored what he called "Computerland." He admitted being awestruck, that something shot one afternoon in his apartment could make its way around the world, just like that. The Brecher video didn't just get hits; it became a hit. It jumped from site to site, as strikers sent it onward to spread his wisdom. Fans forwarded it even further, to TV and movie columnists, where some journalists, tickled, wrote it up, provoking dozens of comments. (To watch Irv's video, visit the website YouTube.com and type in "Irv Brecher." Click!)

Herewith the text of that furious declaration of attack on producers:

It's still the same old story.
I remember the strike of aught-seven.
A tough time for writers, who would prefer to
write than picket.
That was last week...
The producers want to keep all the profits.
Now, it's not as if we were asking for the
whole cash cow.
All we would like is a little squirt of milk.
They won't give a drop!

I'm going to be 94 next month. No gifts please.
But since 1938, when I joined what was then
the Radio Writers Guild,
I've been waiting for the writers to get a
fair deal.
I'm still waiting.
I'm still angry that they took away our
copyrights.
I'm very angry that they took away the
residuals for everything up to 1960.

```
Don't let them take away the internet!
It's our future.

As Chester A. Riley would have said:
"What a revoltin' development this is!"
But he only said it because I wrote it.
I'm Irving Brecher.
And I'm a writer.
```

[*"The Same Old Story" written by Nell Scovell and Irving Brecher. Edited and directed by Rodman Flanders*]

Fifty-thousand hits later, here are some comments that appeared on the YouTube webpage below the video:

What an eloquent spokesperson Mr. Brecher is. Can we get him on the Local One negotiations committee in New York? (IATSE 764 member)

Well done Irving...Well done! Possibly one of the greatest writers ever! (Miss Harpo Marx)

"What a revolt'n development this is!"
So that's who made that up!!...wondering for years about that one.
Good man, Mr. Brecher! I bought **The Shadow of the Thin Man** *on DVD. Did you get a cut of it? Copyright laws are bullshit. Warped by un-talented garbage that is corporate executives. (Yep147)*

Three months later, when I called to tell him the walkout had ended, Irv said: "I can't wait for the next strike. I've got some good insults for the vultures who own TV."
Viva Irv!

The Man Who Outlived America

In the spring of 2008, the Brechers attended a memorial for one of Irv's oldest friends, Seaman Jacobs. "Sy" had died at 96; he was a hilarious fellow who wrote movies and TV, and monologues for Bob Hope, George Burns and Johnny Carson. I met him at a cocktail party at the Brecher's, where I got to ask him about writing shows I loved as a kid, like, "My Favorite Martian" and "I Dream of Jeannie."

"I also punched up the Old Testament," said Sy.

I remember a toast he gave at Irv's 90th birthday party, held at Matteo's Taste of Hoboken restaurant: "If it wasn't for Irving Brecher, I'd be selling beer in Kingston, New York."

Irv got him hired at the Mickey Mouse Magazine. *It was 1935.*

The Jacobs memorial at the WGA Theatre brought out a couple dozen Hollywood figures. Afterwards, Norma said some of the speakers went on for twenty minutes, making lame attempts at being funny. Her husband, not on the program to speak from the podium, did offer brief remarks when he was handed a microphone at his seat.

Irv told a joke he attributed to Sy, about a town that was so primitive they only had one hooker and she was a virgin.

And then he said:

"I feel strange, you know. I came here hoping to be downcast and sad, grieving at a memorial. Instead, I listened to a lot of people auditioning for 'American Idol.'"

Norma said it brought the house down.

I told Irv to be sure to invite me to the next memorial.

"You're like a Boswell," he said.

"How do you mean?"

"Following around an old cocker in the last stages and writing down what you think he says is funny. I hope you're right. You're the sofer."

"The sofer. The Hebrew writer who calligraphies the Torah scroll?"

He paused and said: "Maybe not."

It does feel like it's time to roll up the scroll. Roll credits. Seven years in and out of the chat room that was Brecher's lair—still trying to make a buck run-

ning around town with a tape recorder, stealing some time to phone him, always hoping I'd get the right answer: "Hello, who the hell is this?"—I've listened spellbound to tales of characters he called, "Hollywood's greats and ingrates."

Irv Brecher will never run out of material. The problem with this world is that we run out of Brechers.

He was sitting in the red chair in his study, patting his hands to his left, stretching two bony fingers to pop off the audiocassette playback machine from Braille. I came into the room doing an impression of Jack Benny's butler Rochester ("I'm coming, Mr. Brecherrrr!"), which Irv hated...

You're 94-and-a-half now, Irv.
Yeah?
One of a kind, end of an era—
Get to the point, sonny.
Are you planning on having a big party for your 95th?
No.
That was quick.
Okay then, can you tell the readers, to what do you owe your longevity?
I can't speak for the other museum pieces, but the last hundred yards, what's kept me going is, I suppose, anger. That and my diet. The mainstay of which are twice-weekly injections of corned beef.
And a steady diet of anger?
The anger comes from the realization that almost half the voters in 2004 were stupid enough to keep a man in office who was destroying this wonderful country. People who'd like to name this country in honor of Bush and Cheney, the new name of which will be, "Megalomania."
I had suspected America had contracted a serious disease when Reagan had that airport named after him. But November 2, 2004, was the day America died.
Died?
You're talking to a guy who outlived America.
Whoa. Wait. What about the future?
In fact, I wouldn't have minded checking out the night Bush was re-elected. The thing that kept me going was I didn't want to leave my wonderful wife and daughter and a few friends.
He didn't say anything about the future.
It's a good thing you didn't check out, because now you're booking

stand-up gigs, and different documentarians seem to be beckoning—

Aw shit, it's just their anticipation of me dying. Come on. Get with it. You see, it's a little like fishing. Norma and I used to go fishing on the Rogue River in Oregon, almost every fall until it became obvious: you can't use a walker in a rowboat. What's happening to me is what happens to a male salmon. In their last stage, they leap out of the water and flop back a few times and then it's all over.

What about going on a book tour, doing TV and radio promotion...

Now there's a good reason for dying.

We laugh.

I'm sure gonna miss having these conversations with you.

It's more than conversations for chrissake!

Listen, we've been friends for almost all of that son-of-a-Bush's administration. It's time we wrapped it all up.

I think so. But don't you think you ought to have it printed first?

I laugh.

So we can get going on the sequel?

He laughs.

Lori Champagne

Irv sings, "Hello, I must be going" to Marx Brothers fans at the Max Palevsky Theater/Aero Cinematheque in Santa Monica.

Irving Brecher

CREDITS

Irv would like to thank S. Charles Lee, architect of some of the greatest movie theatres in the United States, and a tremendous patron of Braille Institute. He asked me to write a closing line for a speech he gave when he was being honored for his work at the Institute, something to sum up his devotion. So I wrote: God said, let there be light—and when there is no light, let there be Braille.

Thanks to the Yudelsons who took this project on and stayed positive every step of every year it took to get it to fly. Hank would like to thank Norm and Dulcie Rosenfeld for their enduring support and letting him write some of this in their home when they weren't there watching movies, listening to the radio, reading books or bugging him to finish this.

Additional thanks to: Tom O'Neill, who told me to pitch the original story of the Turner Classic archives to the *LA Times*; to TCM's generous Michelle Rosenblatt and producers Alexa Forman and Maureen Corley (who said *Meet Me in St. Louis* was her favorite movie). To the late, great Midnight Special and Dutton's bookstores, Arnold M. Herr Books, Angel City Books, Strand Books, and First Edition Too in Michigan's Upper Peninsula and the other ageless antiquarian wonders full of floors of knowledge to sit and steal upon; the great new Santa Monica Public Library (more bike racks, please), Ocean Park, Central and Beverly Hills Library; and The Office on 26th Street for the urban retreat. To the following authors: Scott Eyman, for his continuous encouragement and his many books, including *The Lion of Hollywood* about Louis B. Mayer; Jordan R. Young for the chapter on Irv in *The Laugh Crafters*; Lee Server for his interview with Irv in *Screenwriter: Words Become Pictures*; and Joe Adamson for his brilliant *Groucho, Harpo, Chico and sometimes Zeppo*. Other books we used that you might take a laugh at include, *The Marx Bros. Scrapbook* by Groucho Marx and Richard J. Anobile; *Groucho and Me* by Groucho; *The Groucho Letters* by Groucho; *Groucho Marx* by Peter Tyson; *Groucho Marx And Other Short Stories And Tall Tales* edited by Robert S. Bader; *Life With Groucho* by Arthur Marx; *Son of Harpo* by Bill Marx; and the most delightful *Harpo Speaks!* by Harpo Marx and Rowland Barber. Among other sources in the Norma and Irv living room collection were, *Directed by Minnelli* by Stephen Harvey; *The 4th Film Encyclopedia* by Ephraim Katz; *The New York Times Encyclopedia of Film*; *The Best of MGM: The Golden Years* by James Robert Parish and Gregory W. Mank; and *Raised On Radio* by Gerald Nachman. Audio and video interviews with Irv came from the Arclight Cinema with Dennis Michael, Aero Cinematheque from Lionel Herer, Taylor Made Entertainment, Garner Creative Concepts, and Mario Machado on KRLA. Other audio inspiration came from the LP "All Hail Marx and Lennon: How Can You Be In Two Places At Once When You're Not Anywhere At All" by The Firesign Theater, special thanks to Phil and Peter and David.

Much appreciation to Lori Champagne for her spot-on photography; Mary Fitz for excellent transcriptionals; Barbara Bogaev, Jim Gates and Sara Sarasohn and Art Silverman at NPR; Jon Kalish for being such a radio aide; Daniel Mandil and Bob Rees for listening to Irv tales around a campfire in Kings Canyon; Eddie Marx for Langer's Deli treats and tapeage; and Daniel Asa Rose for getting Irv-as-Groucho on the front page of the *Forward*.

Thank you to Martin Smith and Al Martinez at the *LA Times*; the latter sent the Erskine Caldwell line, "You write like you whistle, ya pucker up and blow." To David Greenberger and his DuplexPlanet.com for the quick brilliance of his questions; Darryl Henriques "The Swami from Miami" and Paul Krassner for answers; Lisa Karrer for suggesting we "leave out the Tootie and pitch the Judy;" Annie Randolph for always finding the funny; Flash Rosenberg for long distance inspiration and enduring endearing advice; Liz Ellen Ryan for the new Dictionary and morning brainstorming bike rides up to Back to the Beach; to Nell Scovell for all her time and affection; Kris Strobeck for always calling from North Dakota and Las Vegas and Glendale, and Ridge Tip Tolbert for always reading to Irv; Gary Gordon for his writing hideout in 29 Palms; and Gerry Fialka for showing free movies in Venice and quoting Frank Zappa, "When you're laughing you're learning." Thanks to the writers and/or friends out west: Roni Cohen, Andy Cowan, Ronit Davidyan, Steve Fife, Jeanine Frank, Sally Kaplan, Michelle Kholos, Jason Kramer, Emily Kunstler, Marta Kupesok, Eliza Lewin, Marybugs Menaker, Robin Menken, Nick O'Connor, Randi Pereira, Jessica Portner, Lisa Robins, Scott Rubin, Mort Sahl, Laurie Selik, Terrie Silverman, Michael Simmons, Mark Solomon, Louise Steinman, Susan Van Allen, Suzy Williams, and Chelika Yapa. To you guys back east for seven years of good words: Miriam Ancis, Jane Brenner, Ernie Harwell, the Parlan McGaws, Stephen Ringold, Shelley Roth, Andy and Rocky Ross, Cynthia Ryan, David Tabatsky, Liz Tuccillo, Leslie Udelson, Julius Valiunas, Byron "Otis P. Driftwood" Washington, and Kenny Weinstein; Judith, Kim, Stu and Meredith Zamsky—Thank you.

Much gratefulness goes to the table of wits from Minnesota: Chris Bloch, Dick Dahl, Rob Elk, Don Foster, Fred Haeusler, Heneghan & Staloch, Joel Madison; and the house of dreamers at 241 Marine: Ted, Laura and Elaine Bonnitt, Paul Lyons, Giovanni Natala and "Tutu" Lopez for them there meals that heals; to Eric Roth for telling me to stay home when I needed to and to just send it in when I needed to; Chris Stanley for the job at KNX writing when I was working at a car wash and needed it; Stephen Capen and Susan Wu for undying friendship; and to Ann & Angie & their 4th-grade Rustys and Farfels at Roosevelt Elementary who taught me the word "humorism."

Finally, thank you to Ben and Rose Miller; Billy and Margie and all their Krasnicks; and Liz, Adam, Ben, Harrison, Jill, Evan, Nancy, Chris, Jimmie, and Peggy for they-know-what.

Eddie Montilla—you've been so helpful; thanks go to Oscar and Anna; to Joanna for her hilarious spirit and support, and to Ellen and Jane; and especially to Norma from Iowa, for Irv and everything else. And to Mr. Jan Murray who said during Brecher's comedy act at Cedars-Sinai Medical Center, "I love Irv and respect him as a great artisan. What is he worried?"

Thank you Irv for letting everyone in on the jokes.

As credits fade, Cole Porter's "Friendship Song" from ***Du Barry Was a Lady*** plays. "...If you ever lose your teeth when you're out to dine, borrow mine/It's friendship!"

About the Authors

Irving Brecher is the last living Metro-Goldwyn-Mayer studio writer from the "Golden Age" of the 1940's. His screenplay for *Meet Me in St. Louis* was nominated for the 1944 Academy Award. He wrote seven musicals at MGM, including scripts for Gene Kelly, Lucille Ball, Fred Astaire, and Red Skelton. He wrote *The Shadow of the Thin Man* and two Marx Brothers features. His movie career began by punching up comedy material for *The Wizard of Oz* when the words "punching up" hadn't even been invented yet. He final screenwriting credit was *Bye Bye Birdie*, starring Ann-Margret and Dick Van Dyke. Irv also created "The Life of Riley," the first sitcom ever filmed for TV. He originally wrote "Riley" for the radio, a medium Irv started working in at the age of 19 as a writer for Milton Berle. He wrote for numerous vaudeville acts. He forged storied friendships with many of the comedians he wrote for: Berle, George Burns, Jack Benny, Ernie Kovacs, Groucho, Harpo, Chico, and Cleo the bassett hound from "Peoples' Choice," a sitcom Irv created (starring Jackie Cooper) in 1953. He lives in Westwood, California.

Hank Rosenfeld wrote comedies for the Bond Street, DaK, and H.E.A.P. theatres in New York, touring with productions to the Netherlands, Berlin and New Jersey. Hank was on staff at *Spy Magazine* in NYC. He has written for the *Los Angeles Times*, *Los Angeles Magazine*, the *NY Post*, *Premiere*, *PAPER*, the *Jewish Forward*, and the *Shambhala Sun*. Currently a storyteller on NPR's "All Things Considered," "Marketplace," "Weekend America" and "Off-Ramp," he has produced comedy shows for KSAN in San Francisco and K-ROCK (WXRK) in New York. He wrote jokes for the long-running Broadway show, *Catskills on Broadway* at the Lunt-Fontanne Theatre, and lived as a deejay on the pirate-radio ship, The Voice of Peace, broadcasting "from somewhere in the Mediterranean." While writing for the *Athens Times*, Hank was arrested for robbing the National Bank of Greece. Found innocent, he was kicked out of Greece after receiving a beating and a wonderful recipe for tzatziki.

Lori Champagne

Ben *Yehuda* Press
Experience the weekly Torah portion

Discuss Torah at your table
TORAH & COMPANY
by Judith Z. Abrams

"Reveals the power and relevance of each weekly Torah portion. A Shabbat treasure for every home." —Rabbi Goldie Milgram, author, *Reclaiming Judaism as a Spiritual Practice*

This useful book offers brief excerpts from each Torah portion, along with appropriately related selections from the Mishnah and Gemara—the "oral" Torah. Discussion questions for each selection are provided to spark open-ended conversation around dinner tables, and wherever else Jews gather to learn and argue.

The texts are short and provocative—the questions even more so. This book promises lively debate, where the deepest text of all is your learning partner.

Discover a unique Jewish poet
FROM THE COFFEE HOUSE OF JEWISH DREAMERS:
POEMS OF WONDER AND WANDERING /
POEMS ON THE WEEKLY TORAH PORTION
by Isidore Century

"Isidore Century is a wonderful poet," says the *Jewish Week*, "funny, deeply observed, without pretension."

Says a reviewer at Librarything.com: "When I read the 'Poems of Wonder and Wandering,' I was awash in a sea of sadness and longing. Flip the book over and read 'Poems on the Weekly Torah Portion', and it is laugh out loud funny, full of tongue in cheek wit. It is the balance between sadness and humor, anger and joy, longing and acceptance, which makes this collection such a treasure."

Another reviewer agrees: "I am not a sophisticated reader of poetry. However, I absolutely love Isidore Century's collection. A treasure."

Ben Yehuda Press
Women who challenge the status quo

BESSIE SAINER. Bessie's "career" is full of hazards. At the age of twelve, she is exiled to Siberia because of her brothers' anti-czarist activities. At twenty-five, she loses her husband and baby girl to the ravages of civil war in revolutionary Russia.

At forty, she faces down Nazi hoodlums as she tries to disrupt a pro-Hitler rally in Madison Square Garden. At fifty-five, she is driven underground by McCarthyite persecution. At sixty-two, she squares off against racists in the South—and nearly loses the loyalty of her beloved daughter.

At eighty-eight, she is still making trouble and still making jokes.

A profoundly optimistic novel about a remarkable heroine—a rebel, a lover, a mother, a grandmother, a Jew, and an extraordinary human being.

Bessie: A Novel of Love and Revolution by Lawrence Bush.

KARIMA AL-TUSTARI. Charming and headstrong, Karimah is a young Karaite Jewish woman in 11th Century Egypt who follows her heart to live a life of adventure. Although unpredictable, Karimah is guided by her own steadfast ideas of honor and tradition.

Devastated, Karimah's father seeks comfort from Rabbi Nissim of North Africa, who responds with tales from classical rabbinic literature. Karimah, writing home to her brother, quotes not only from traditional Jewish texts, but also from the Arabian Nights.

As events unfold, the storytellers become lost in their own stories which begin to entwine and take on a life of their own. The storytellers learn that their tales are mirrors; the more they are told, the more they reflect the teller.

A Delightful Compendium: A Fabulous Tale of Romance, Adventure & Faith in the Medieval Mediterranean by Burton

Ben Yehuda Press
Rediscovering classic Jewish thought

THE ESSENTIAL WRITINGS OF RABBI ABRAHAM ISAAC KOOK

Edited and translated by **Ben Zion Bokser**
"This work excels both in its judicious selection of texts and the quality of the translation. The reader is treated to Rav Kook's views on such topics as culture, evolution, scientific change, Torah study, holiness, morality and the Zionist revival. This volume enables readers to feel the pulse and power of this remarkable thinker."
—David Shatz, professor of philosophy, Yeshiva University

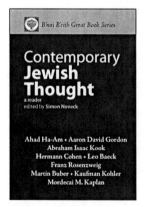

CONTEMPORARY JEWISH THOUGHT
THE B'NAI B'RITH GREAT BOOK SERIES
edited by **Simon Noveck**

Ben Yehuda Press is proud to bring this classic anthology of nine Jewish thinkers back into print. Featuring translated selections from the writings of Ahad Ha-am, Aaron David Gordon, Abraham Isaac Kook, Hermann Cohen, Leo Baeck, Franz Rosenzweig, Martin Buber, Kaufmann Kohler and Mordecai Kaplan. Published in cooperation with B'nai B'rith International.

AHRON'S HEART:
THE PRAYERS, TEACHINGS AND LETTERS OF AHRELE ROTH, A HASIDIC REFORMER
by **Rabbi Hillel Goelman and Rabbi Zalman Schachter-Shalomi**
For the first time, the writings and life of one of the 20th century's most important Hasidic thinkers are made available to a non-Hasidic English audience. To be published in Winter 2008.

Ben Yehuda Press
Discover new Jewish spirituality

TORAH JOURNEYS: THE INNER PATH TO THE PROMISED LAND
by Rabbi Shefa Gold

Week by week, **Torah Journeys** makes the Torah personal, and the personal holy. Following the weekly Torah portion, readers are challenged to think about the Torah in terms of their own lives, and are guided to implement their own spiritual and personal growth.

Hailed as one of the best Jewish books of 2006 by Beliefnet, and designated "the first Jewish Renewal Torah commentary" by the *New Jersey Jewish News*, **Torah Journeys** draws from diverse sources to create a new path of Divine challenge and blessing.

IN THE FEVER OF LOVE
AN ILLUMINATION OF THE SONG OF SONGS
by Rabbi Shefa Gold

"Shefa Gold, songstress and prophetess, here dares to reveal her heart, soul, and body in an intimate, erotic elaboration on the Song of Songs. But more than that: she audaciously proposes a Judaism whose ten commandments are mandates to love. **In the Fever of Love** is personal, daring, and drunk with God." —Jay Michaelson, author of *God in Your Body: Kabbalah, Mindfulness and Embodied Spiritual Practice*

"An amazing, loving and poetic commentary on this sacred text of the Song of Songs. A wonderful and awakening experience."
—David Cooper, author of *God is a Verb*

It is said that the whole of Torah could be derived from the Song of Songs. **In the Fever of Love** provides a poetic response to the Song of Songs, moving from the Biblical verses to a deeply personal, highly erotic meditation of love of God. A Jewish work of ecstatic religious literature in the tradition of the mystical poetess Mirabai.

Ben Yehuda Press
Bold Jewish Books

The Cabalist's Daughter:
A Novel of Practical Messianic
Redemption
by Yori Yanover

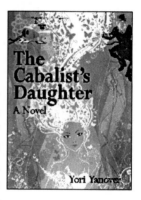

Nechama Gutkind is the clone of the late, great Cabalist of Brooklyn. She's a gorgeous, gifted miracle worker just trying to fill her father's shoes and save the world. But with the highest reaches of the U.S. government and the deepest pits of Hell determined to stop her, will she be able to complete her mission? Luckily, she's not without friends, including a 130-year-old mystic, a hunky counter-terrorism officer, a Ghanese warrior witch and a luscious succubus who band together to keep her in one piece.

"A wildly-fun, fantastical Jewish Hitchhiker's Guide to the Galaxy." —Laurie Gwen Shapiro, author of *The Matzo Ball Heiress*

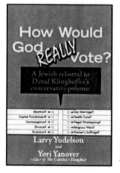

How Would God REALLY Vote?
A Jewish Rebuttal to
David Klinghoffer's
Conservative Polemic
by Larry Yudelson & Yori Yanover

Do Jews belong with the likes of Sarah Palin and Pat Robertson on the "family values" bandwagon? No way! argue the authors of this provocative volume which unapologetically returns the salvos from the Right of America's religious culture wars. Focusing on the arguments made by David Klinghoffer in his book, *How Would God Vote: Why the Bible Commands You to be a Conservative*, How Would God REALLY Votes highlights errors of logic, selective readings of the Bible, and denial of the post-Biblical Jewish tradition.

Yudelson and Yanover argue for liberal positions on issues such as contraception, feminism, gay marriage, health care and even tax policy.

Printed in the United States
139131LV00005B/9/P

9 781934 730232